American
Costume Jewelry
Art & Industry, 1935-1950

A-M

Roberto Brunialti
&
Carla Ginelli Brunialti

Schiffer Publishing Ltd

4880 Lower Valley Road Atglen, Pennsylvania 19310

CREDITS

Photographs: Douglas Congdon-Martin.
English translation (revised by the author): Globostudio Como.
Posters Reproductions courtesy of: URL and Northwestern University Library, Curtis Publications Inc., USA Navy Archives.

Designed by John P. Cheek
Cover design by Bruce Waters
Type set in Tiffany Lt BT/Souvenir Lt BT

ISBN: 978-0-7643-2982-1

Printed in China

Schiffer Books are available at special discounts for bulk purchases for sales promotions or premiums. Special editions, including personalized covers, corporate imprints, and excerpts can be created in large quantities for special needs. For more information contact the publisher:

Published by Schiffer Publishing Ltd.
4880 Lower Valley Road
Atglen, PA 19310
Phone: (610) 593-1777; Fax: (610) 593-2002
E-mail: Info@schifferbooks.com

For the largest selection of fine reference books on this and related subjects, please visit our web site at
www.schifferbooks.com
We are always looking for people to write books on new and related subjects. If you have an idea for a book please contact us at the above address.

This book may be purchased from the publisher.
Include $3.95 for shipping.
Please try your bookstore first.
You may write for a free catalog.

In Europe, Schiffer books are distributed by
Bushwood Books
6 Marksbury Ave.
Kew Gardens
Surrey TW9 4JF England
Phone: 44 (0) 20 8392-8585; Fax: 44 (0) 20 8392-9876
E-mail: info@bushwoodbooks.co.uk
Website: www.bushwoodbooks.co.uk
Free postage in the U.K., Europe; air mail at cost.

CONTENTS
Volume 1

FOREWORD

This book, the fruit of twenty years of collecting, research and study of American costume jewelry dating from the years 1930-1950, has been conceived to offer lovers, collectors and dealers a meticulous, reliable instrument to knowing and understanding these gems which are often true and proper little works of art.

It follows the line of the two previous works, *American Costume Jewelry*, Milan 1997 and *Tribute to America*, Milan 2002, presenting the results of new studies and researches as well as three hundred new pieces, many never published before, and which are often quite exceptional in their rarity, quality and beauty.

A general section is followed by the profiles of the individual manufacturers; this is then followed by color plates with an accurate description of the pieces. The first two parts are fit with appropriate illustrations, most never been published before and which have been drawn from sources of the times.

In the descriptions of patented pieces, the drawings found in the reference patents are included along with indication of the title holder, number, date of issue and request reported in the text.

The holders of title or patentees continue to be called "designers" even if the two qualities do not always coincide. The reason for this choice is fully explained in the text, in the chapter on dating and attributions, and as regards the two main cases, Katz/Verrecchio and Nathan/Kamke, even in the chapters dedicated to Coro and Eisenberg. As a general rule it must be said that the patentees were never simple directors or employees who did nothing but "sign the patent application papers"; they were either the owners of the company or the person responsible for design and style, and they had the last word in the choice of subjects and styles to be produced. Therefore, if the material author of the design is not known with any certainty, it is not incorrect to define the patentee as designer.

In the description of unpatented pieces, on the other hand, where available, reproductions are included of the objects drawn from magazines and publications of the times as they provide certain indication of the date, often the producer (particularly for the minor companies) and, at times, even the name used to identify the piece.

The plates reproduce the pieces in their natural size and are numbered so that the descriptions can easily be related to the pieces. Where dimensions are given, they are indicated in centimeters: the initials preceding the numbers indicate the manufacturer or the type (e.g. C = Coro; JB = Jelly Bellies; P = Patriotic) and they are explained in a list of abbreviations.

Evaluation of the objects is expressed in stars, from * to *****, set at the beginning of the description.

The stars indicate not so much the price of an item as its rarity and its importance for collecting and, often (but not always, particularly for unsigned pieces) a higher number of stars corresponds to higher market sectors. Moreover, even in the past, it was always difficult to provide reliable indications on the market value while today to get an idea of the market value, all one has to do is log onto the internet and, for example, consult the costume jewelry section on eBay.

All the jewelry presented belongs to the Ginelli – Brunialti collection.

The book rightfully continues to bear the name of my wife, Carla Ginelli Brunialti (1951 – 2002), coauthor of the first two and, ideally, of this volume as well.

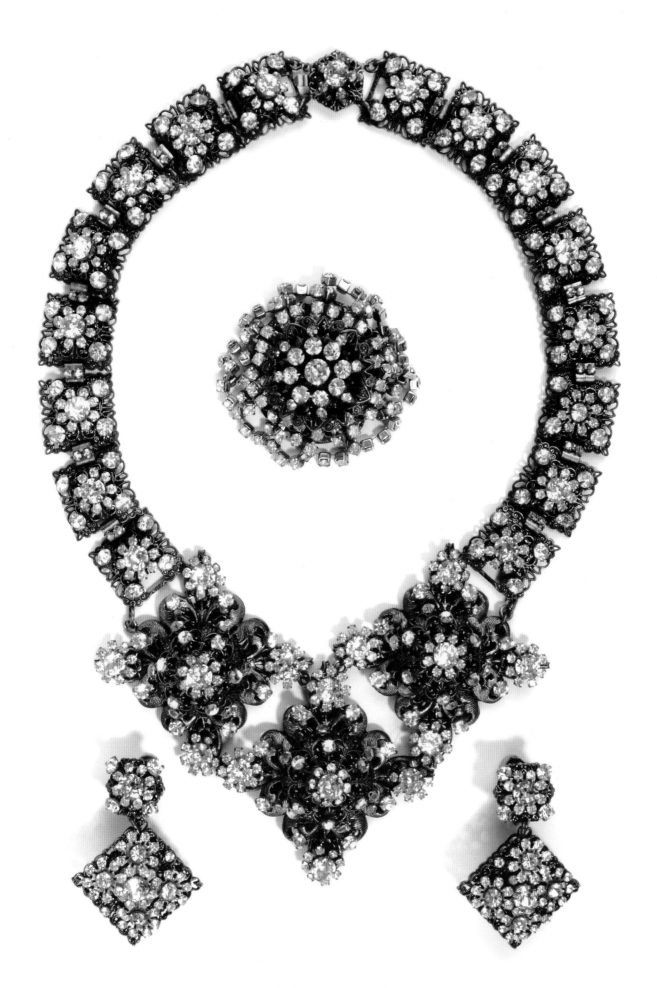

INTRODUCTION

1
COSTUME JEWELRY

The origin of the expression "costume jewelry" is uncertain. It probably dates from the last years of the 19th century or the very first years of the 20th century and, according to a reliable interpretation, it referred to fake jewels originally made for the stage (jewelry for stage costumes) and then habitually worn in everyday life.

This is the serious version, whereas pure myth – a good example of the legends surrounding these items, which are passed around from one book to the next, without any critical checking of sources, and from collector to collector as well as from seller to seller – is the anecdote ascribing, if not the invention, at least the acknowledged use of the expression to the great Broadway impresario Florence Ziegfeld (1868-1932). One day Ziegfeld told William W. Hobé that he absolutely needed jewelry matching the patterns and style of his "costumes," i.e. the dresses worn on stage. From then on, apparently, Ziegfeld constantly used the expression "costume jewelry" to indicate the jewels made for his "follies."

Actually the term had already been in use for a long time. Already at the beginning of the 1900s *Women's Wear Daily* (*WWD*) had given the title "Costume Jewelry" to a column dedicated to these accessories.

Another fully unfounded version ascribes the creation of the expression to Gabrielle Chanel: this version is probably due to the fact that the famous French fashion designer gave the final seal of approval to the use of fake jewelry.

As to the definition of costume jewelry, one given in *An Illustrated Dictionary of Jewelry* by Anita Mason, Harper & Row, New York 1974 defined it as: "Mass produced jewelry made of non-precious metal and not designed to last – made for a prevailing fashion." A definition which, in the light of today's craze for the pieces made in those years that have become much sought after collection items, appears only partially true.

In any case, an aspect of costume jewelry we should always keep in mind for a correct evaluation of the jewels, their designers, and manufacturers, is that it was fashion-bound, "seasonal," and mass produced.

Experts disagree also on the time and place where the American industry of costume jewelry began and, as usual, myth mingles with reality. The most myth-based theory maintains that the first American manufacturer of costume jewelry was a French jeweler, a soldier in the army who fought during the American revolution under the orders of the Marquis de Lafayette (1777-1781). After the war, he settled down in Attleboro, Massachusetts, where he set up shop. A more reliable theory maintains that the father of the industrial production of costume jewelry was Seril Dodge or, rather, his step-brother Nehemia Dodge, who opened a workshop in Providence, Rhode Island, in 1784 or 1794 as "goldsmith, watchmaker and jeweler." As a matter of fact, both were real jewelers. However, Nehemia Dodge was apparently the first to develop a type of rather crude gold plating process for non-precious metals. After this uncertain beginning, in Providence there were already 143 businesses with more than 2,500 employees in 1875, and a turnover of about $5,400,000. They manufactured both precious and costume jewelry, the latter consisting mostly of camisole brooches and earrings.

NEHEMIA DODGE, the father of costume jewelry.

Until the 1939 Census of Manufacturers, there are no separate statistics for jewelry and costume jewelry. In that year there were 299 firms with 12,228 employees and an estimated production of $38,761,000. The mean annual salary of workers was $827. At the time production was already concentrated in four states: Rhode Island (particularly in Providence), accounting for 41.1% of total production, New York (mainly in New York City and Newark, New Jersey) with 32,4%, Massachusetts (especially Attleboro near Providence) with 20%, Illinois (particularly Chicago, with, among others, Fred A. Block, Eisenberg, Elgin American, Morris Mann & Reilly, Inc., and Staret) accounting for 3.5% of total production. Another area of growing importance for the production of costume jewelry was the Los Angeles area, California, with companies such as California Accessories, Elzac, Alice Johnson, Joseff Hollywood, and Hollywood Jewelry Products

Inc., alias "Ricarde of Hollywood".

The figures reported in the 1947 Census of Manufacturers give us an idea of the growth experienced by this industry in the following years, in spite of part of the plants being used for war production during the war: 859 plants (400 of which in the Providence-Attleboro area) with 22,265 workers and a yearly production estimated at $170,294,000. With the exception of Coro, this was mostly the work of small and very small businesses outsourcing a substantial part of production to private persons working at home. In the case of firms specializing in the production of very cheap items aimed at those on lowest-income, who could not afford the more expensive professionals, the design of jewels was also outsourced to amateurs, such as the students of the Rhode Island School of Design.

It was common practice with these occasional designers to purchase single designs at an all-inclusive price which never exceeded $ 25. Although it is impossible to estimate the actual yield of this outsourced production, it probably increased the official figures significantly. Until 1950 the number of businesses remained substantially stable and global sales increased to $ 250,000,000.

2

1935 to 1950

The oldest American manufacturer of costume jewelry, Napier, was established in 1878 at North Attleboro, Massachusetts, first with the name of Whitney & Rice, later changed to Carpenter & Bliss, Bliss Company, and then, with the arrival of James H. Napier in 1920 as chairman and general manager, to Napier-Bliss first and, finally, to Napier Co. in 1922, under which name it still operates today. Many other important firms, established during the 20th century, are still productive or were until recently, some of them under different owners: for example Coro (1901) is still active in Canada, Trifari (1925) and Monet (1937), after experiencing some difficult periods, were operating until 2000, when they were purchased by the Liz Claiborne group, Miriam Haskell (1924), Eisenberg (1937 for jewelry), Hobé (1927) and many others.

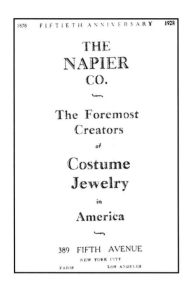

WWD, September 20 1928: Napier fiftieth anniversary.

In the years since 1878, the period in which the industry reached its peak in terms of design, materials, stones, and manufacturing quality, can be pinpointed as being the years between 1935 and 1950.

In fact, until 1935, costume jewelry, apart from being ancillary to the production of other accessories such as combs and other hair accessories, compacts, tie-pins, and cigarette holders, was strongly influenced by the style of European fake jewelry, and in particular by the production of French fashion designers (Chanel, Lelong, Patou, etc). Some important firms, such as Cohn & Rosenberger, Calvaire, Lisner, Mazer, and Miriam Haskell, in addition to being themselves manufacturers, were importers of French costume jewelry. In particular, they manufactured necklaces, bracelets, earrings, and small clips, in keeping with the fashion of the so-called wild, Charleston years that featured short dresses with generous necklines and short hairstyles *à la garçonne*. However, some original features started appearing in some jewelry lines by Coro, Trifari, Mazer, and Leo Glass that would grow to their full extent in the following years. A strong impulse to costume jewelry production came from the will to react to the years of the Great Depression and that same impulse resulted in the so-called "novelty jewelry," which consisted mainly of brooches made

of the most disparate materials and with the wildest subjects. Another constant was represented by the imitation of precious models by the great jewelers, such as Boucheron, Cartier, Maubussin, Tiffany, Van Cleef & Arpels etc.

A useful guide to following the development of costume jewelry in a given period is represented by the pictures and advertisements of jewels in the magazines of the time, and by the patents of the various designs, which were few initially, but became more and more frequent in the course of the years. In the years between 1935 and 1950, including also a few patents made before and afterwards, a total of about four thousand designs were patented.

The subject of patents is dealt with more extensively in the following paragraph. Just a few examples of the very first patents will be mentioned here. The designs for a brooch and a bracelet with the Zodiac signs of Libra and Virgo, respectively, were patented by Oreste Pennino, founder of the firm with the same name, on January 14th, 1928 (des. pat. n° 76,039 and 76,040). In the same period Pennino also registered a trademark with the ten remaining Zodiac signs.

Since 1930 this is one of the only two patents registered for Napier: it is a "metal unit for jewelry," i.e., a chain link for a bracelet or a necklace designed by F. W. Rettenmeyer (des. pat. n° 80,741 18th March, 1930). Frederick W. Rettenmeyer had been the firm's head designer since 1913, after succeeding his father, William R. Rettenmeyer, who had gained great experience as a goldsmith at Tiffany's, had studied at the Cooper Union and had been hired by Napier as head designer in 1893. Frederick Rettenmayer worked for the company until his retirement in 1964. The other design patented for Napier, however after the period we are considering, is a brooch by Eugene E. Bertolli dating from October 11th, 1955 (des. pat. n° 175,757).

The only design by Royal Marcher, the legendary Coro salesman, was patented for the same company on December 2nd, 1930 (des. pat. n° 82,685). It is a brooch shaped like two golf irons on tees. The brooch also features a small clamp that can hold a handkerchief. The first design by Adolph Katz, who at that time was head of production and in 1937 also became Coro's head designer, is a rhinestone-paved brooch complete with closure mechanism, that was patented as a mechanism with the definition of jewelry (des. pat. n° 1,937,347 of November 28th, 1933).

The choice of 1935 as the date marking the beginning of the best period of costume jewelry coincides with the launch, in the same year, with an advertisement in *Vogue America*, i.e. nationwide, of the Coro Duette, two clips that could be worn separately or as a single brooch thanks to a special mechanism that was patented by Gaston Candas of Paris on March 31st, 1931 with n° 1,798,867. Between 1935 and 1940 the clips made to be worn as a single brooch using the Duette mechanism often featured a mechanism that had been patented by Elisha A. Finney of South Attleboro, Massachusetts on April 5th, 1932 with n° 1,852,188 for Geo H. Fuller & Son Company of Pawtucket, Rhode Island. The use of this second mechanism was abandoned towards the end of the 1930s, whereas Candas's mechanism remained in use for as long as Coro continued to manufacture its Duette brooches (1954?).

Vogue, October 1, 1935: the Coro Duette.

After 1936 the patenting of designs kept growing until 1942, then decreased in war time and resumed on a huge scale in 1946. It peaked in the years 1947-1949, and began to drop in 1950, reaching an all-time low in 1952 and in the following years contextually with the extension of copyright to costume jewelry designs (1955).

January 7th 1936, is the date of the first of the only two designs by Ralph De Rosa, founder of the company with the same name, a butterfly-shaped "ornament" (DR8.), which was at the same time a brooch and a mechanism (des. pat. n° 2,026,934.) This number also appears on pieces that were not marked De Rosa, allowing for the conclusion that the patent had also been transferred to other manufacturers. In fact, it also appears on a brooch marked Ora. August 11th, 1936 is the date of the first design to be patented for Trifari by Alfred Philippe, the company's head designer: it is a brooch mechanism, designed to join together two detachable clips (or clips mate – des. pat. n° 2,050,804), and obviously Trifari's response to Coro's Duette.

From this time onwards, as already mentioned, design patents were registered at an unprecedented frequency of two lines per year: spring-summer and autumn-winter.

Apart from a few significant exceptions that are examined in more detail later on, a great part of the most beautiful pieces manufactured in the period being reviewed, was made on the basis of patented designs. Many designs were signed by Alfred Philippe for Trifari and by Adolph Katz for Coro, but many other designers worked both for Coro and Trifari and their work is described in the sections dedicated to these firms and their jewelry. Other important names in costume jewelry were Marcel Boucher for his firm, Louis Mark for Rice-Weiner, Louis Mazer and Joseph Wuyts for Mazer, Nicolas Barbieri for Uncas, Willard Markle for Castlecliff, William and Sylvia Hobé for Hobé, Florence Nathan (of Fallon & Kappel) for Eisenberg, Murray Slater for Urie F. Mandel, Solomon Finkelstein for Réja, and Jules Hirsch and Jacques Leff for Du Jay and many others.

On the other hand, it should be borne in mind that even the firms most likely to apply for the patenting of designs, such as Coro and Trifari, manufactured many pieces based on designs that had not been patented, for both low-priced lines and high-quality lines. Such was the volume of production that some companies patented only a few designs and many other companies, including some famous ones, did not patent any.

Thus, for example, only about thirty designs were patented for Eisenberg, all in 1942, in the name of Florence Nathan of Fallon & Kappel, whereas none was patented in the name of Ruth Kamke, also of Fallon & Kappel, the author of most designs for Eisenberg manufactured by Fallon & Kappel between 1940 and 1972.

Very few designs were patented by Pennino, just four were patented by Solomon Finkelstein for Réja, and very few by Mazer, in spite of the hundreds of models actually manufactured.

No patent (or copyright) can be found of Miriam Haskell's jewels, none was ever ascribed to Hattie Carnegie and Nettie Rosenstein, and practically none to Eugene Joseff: the only patent found in his name is an insignificant design of a ring (des. pat. n° 143,596 of January 22nd, 1946, filed September 4th, 1945), obtained for Breakfast in Hollywood of Los Angeles, a firm in which he had a partnership. No patent was found for Staret either.

Thus, this was the time in which costume jewelry achieved not only its best quality, but also its most particular identity and greatest creative results, even when it imitated the models of European or American precious jewels.

In order to give an even more accurate analysis, it could be stated that the very best costume jewelry was manufactured in the years between 1938 and 1946, and particularly from 1939, when Europe entered the war. The subsequent isolation of the USA, combined with the rationing of materials, spurred the best designers and manufacturers to find more original solutions.

Beginning in 1947, with the abandoning of the use of sterling and the debut of new fashions (especially Dior's new look), a progressive worsening in quality and a decrease in inventiveness is evident, albeit with many noticeable exceptions, in sterling and in the new alloys created in those years (such as "Golden Trifanium" invented by Gustavo Trifari and introduced in 1947).

Beginning in 1950 the quality pieces brought to the market by the most important firms were less and less numerous and in 1951-52 their number dwindled to almost nothing, while the new companies established at the end of the 1940s never reached the high level of their predecessors. Bogoff (established in 1930 in Chicago by Henry Bogoff, who died aged 51 in 1957), De Mario (established by Robert de Mario in 1945 and closed in 1960), Eugene (1950-about 1960), Kramer (established by Louis Kramer in 1943 and, until 1956, manufacturer of the jewels designed by Christian Dior for the American market, based on an exclusive right of production agreement signed on June 1st, 1952), Robert – Fashioncraft (established in 1943 by Robert Levey, David Jaffe and Irving Landaman. Robert Levey left Fashioncraft in 1960 to establish his own firm, Robert Originals Inc. 20 West 36th Str. NY. NY., closed in 1975), are some of the best manufacturers in the first years of the 1950s and also other firms, such as Haskell, Castlecliff, Napier, Rosenstein still offered good quality products. Trifari and Coro have not been mentioned on purpose: although their primacy continued throughout the 1950s, the discrepancy between their later production and the level of their products of fifteen years before, is too great to make them worthwhile mentioning.

Among the manufacturers who made their debut in the second half of the 1950s, and whose quality products might tempt collectors to make exceptions, are: Har (trademark of Hargo Creations of New York established in 1955 by Ioseph Heilbronner and Edith Levitt, who were also the firm's designers), Kenneth J. Lane (particularly his early production), De Lillo – Clark.

3

PATENTS AND COPYRIGHT

There are three different types of patents issued by the United States Patent and Trademark Office (USPTO) in Washington, DC:

- Utility patents
- Design patents
- Plant patents

In the case of jewelry, both precious and non-precious, only the first two types apply, the utility patents and the design patents. The difference between the two categories is the following: a "utility patent" protects the way an article is used and works, a "design patent" protects the way an article looks. The two types of patents have separate numbering and utility patents outnumber design patents. Both types obviously refer not only to jewelry but also to any kind of utility or design.

The USA Patent and Trademark Office: frontispiece of a 1944 patent.

Already in 1930 the number of utility patents was nearing two million, while design patents were fewer than one hundred thousand. For example, the patent for the mechanism by Gaston Candas, used for Coro's Duette, is from 31st March 1931 and bears the progressive number 1,798,867 whereas a design by Oreste Pennino of a brooch depicting the Libra zodiac sign, of 14th August 1928, bears the number 76,039. The result is that if the item bears a patent number, it is easy to verify what type of patent it is. In addition, a utility patent number usually appears on the device it refers to, as with the mechanism of the Duettes or the clips of the

brooches or earrings. Another difference, which is also very important for the dating of the items, is that utility patents have a duration of seventeen years, while design patents have a maximum duration of seven years and a standard duration of three and a half years. Therefore, in order to date the items, the design patent is essential, while utility patents can be used for years after being issued and are not therefore a decisive element in the dating process. In this way the patent of the Duette by Coro appears for the whole period that Coro produced this type of brooch, and therefore at least until the end of the 1950s, more than twenty years after the patent was issued even if the patent was no longer effective. In the case of the designs, however, the items were produced as soon as the patents were issued or even before, when the patent was pending, and therefore it is appropriate to assign the date of the patent to the items.

Some companies, especially Trifari but also less frequently Coro, stamped the patent number on the items, usually with the mark "des. pat. n°." or, if production was started before the issuing of the patent, as was often the case for sample items, with the mark "pat.[ent] pend.[ing]".

However, the procedure for obtaining a patent was and still is the same in both cases. The inventor of the utility or the design presented an application form along with the necessary documents to the USPTO. In the case of utility patents it was necessary to present the design along with all the individual components with relative technical details, whereas in the case of design patents it was necessary to present the design of the object from at least two different angles, usually one seen from the front and one from the side and a declaration that indicated the article it referred to (for example a brooch or a similar article), and vouched for its originality. The application was filed indicating the date that it was presented and was registered with a temporary progressive number. Referring to the examples stated, the application of Candas was presented and registered on 31st May 1930 with the number 457,914, and that of Pennino on 2nd February 1928 with the number 25,153. After the application was made, a USPTO attorney would examine it, and if it was accepted, usually within a few months, but sometimes longer (in the above examples the final patent was granted to Pennino after a period of six months and to Candas after ten) the patent was issued. The patent was then published in the "Official Gazette" with the publication date and the definitive number.

Another important aspect to keep in mind is that inventors could only apply for and obtain a patent in their own name, which also meant the preservation and exploitation of the relative rights, or on behalf of a third party (an assignee), usually a company whose name was on the patent and to which the inventor was assignor.

The procedure was quite expensive. In 1958 the cost was $30 for registering the application and a further $30 when it was granted plus $1 for each additional claim of what the item was or could do, after the first 20 claims which were free (WWD, 17th January 1958).

Design patents were mainly resorted to as a deterrent in an attempt to discourage copying, at the time called "style piracy," which was a very frequent occurrence right from the start, even though lawsuits based on patent right disputes were, as is still the case today, very difficult because a few minor changes were enough to avoid being charged with "infringement of patent rights." For this reason companies were reluctant to take legal action despite sometimes successfully doing so.

There was a turning point in the protection of designs in 1955 after the victory of a lawsuit launched by Trifari.

In April 1955 the company took Charel Co. and Charel Jewelry Co. to the USA District Court of New York, accusing them of infringement of design and copyrights in its "Bolero" costume jewelry. In October of the same year judge Alexander Bicks granted Trifari a preliminary injunction according to which "a piece of costume jewelry can be considered a 'work of art' under the copyright laws and is entitled to the protection of these laws. Costume jewelry may express the artistic conception of its author no less than a painting or a statue.... and is entitled to copyright protection."

A few days later, on the 14th October 1955, WWD commented: "the first court decision allowing costume jewelry design protection under the United States copyright laws has started a chain reaction in the trade. The idea of having jewelry designs copyrighted is not new. Some manufacturers have had various items copyrighted in the past. The strength of this protection however, has never been tested in court prior to the preliminary injunction obtained recently by Trifari, Krussman & Fishel. Jewelry manufacturers have attempted to protect their original designs by obtaining design patents. Since this took up to eight months after application any protection was purely academic as by that time the item involved was out of season. Under the design copyright, which can be obtained in about two weeks, manufacturers can now have quick protection against style piracy."

In June 1956 an article in WWD had the following title: "Use of copyright spreading, style piracy under fire."

The lawsuit between Trifari and Charel concluded in October 1956 when the Federal Judge Irving R. Kaufman approved a consent judgment enjoining Charel Co., Inc. and Charel Jewelry Co., Inc., not to infringe the copyrights of Trifari, Krussman & Fishel, Inc. The decree held the copyright valid and infringed. The Charel companies were also directed to pay Trifari $1000. Carlton Fishel, vice president of Trifari, said that while the settlement might appear small, the basic principle of the copyright law was achieved.

From that moment on the use of design patents, while not falling into complete disuse, dropped considerably, so much so that the copyright insured better protection at lower prices. In fact, in 1958, the cost of copyrights issued by the Copyright Office of the Library of Congress was $4 and copyrights were valid for twenty five years after which time they could be renewed by payment of the same fee again.

From 1955, the copyright symbol © appears next to the mark on the items of the producers, which allows for dating the items after that year if they are stamped with this symbol. This means we can be certain that articles marked for example ©Trifari, ©Boucher etc., were produced after 1955.

4

MARKS AND TRADEMARKS

A distinction should be made between the names, hallmarks, symbols, *etc.* actually marked on jewels, and the names, words, symbols, slogans, *etc.* patented as trademarks by the USA Patent and Trademark Office. It is an important distinction because, more often than not, what a manufacturer stamped on the jewelry as his mark of distinction (usually the company name or an acronym) was not a registered trademark and, vice versa, most, if not all registered trademarks of a given company, never appeared on the actual jewelry, but were used instead for the packaging, labels, billboards, or other material exhibited on shops and store counters, and, above all, in press advertisements.

Besides, it was common practice to register a trademark covering the whole range of products of a firm, *i.e.* not only jewelry (brooches, necklaces, bracelets, rings, *etc.*), but also combs, compacts, cuff-links, and tie-pins, although it was not necessarily used for all products.

Evidence of this terminological confusion is apparent already in the first edition of Maryanne Dolan's book, *Rhinestone Jewelry*, which includes – as it states on the cover – "a comprehensive section on designers' marks," where hundreds of marks are listed in alphabetical order, if rather haphazardly, with the result that the reader could confuse an item with a designer's mark, and many famous marks actually stamped on the items are not mentioned at all. It is true that, before supplying this list, the author warns that most costume jewelry was unmarked and that several marks appeared on labels or similar items. However, the confusion remains and the list is practically unusable, unless one can add information from another source, as will be seen later on.

An improvement is represented by the section entitled "I produttori e i loro marchi" (Manufacturers and their marks) in the volume entitled *I Gioielli della Fantasia (Jewels of Fantasy)* (page 210-221), where the marks actually stamped on the jewels are reported. In addition, the author indicates whether the marks correspond to the registered trademarks or not. However, even in this case, the author starts enumerating other trademarks that were never stamped on the actual jewels, such as, for example, "*De Rosa Designed* JEWELS," "Black Magic" by Elzac, "Courtly Jewels" by Leo Glass, and "Jewels by *Trifari*" by Trifari.

In any case, it is always advisable to mention what is, or, in the case of several marks, what are the marks actually stamped on the pieces. Any other trademarks registered by a company (sometimes hundreds of them, as in Coro's case) are useful if they allow us to trace – through newspaper advertisements or articles in the specialized press – the pieces they refer to. In this case the trademarks are useful tools that allow us to date the jewels and to know the names the manufacturers had given them.

A brief review may help explain these concepts.

The firm Marcel Boucher registered all the marks stamped on their jewels beginning with the famous MB topped by a Phrygian cap (because *it is* a Phrygian cap – the symbol of France and hence of Boucher's origins – and not, as sometimes surmised, a stylized bird's head – hawk, cock, eagle, *etc.*) that was used from the start to the end of the period being dealt with in this book. On the other hand, the names of other pieces such as "Columbine," "Punchinello," or "Cambodian" (1940), or of whole collections such as "Ballet of Jewels" or "Carnival" (1949) were never registered as trademarks. It is an interesting fact that, right from the start (1937), the firm used the registered trademark "Marboux" which, in the period being investigated, was used as the firm's telegram address.

As far back as 1938 Hattie Carnegie had registered a trademark reproducing her signature. This trademark appeared on advertisements, while, in that same period and for many years afterwards (probably until the first half of the 40s), the mark stamped on the jewels consisted of the letters HC inscribed in a lozenge, which was never registered as a trademark.

Cohn & Rosenberger, better known as Coro, registered all the marks stamped on their jewels and also, as already mentioned, scores of trademarks. Just a few examples are given here since, later on, an important section of this book is dedicated to Coro, whose production will be examined in detail. For instance, it may be surprising to know that there is no "Russian Antique" trademark, the famous line created in the second half of the 20s, which was still mentioned as a must by its creator, Royal Marcher, as late as 1948. Vice versa, there is evidence to confirm what has previously been stated: the trademark "Thorobreds," registered in June 1942 to cover the entire range of products, has actually little meaning and could refer to any one of the many Coro pieces representing horses, or even to other items that have little or nothing to do with jewels. However, in an advertisement that appeared in *Harper's Bazaar* in December 1943, "Thorobreds" was used with explicit reference to one of the best known Coro Duettes, the

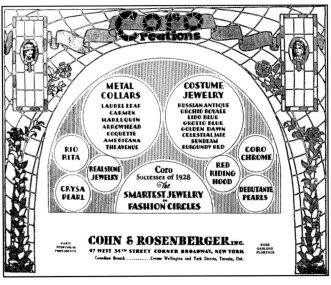

WWD, December 12, 1928: Coro's Trademarks.

one reproducing two horse heads. Therefore this item can be called Duette "Thorobreds" with absolute certainty.

The mark "R. De Rosa" with the addition, whenever it was the case, of "Sterling," that appears on the jewels of this firm, was never registered, while the above reported registered trademark appeared in the advertisements published, for example, in *Vogue*.

The most famous mark of the jewels by Eisenberg, i.e. "Eisenberg Original," which, as stated by the firm in an advertisement appearing in the *Vogue* issue of

November 1st 1941, was stamped on each item identifying it as an "original" Eisenberg item, had never been registered. On the other hand, the trademark "Eisenberg Ice," used for advertising purposes since 1941 (*Harper's Bazaar*, December 1941) and registered in 1945, was never actually stamped on the jewels dating from the years being reviewed (1935-1950).

The Leo Glass mark, the only one stamped on the jewelry, was never registered as a trademark, similarly to the marks of the Haskell jewels manufactured in the years 1935-1950.

Several marks have been attributed to Hobé from 1868 to date, however the only mark actually stamped on jewels dating from 1935-50 is "Hobé," which was registered as late as 1948.

The mark "Joseff Hollywood" written in block letters that appeared on the oldest jewels by Joseff of Hollywood Inc. was not a registered trademark, whereas the mark reproducing the designer's signature, though registered as late as 1947, had been in use since 1938 for the retail sale lines.

The marks "Mazer" and "Mazer Bros." that were stamped on the items of this company in the period considered in this book, were not registered, whereas a signature mark with a lily above the letter "M" was registered in 1949, but used only for advertising purposes.

The marks stamped on Monet's jewels are all registered trademarks, although there are other trademarks referring to the same items, which were never actually stamped on them. Napier's marks were registered trademarks, but Napier was also the holder of other registered trademarks such as "Naco," the trademark of a particular metal lacquering method that made the jewels rust- and wear-resistant (1933).

In the period being reviewed, the Pennino mark was not registered, whereas the designs of the zodiac signs had been registered as trademarks for the same company (Pennino Brothers).

Nettie Rosenstein never registered either jewelry marks or any other marks.

Réja Inc. registered both its previous trademark "Déja," and the trademark "Réja" that was stamped used for the launch of sterling jewels with opal rose cabochons, such as those appearing in the above mentioned *Vogue* advertisements: a set including a necklace, a brooch and earrings. In the same year, the trademark "Jack in the Box" (also separately advertised with this name) and the brooch in the shape of a hobby horse, named most appropriately "Hobby Horse" were also registered. Also in 1946 the trademark "Artistry in Jewels" used for the Fall collections, was registered. The name "Africana by Réja" used to advertise (*see Harper's Bazaar* February 1946) the three sterling African masks with black enamel faces, the only design, in addition to the "Jack in the Box," to be patented by Solomon Finkelstein for his company, was never registered. A fourth African mask, also in sterling and black enamel, called "Congo Belle" completed the series.

The "Sandor" mark, stamped on the jewels manufactured by the firm Sandor Golberger Inc., is not a registered trademark. Whereas the trademark "Regimental Crests" of 1939 was registered for the same manufacturer. An article accompanied by a picture published in *Women's Wear Daily* of February 8th, 1939, describes brooches, bracelets and medallions with military subjects.

Trifari, on the other hand, registered all their marks. The initials "KTF" were used from the start (1935), with the T for Trifari slightly higher than the other two letters (for Krussman and Fishel), as well as the later mark, "Trifari" with a small crown over the T (1938), which remained in use until the end of the period being reviewed and thereafter. The trademark "Jewels by Trifari" registered in 1938 was the one most often used for advertising purposes. Trifari also registered other trademarks especially before and after the period being considered.

From this brief summary another general conclusion can be drawn: the marks stamped on the jewelry, even when they changed in the course of the history of a jewelry manufacturer, are not in themselves decisive elements for the dating of items, unless the dates are known with certainty of the start of the use of a given mark and the start of

the use of the successive mark. In this case we know at least in which period a piece was manufactured. Such periods can be short or long. For example, a Trifari piece marked "KTF," if there are no other elements hinting at its date of production, may have been manufactured between 1925 and 1937, i.e. a period spanning 12 years. In the case where a patent or other material from the same period is lacking, it is possible to narrow down the search for a more precise date by looking at the stylistic and material characteristics of the jewel in question. However, it is, nonetheless, practically impossible to indicate a precise year.

5

MATERIALS AND TECHNIQUES

In this section very intricate, technical explanations will not be made but a few indications will be given on the subject that could be useful for a correct identification of the items.

1. *Metals*

In the period under review and for the most valuable pieces, the following metals were used:

a) 1935 – first half of 1942. Metal alloys with a prevalence of copper, tin, zinc, and nickel, such as white metal (75% copper, 25% nickel) and pewter or Britannia metal (tin, lead, antimonium with a small added quantity of silver or copper).

b) Second half of 1942 – 1947. Even before the actual participation of the USA in the war, there had been a rationing of strategic materials (shortage), including the base metals used in alloys, and, in particular, copper, which was essential for the manufacturing of cartridges. With the official entry of the US in the war, on December 7th, 1941, prohibition of the use of base metals became practically complete and, at the same time, the plants engaged in the manufacturing of costume jewelry were largely used for the production of war materials, such as cartridge cases or weapon components. Lead and silver were part of non-prohibited metals, and for this reason most companies started using silver for their quality production. Silver had also been used in previous years, but only sporadically and in small quantities compared with other metal alloys. The actual date on which this new fashion began, coincides with March 20th 1942, when an article appeared in *Women's Wear Daily* stating that companies "have just started presenting some small lines of sterling silver jewels [...] that are not much more expensive than their metal counterparts [...] also in the 'novelties' sector, since sterling silver can be used in finer ways than white metal."

Soon after silver became the only metal used for the more expensive lines and was also largely used for the manufacture of cheaper items. The first company to convert to silver for their Corocraft line were Coro, which publicized this in a whole-page ad in *Women's Wear Daily* of May 22nd, 1942, where they claimed to have "met the challenge" for their fall collection. Trifari followed, beginning in the fall of 1942, and soon other companies followed suit.

Sterling silver is an alloy used in English-speaking countries which is made up of 92.5% silver and 7.5% copper. Each silver piece, regardless of whether or not it bears the manufacturer's trademark, should bear the sterling hallmark, then as now. The use of sterling also continued massively after the end of the war, until the end of 1947. During the war, use of sterling silver was subjected to the decisions of the War Production Board which decided what quantities should be put at the manufacturers' disposal.

However, it should be noted that in 1946 there were great difficulties in purchasing sterling, due to the liberalization of the sale of metals and the ensuing market adjustment. This accounts for the presence of metal jewels in the production of companies that in the following years favored the use of sterling silver.

From the second half of 1947, with the creation of new metal alloys, the use of silver gradually decreased, until it finally disappeared in 1950, mainly due to its cost. Partial exceptions to this trend were Monet and Nettie Rosenstein, who continued to produce a significant number of silver lines throughout the first half of the 1950s. As far as we know, Coro made no sterling pieces after 1948. Trifari made an exception for its 25th anniversary with the production of a few sterling pieces. The last known sterling jewelry made by Trifari dates from 1952. Sterling made a comeback at the beginning of the 1950s. This revival was a direct consequence of the Korean war (1950-1953), during which base metals were again rationed, though not so strictly as during WWII.

c) Second half of 1947 – 1950 and later. During this time metal alloys made their comeback. They were basically made of the usual components, though in the meantime the composition had been greatly improved. A perfect example is offered by the so-called Trifanium or Golden Trifanium. This was a new alloy created by Gustavo Trifari, which was presented by the firm during the third week of July 1947, at the same time as the presentation of their summer-fall collection. Though its composition had not been revealed, the firm maintained that it was as suitable for gold plating as sterling, from which it differed only for its lower cost (*WWD* July 18th, 1947). Its name is a compound word in which "Tri" stands for Trifari, "fa" for "famous" and "nium" is the usual English suffix for metals (*WWD*, December 30th, 1947).

2. Other Materials

Apart from metal, many other materials were used for the production of costume jewelry, especially during the war for the above mentioned reasons. Ceramic, wood, leather, plastic, and even fabrics, among others, used alone or in combination, sometimes with the addition of enamel, rhinestones and other imitation stones.

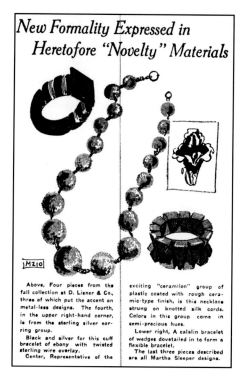

New Formality Expressed in Heretofore "Novelty" Materials

Above, Four pieces from the fall collection at D. Lisner & Co., three of which put the accent on metal-less designs. The fourth, in the upper right-hand corner, is from the sterling silver earring group.

Black and silver for this cuff bracelet of ebony with twisted sterling wire overlay.

Center, Representative of the exciting "ceramilon" group of plastic coated with rough ceramic-type finish, is this necklace strung on knotted silk cords. Colors in this group come in semi-precious hues.

Lower right, A calalin bracelet of wedges dovetailed in to form a flexible bracelet.

The last three pieces described are all Martha Sleeper designs.

WWD, June 19, 1942: Wartime alternative materials. Jewelry by D. Lisner & Co.

3. *Fake Stones and Imitation Pearls*

Almost all metal jewelry manufactured in the period under review, except for the small production of so-called tailored jewelry that was made of metal only, was ornamented with fake stones and/or imitation pearls or glass beads. Among fake stones the most widely used, with a pavé arrangement (i.e., where the stones are fixed to the jewel surface in such close proximity that they form a sort of carpet that totally hides the metal underneath) or to emphasize the contours or other details of the jewels, were "rhinestones" (known in Europe as "strass"). These were diamond-imitation crystals whose name "Rhine stones" derives from the German word "Rheinkiesel" with the same meaning. The crystals used to make rhinestones had the characteristic diamond cut and an extremely thin metal sheet (a mixture of mercury and tin) applied to the back in order to emphasize their glitter. The term is sometimes incorrectly used to describe other small non-precious stones; however, in that case, it is more correct to speak of glass or synthetic stones.

Glass or synthetic stones imitate in color and cut all precious or semi-precious stones used in "real" jewelry: rubies, emeralds, sapphires, quartz, amethyst, rock crystal, opal, onyx, aquamarine, alexandrite, topazes, and moonstones to mention just the most frequent imitations. Other frequently imitated stones and materials were coral, jade, garnet, mother of pearl, lapis lazuli, and turquoise. These imitations ranged in size from the very tiny to the extremely large.

Imitation pearls are glass beads covered with a special substance called pearl essence or essence d'Orient (a mixture of compounds derived from fish scales, cellulose, acrylic resins) that makes them look like real pearls. Naturally the final result depends on the purity of the essence and the number of layers applied.

Rhinestones and other synthetic stones were almost totally imported from Austria, Czechoslovakia, and France. At the outbreak of war in Europe in 1939, imports to the USA began to decrease, following the Nazi invasion of those countries, until they stopped almost completely when the United States entered into the conflict. As in the case of metals, costume jewelry manufacturers had to find alternatives, on the one hand by economizing on their rhinestone stock, on the other by trying, rather unsuccessfully, to become rhinestone producers themselves. However, technology and over a century of experience gave European manufacturers a great advantage over their American counterparts. In fact, the American products could not compete with European rhinestones.

Better results were obtained in the domestic production of synthetic stones, especially the larger ones. Often jewelry was practically built around a stone. Since jewelry at the time was made of sterling, the use of large stones offered the additional advantage of allowing to save on the amount of sterling used.

A peculiar characteristic of the war years was the use of large rock-crystal imitation Lucite cabochons that were used as the center of – mostly – animal-shaped brooches. These jewels are dealt with in greater detail in the section dedicated to jelly bellies (found in Volume 2).

After the war the import of stones resumed vigorously, but the use of Lucite and imitation pearls continued or, as in the case of pearls, even increased.

Stones and pearls were set in the jewelry mainly in two ways, that were contextually used in the various parts of the jewelry: prong setting, i.e. the mounting of the stones or pearls in settings fitted with prongs that were hammered on the stone to keep it in place (in the prong setting of large stones or Lucite cabochons, the prongs are directly connected to the metal piece); gluing, a technique used especially for the mounting of small stones, consisted of fixing the stones to the base of the setting with glue; it was important to use the right amount of glue in order to preserve the stone light and glitter. The same techniques were used for the setting of pearls.

A special type of setting deserves a special mention. "Invisible setting" was invented by Van Cleef & Arpels for precious jewels. This technique was imitated by Philippe for Trifari already in 1937. In this type of setting each stone is individually mounted, however the metal framework remains invisible. The wall-to-wall effect obtained completely obliterates the setting from view and gives the impression of a larger single stone. The use of a great number of types of glass beads in all sorts of pieces, especially necklaces should be mentioned.

In the period being considered, the setting of stones was done completely by hand, by highly specialized craftsmen who were sometimes identified, for in-house purposes, by a number or a letter stamped on the jewel.

4. *Manufacturing techniques*

There are basically two methods for the manufacture of costume jewelry: casting and stamping.

a) Lost wax casting is the method used for the manufacture of the most valuable pieces, since it allows for the use of finer designs and textures, and the resulting jewels are heavier, more compact and three-dimensional.

The designer makes a detailed drawing of the jewel, including the stones, enamel, and whatever else is a part of it. Then, the drawing is passed to the model maker, usually a specialized goldsmith who makes a detailed metal (silver, white metal) model of the jewel. The model is somewhat larger than the finished item, to make up for the loss of volume occurring in the course of manufacturing. The model is used by the mold maker to make a

vulcanized rubber mold, obtained by coating the metal jewel with raw rubber which is then vulcanized (heated under pressure at about 150°C for 45 minutes), and cut in half, thus obtaining a positive and negative mold of the jewel. The mold is injected with liquefied wax. When the wax has hardened, the half of the mold that is easier to take off, is removed and the wax model is extracted from the mold. This procedure is repeated as many times as the number of pieces to be produced. Then the wax models are coated with an investment made of plaster mixed with water. When the plaster has hardened, it is slowly heated so that the wax melts and flows out ("is lost") and the shape remains impressed in reverse in the two cavities of what has become a heat resistant ceramic mold. Finally, the metal is poured into the mold.

Another, less costly, casting technique, which was rather popular in the 1930s and until the beginning of the 1940s, is sand casting. In this technique, the side of a hand-engraved model is pressed into a box completely filled with slightly damp sand. When the sand has dried, the model is taken out and pressed on the other side into another sand box. Then, a groove is dug into each sandbox from the top of the box to the impression left by the model. The two boxes are joined together and the molten metal is poured inside from a hole in the box. Running along the groove, the metal fills the two halves of the model impression in the sand. When the metal has dried, the two boxes are unhinged and the piece is extracted and cleaned, polished, and sometimes filed to leave the margins raw. The metal at the back of pieces made with this technique is granulose, and often presents a rather raw appearance.

b) Stamping is mainly used for the production of large quantities of low cost pieces. In this process the drawing is given to a sample maker who manually crafts a sample of the jewelry and then passes it to the tool maker who prepares the steel stamps. These "positive" matrixes are then pressed into a soft steel block that represents the negative matrix. Stamping is carried out by presses in which the positive matrix is fixed to the hammer, while the negative matrix is fixed to the press bench. Metal sheet ribbons are continuously fed to the press. Whenever the press hammer is lowered onto the metal sheet, the metal is compressed between the two matrices and the jewelry is stamped. This technique allows for the rapid manufacture of hundreds of thousands of pieces with the most disparate shapes. However, the pieces are "flatter," lighter, and less elaborate than the cast jewels and the difference is visible even to an inexpert eye.

The finishing of the pieces, regardless of the manufacturing technique used, was basically the same, though, often, in the case of stamped pieces, it was less accurate.

First of all the surface of the pieces was accurately polished. This operation was carried out by hand on cast pieces, while, in the case of stamped items, it often consisted of stirring them inside barrels full of water and steel particles. Then, the items were "invested" i.e. coated with a layer of another metal for protection and/or decoration. The method habitually used was electroplating, i.e. the coating with metal by electrolysis. The pieces were coated with a layer of copper, then one of nickel (nickel plating) or chromium (chromium plating) and finally with a precious metal layer. In the case of costume jewelry this metal was usually rhodium (a grey-whitish metal of the platinum group), in which case the coating was a glossy silver color (period 1935-1942, when rhodium was also rationed); or gold (especially from 1942 onwards), and, rarely, silver.

When gold was used, the items were said to be gilded if the gold layer was thinner than 0.000007 inch, and gold-clad if the layer was thicker. In this case the gold titer was never less than 10 carat. A typical example is the sterling items by Hobé, in particular those manufactured between 1942 and 1947, in which a small plate at the back of the items indicated that they had a 14 carat gold cladding. The gilding or gold cladding of the first half of the 1940s, especially of sterling items, was made of pink or yellow gold and was more delicate and shaded, and generally less yellow than that made after the war, from the second half of 1947, on a base made of the new metal alloys. An exception was represented by the gold plating of Trifari's jewels made of the alloy called Golden Trifanium which, though different from the sterling items by the same manufacturer, was outwardly very similar.

Plating had not only a decorative function, but also a protective one. In particular it would preserve the jewels from scratches and rust and the manufacturers constantly strove to improve these characteristics.

Then, the items could be enameled in several bright colors and actually, the presence of enamel, independently of the metal and plating of the jewels, was almost the norm, not only for novelty brooches, from the beginning of the period under review to 1946, with several revivals afterwards. The enamel was applied by hand and fused under very high temperatures.

The successive operation was the setting or gluing of stones, as previously described.

During the last manufacturing step, the missing components, such as pins, springs, clips, brooch and bracelet fastenings, etc. were assembled. Often these components were supplied by specialized manufacturers, sometimes with the patent number already stamped on the back. This means that items from the same manufacturer were used by different companies.

Finally, the items had to pass the inspection of quality control.

6

DATING AND ATTRIBUTION

The dating and attribution of jewelry are of fundamental importance both for a scientifically reliable treatise on costume jewelry, and for the collector. It is obviously important to know with certainty the name of the designer and the manufacturer as well as the manufacturing date of a given item. Often the attribution of a piece of jewelry is a complex, sometimes insoluble issue, while the dating is approximate at best. However, it is less complex than it seems or is claimed to be, provided extensive research is willingly undertaken.

The right way to do this was indicated by Deanna Farneti Cera in the section "Il lusso della libertà e la libertà del lusso" (The luxury of freedom and the freedom of luxury) of which she is the author, in the book *I Gioielli della fantasia* (*Jewels of Fantasy*) which she edited. Farneti states (p. 155) that the best criterion for dating (and also, for attribution) is the one based on certain data, meaning "the patent number stamped on the main structure of the object (and not on one of the components welded to it, because this number might refer only to that component) or an advertisement or article in a magazine of that time." These are the foundations on which this research has been built:

• The study of all costume jewelry designs patented by the USA Trademark and Patent Office of Washington (USPTO) from 1928 to 1950 (about four thousand designs, including the most important patented mechanisms) with a few digressions, limited to the most significant designs, into 1954.

• The comprehensive study of the copyrights of costume jewelry designs filed with the USA Copyright Office of the Library of Congress of Washington (USCO) from 1928 to 1970. Copyrights were very scarce until 1950 and mainly held by Coro and Trifari. They became the norm beginning in 1955 after a decision in favor of Trifari which has been extensively dealt with in the section Patents and Copyrights.

• The comprehensive study of the weekly column "Costume Jewelry" published in *Women's Wear Daily* from 1925 to 1975.

• The comprehensive study of *Vogue America, Harper's Bazaar, The Jewelers' Circular Keystone, Mademoiselle, Town & Country, Life, Ladies' Home Journal, Glamour, Modern Plastic,* and of the Sears & Roebuck catalogs from 1935 to 1950.

• The perusal of all available books on the subject.

• The consultation of the main press articles of the time on costume jewelry.

• The constant surfing of the relevant eBay section and of websites dedicated to costume jewelry.

Our research proved very rewarding, since it allowed for the attribution and dating of a great number of pieces, some of which were totally anonymous, in addition to the near totality of the most valuable items. Some uncertainty is still present regarding some manufacturers, such as Miriam Haskell, who did not patent their designs and did not register any copyright, and also made a

relatively limited use of advertising in magazines and newspapers.

The results obtained are absolutely certain and allow collectors to reject such dubious methods as the so-called stylistic analysis which, in the field of industrial production, as in the case of costume jewelry, can be misleading and lead to wrong conclusions. For example, it is difficult to maintain the thesis according to which, in case of apparent contrast between the publication date of a non-precious jewelry and its style, the latter should prevail, since the manufacture of the jewelry could have taken place years after its conceptual creation. On the contrary, the rule is that an item was manufactured immediately after the realization of its design (patented or unpatented), since designs, which were always technical drawings, were made for production. What could happen was that, if an article did not achieve the expected success in the sampling phase, its production would be discontinued in order to concentrate on the more successful models.

If there is a patent, its date or, even better, the date of registration of the patent application, represents the most certain reference point.

It is not possible to object that the patent number stamped on an item could be misleading, since it could refer to the clip of a brooch or earrings or to the clasp of a necklace or bracelet, and the patents could have been granted years before the actual production of the pieces. This might be true for the patents on mechanisms (utility patents), but not for the patents covering the design (design patents). In the section on patents the difference between the two has been explained and an indication made of an empirical but safe indicator: utility patents are always made of seven figures, design patents of six. In addition, mechanisms do not change with the changing of fashion and therefore it is absolutely normal that a good mechanism, such as Coro's Duette, should remain in use for about twenty years as the support of the most disparate types of clips. The same applies to the clips of earrings or the clasps of necklaces and bracelets.

It could be argued that the most successful items could remain in production forever, since the molds can be used over long periods of time. Though containing a nugget of truth, such a position is also wrong, if taken literally, especially with regards to the period in consideration, i.e. between 1935 and 1950, and to cast jewels. First of all it should be borne in mind that costume jewelry is fashion-bound and therefore can not outlive the fashion for which it has been created. And indeed, costume jewelry manufacturers were used to producing two collections a year, a spring-summer and a fall-winter collection, to suit the fashion of the time not only in terms of shape and type of jewelry, but also in terms of colors of the stones. As a consequence, even successful items could not be manufactured for more than a few seasons, or years. Another convincing argument further supports the thesis regarding the period considered. As already stated, basically three types of metal were used for costume jewelry: white metal before the war, silver (or non-metal materials) during the war and up to the first half of 1947, and the new alloys, mainly gold-plated, from 1947 onwards. Now, if a piece manufactured before the war, had remained in production during the war, it should be possible to find two versions of the same item, one made of white metal and one made of sterling (as is the case with some pieces by Eisenberg), and this would allow to date precisely the two versions of the same jewel. Similarly, if a model had remained in production after the war, it would be possible to find sterling and metal versions of it. In both cases, however, if there is a patent or another reproduction of the time, it is correct to date the item with reference to the patent or reproduction, since, even if made of a different metal, if the model was unchanged, it would still resemble the original. In this case it is important to point out that the item remained in production or was reproduced after the change of metal, which means that the item in question had actually been manufactured after the new metal had been used in production.

A separate case is represented by the "remakes" after many years of a given item or series of successful items by the same manufacturer. Such remakes, though accurate, as in the case of Trifari, were still "reproductions" that had nothing in common with the actual original production, with which they cannot be mistaken, even at first glance.

Here are a few examples to clarify this concept: the famous Trifari crown, designed by Philippe and patented on 28th March 1944 with No. 137,542, was such a huge success at the time, that it appeared again in an article by Elsie McCormick in the *Saturday Evening Post* of 31st March 1947. In the article a statement by a Trifari manager is reported, according to whom, "if we had manufactured nothing else, but those crowns (meaning the above mentioned crown and its smaller or 'queen' version) in the last three years, we would still be processing the orders." Therefore, the crown remained in production with the same characteristics (sterling silver and large green, white, red, and blue cabochons) for three years. In this case it is not possible to establish whether the crowns with these characteristics, marked Trifari sterling des. pat. n. 137,542 were actually manufactured in 1944, 45, 46 or 47. However, the matter is irrelevant, since all crowns of this type can be dated 28th March 1944. Beginning in the second half of 1947 Trifari introduced the new alloy called Golden Trifanium: as a consequence the crowns made of Trifanium instead of sterling can be described as being the 1944 model, produced between 1947 and 1950. At the end of the 1980s and, precisely, in 1988, in the framework of its "Retro collection," Trifari manufactured a remake of the crown, which cannot possibly be mistaken for a period one, both for its characteristics (metal, gold-plating, stones), and because it correctly displays the date 1988 at the back.

The same applies to the famous "Hoots" Duette in which the large eyes of the owls are made of a single faceted stone, designed by Adolph Katz for Coro and patented on 3rd October 1944 with pat. No. 138,960. The same Katz, in the article by Irwin Ross entitled "Every Woman a Queen" and published in *American Magazine* of February 1948, refers to the brooch as one of his greatest successes. Also in this case, there is a sterling version of the brooch that can be correctly dated based on the 1944 patent, whereas the gold-plated metal version may be defined as a 1944 model, possibly manufactured in 1948, since Katz's reference to it was probably not a casual one.

However, these are exceptions that confirm the general rule, according to which most pieces remained in production for one or few seasons.

Recently, especially with reference to Adolph Katz and Florence Nathan of Fallon & Kappel, holder of some 1942 patents (which were the only ones granted to Eisenberg), doubts were raised as to whether the holder of the patent and the designer were actually one and the same person. Apart from the fact that, in this case, it would be almost impossible to discover the actual author of the designs, in the case of Katz (or Alfred Philippe) nobody ever maintained that he had actually designed the hundreds of designs patented for Coro in his name. Nevertheless Katz was responsible for the style of the jewels and he had the last word on each and every design. Moreover, in the above mentioned interview, Katz is described as "Coros' top designer and factory manager" and he described himself as being the author of many designs, among which the above mentioned "Hoots" and "Rockfish" of 1944 and there is no reason why he should have lied about that.

To give a modern example, nobody thinks that Giorgio Armani personally designs all the items bearing his trademark; however he is certainly responsible for the special style that makes an Armani a Giorgio Armani design, irrespective of whether or not it has been designed by someone else. The same applies to Adolph Katz and Alfred Philippe who employed dozens of in-house and free-lance designers and who were themselves designers and, personally chose the designs or had them changed by their collaborators, before using them for production. Therefore, due to lack of any other certain information, it would be correct to consider Adolph Katz or Alfred Philippe the authors of designs patented in their names. This also applies, more or less, to Florence Nathan, especially because at the time, Ruth Kamke, the main designer for Fallon & Kappel, was only seventeen (this subject is dealt with more extensively in the section on Eisenberg).

A rather unreliable source is what could be described as the "oral tradition," i.e. information on the older productions supplied by still active company representatives or former employees. In fact, archives that still exist, are often scarce and full of blanks and memory can be tricky, especially in the States where "ten years old" events rate as ancient history, and fifty years old events as prehistory

or "myth" to be told with the obligatory opening words: "once upon a time..."

Finally, for the keen observer, the fact that certain styles, Victorian, Egyptian, Renaissance, Art Deco, Art Nouveau, the so-called "Empress Eugenie" style (the name of Napoleon III's wife), and, in general, a "retro style," periodically return, even in the relatively short period under review, creates no uncertainty in dating, especially in the case of marked and/or patented pieces, and/or items reproduced in publications of the time.

But also in the case of completely anonymous pieces, only a total layman or someone trying to exploit the situation, could mistake a "Victorian" piece made in the 1940s, for one in the same style made, for example, in the 1920s. First of all, any "revivals" of style always imply a certain degree of adjustment to the current fashion; secondly, the metal, manufacture, stones, and design are manifestly different.

With this premise, it is possible to proceed with the dating and attribution of pieces in the following way:

a) An item bears the manufacturer's name and the design patent number. This is the case of most Trifari jewels from our period, of a few Coro and Boucher pieces, and of a few others. In such cases the riddle is easily solved, because the manufacturer's name is known and, through the patent number, it is possible to discover the designer's name and the dates of patent application and issuing. Thus the item is neatly dated and attributed. If, in addition, it is possible to find an advertisement or other publication of the time featuring the jewel, it is also possible to learn the name the manufacturer had given to the piece or collection.

b) An item bears the manufacturer's name and "pat. pend." (patent pending). Since there is no patent number (which can be found on pieces manufactured only after the granting of the patent), the dating of the piece can only be done approximately and then the item patiently compared with designs patented in that period. If the patent had been granted, it would be possible to find the corresponding design, and the procedure would be the same as that described in a), with the additional notation that the piece had been probably manufactured in the time between the patent application and the actual issuing of the patent. Sometimes however, no patent follows, either because the design did not possess the originality features required, or, more frequently, because it had not fared well in the sample sales, leading the manufacturer or designer to withdraw his application.

In this case it will be difficult to identify the designer or the date with certainty, unless the latter can be found in a period publication (it is highly improbable that the designer's name would appear in advertisements or specialized press articles).

c) An item bears only the manufacturer's name. Again, in this case, the item might have been manufactured on the basis of a patented design. This was the case with some famous pieces by Trifari (such as the greyhound and the stork fishing in a pond made from a single large stone), most Coro items, several Boucher items, the only four patents of Réja, and others. In this case, after approximately fixing the date, the procedure is as described in b).

d) An item bears no manufacturer's trademark, but it exhibits a "pat. pend." marking or a design patent number. In this case the procedure to follow is as in a) and b). Two possibilities are likely: after finding the patent, the designer's name and the manufacturing date will be definitely known. However, if the designer is not the assignor of the patent on behalf of the company indicated in the patent, it will be impossible to find the manufacturer, unless other period documentation containing this information is uncovered.

e) A jewel bears no marking at all. Also in this case, it cannot be excluded that the design is covered by a patent. Therefore the procedure to follow is as in a), b) and d).

f) A jewel bears no marking, there is no patent covering the design and no other documentation is available. In this case, it may be possible to attempt to date the item based on its characteristics. Any attribution to a given designer and/or manufacturer

on the basis of "stylistic" criteria is absolutely unreliable and therefore the item must be correctly classified as being of unknown manufacturer and designer. This does not mean that unidentifiable pieces cannot be of high quality both in design and manufacture.

It has already been established how many manufacturers and professional as well as amateur designers were active at the time, both as employees or freelancers. Many of these companies were "specialists" at copying the models of the most famous and successful manufacturers, since it was easy to avoid the infringement of patents and trademarks by means of small, clever changes to the design and even to the trademark. Indeed, some companies manufacturing costume jewelry on behalf of third parties, marketed the items made for their more famous counterparts without the trademark.

At the time there was already an ongoing discussion on the subject of "style piracy," and in March 1939 Trifari, with Leo Krussman, tried to establish an association against copycat. The project participants were representatives of the costume jewelry elite. In addition to Trifari, represented by Krussman and Fishel, there were Harry Levy of Ben Felsenthal Co, Michael Cernow of Monet Jewelers, Saul Ganz of D. Lisner & Co, M. Rosenblum of Albert Manufacturing Co., Leo Glass of Leo Glass & Co., Carl Rosenberger of Cohn & Rosenberger. Other participants in the meeting, though on the fringes of this meeting, were B.J. Foster of Bowman, Foster & Wurzburger, Irwing Ciner, of Ciner Manufacturing Co., Clifford Furst of Castlecliff, Marcel Boucher and Arthur T. Halberstadt of Marcel Boucher Ltd., Joseph Mazer of Mazer Bros., Ralph De Rosa of Ralph De Rosa, Sol Weinreich of Weinreich Bros., Jules Hirsch and Jacques H. Leff of Du Jay Inc., and Jules Schwab of Jules Schwab & Co. In a word, the upper crust of the industry were present. However, after the initial enthusiasm, in the following years no trace of the association can be found and it petered out, if it was ever really established, on account of the war. However, the effort was not insignificant.

An opportunity is being taken here to firmly reject an observation frequently made concerning unidentifiable pieces that are attributed to this or that famous manufacturer or designer, without any real evidence at all. "They did not always sign…"

In the world of costume jewelry, the use of the word "signature," as in the contemporary world of fashion, is wrong and misleading. Here, there is no reference to signatures, but to trademarks, often registered, stamped on the items to protect the manufacturer more than the customer. If there is no trademark or any other identification marking on a jewel that seems to belong to a manufacturer used to mark his pieces, the only hypothesis, in the presence of evidence confirming the attribution, is that it is a rare case of a punching mistake.

Or it is a piece belonging to a set in which only one of the pieces was marked. The manufacturers who used labels instead of markings, cannot be identified for lack of reliable documentary evidence. Whereas a piece marked "differently" from a similar one by a famous manufacturer and/or designer, probably is one of the period copies about which we have already talked. For example, there are several period copies of the wonderful bird by Boucher, which was patented on 7th October 1941 with No. 129,843 (B21.), some of which were unmarked whiles others were marked Reinad.

7

CINEMA, THEATER AND COSTUME JEWELRY

Definitions such as "Hollywood jewels" or "stars' jewels," etc., establishing a very tight connection between costume jewelry and showbiz, especially the cinema, are misleading.

In fact, almost all companies made jewels for the cinema or the revue; however only Eugene Joseff made his products initially exclusively and afterwards almost entirely for the cinema. In 1938, i.e. three years after establishing his firm, he had started an important commercial production partly consisting of reproductions on a smaller scale of designs made for the screen and partly based on new designs (it should be borne in mind that the jewels made for the screen had to be particularly large to be well visible). This subject is analyzed in greater depth in the section dedicated to Joseff. For the time being, suffice it to say that most jewels initially made by Joseff for the cinema, were used in costume movies and were therefore unsuitable for use in daily life by the average American woman. Otherwise the relationship between real life and life on the screen was totally reversed, meaning that actresses playing the main roles in comedies, musicals, and gangster movies, i.e. contemporary characters, often wore the same costume jewelry worn by women in real life: for example the jewels (probably made mostly by Eisenberg) worn by the leading stars in "The Women" by George Cukor (1939).

Judging from an article in the *Saturday Evening Post*, "Merchants of Glitter" by Elsie McCormick of 31st May 1947, costume jewelry manufacturers, though aware of the publicity given to their products by their use in movies, to the point that they sometimes showcased their collections in the movie houses where films were presented (this is the case with Coro's "Carnegie Jewelry" collection of 1947), nonetheless feared the negative effects of close-ups in which the jewels sometimes looked like neon lights because of bright lighting. For this reason Joseff's stage jewels were made of matte metal, which was also used for the manufacture of jewels for retail sale.

Thus, it was real life that inspired the cinema and not vice versa, although the cinema undoubtedly influenced the habits and customs of the population.

The relationship between cinema and real life should be examined in individual cases, without hazarding general statements. The jewelry made by Trifari for the Broadway musical *Roberta* (1933), due to the wishes of Carl Fishel, one of the company partners, deserves a special mention, because it was the first time that the name of jewelry appeared in the program of the show.

Slightly different, but of equal importance, was the case of jewelry more or less freely inspired by successful movies and usually manufactured by license from the producers. Many of these items bear the copyright symbol much prior to its widest diffusion. In this case copyright did not cover the design, but was referred to the purchase of the rights for the reproduction and use of names (usually the movie title). The production of such firms as Coro, Trifari, Albert Manufacturing, Rice-Weiner, Wertheimer, and Mazer are analyzed in the relevant sections or in the jewelry monographs.

Harper's Bazaar, October 1947: Mazer jewelry inspired by the film "The Swordman".

Within this framework, a little known manufacturer, whose products are rarely seen, should be mentioned: Ricarde of Hollywood.

Ricarde of Hollywood was the trademark and also the marking of the jewelry made by Hollywood Jewelry Products Inc. 6636 Hollywood Boulevard Hollywood, California.

In 1939, according to the articles, advertisements and pictures published in *WWD* on 3rd February, 3rd March, 21st July, 4th and 11th August, respectively, the firm made jewelry inspired by the films "Juarez" and "Gone with the Wind," both presented in that same year.

In "Juarez," Bette Davis, who played the role of Carlotta, emperor Maximilian's unlucky wife, wore 17 different sets of jewelry designed by Orry Kelly, the movie costume-maker. The jewelry was inspired by the real jewelry of the empress, which were kept in Mexico City. Based on this source of inspiration, and with Kelly's approval, five sets, each composed of six pieces, were made: "The Empress Carlotta," "The Maximilian," "The Phantom Crown," "The Miramon" ("Il Miramare"), and "The Hapsburg."

From "Gone with the Wind," whose jewelry had been designed by Walter Plunkett and manufactured by Joseff, five sets, each composed of six pieces, were derived: "The Melanie," "The Scarlett," "The Sue Ellen," "The Tara," and "The Robilard" (Scarlett's mother's name). Two brooches were called "The Twelve Oaks."

The jewelry designer and owner of the firm was Richard C. Baxt, a jeweler's son who had been working for thirty years, signing his pieces "Ricarde of Hollywood."

After these two achievements no further information about the firm is available, due to a possible cessation in its activity or because it was used for other purposes during the war.

WWD, July 21, 1939: "Gone With The Wind Jewelry" by Ricarde of Hollywood.

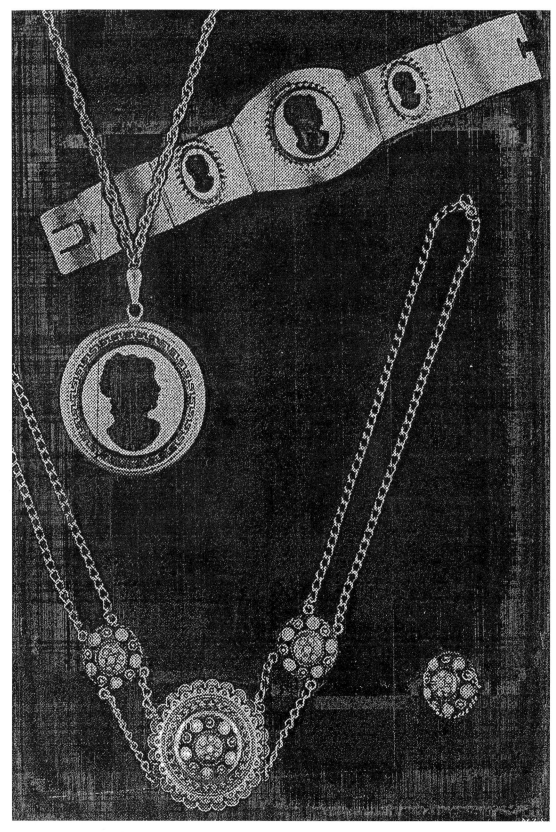

WWD, August 11, 1939: Period Jewelry From the Film "Gone With The Wind" by Ricarde of Hollywood.

8

FASHION AND COSTUME
JEWELRY

Fashion is an expression of the social, economic, and political environment and follows, or often anticipates, changes in taste and lifestyle. Women have always dressed and adorned themselves according to their way of life and social status.

Costume jewelry is a fashion product. In fact it was created as a complement to clothing collections. This is the reason why costume jewelry manufacturers made two collections a year: a spring-summer and a fall-winter collection, whose items harmonized with the lines and colors of clothes. Fashion in clothes (models, necklines, fabrics) also determined what type of jewelry would be more successful in a given season. The same applied to fur coats and coats that were ornamented with large brooches and clips (fur clips), and to hats.

Thus the simple, rigorous shapes of the 1920s called for long necklaces and earrings, the soft and flowing shapes of the 1930s were ideal for clips and large bracelets, whereas the more structured clothes that appeared at the end of the 1930s and, with few changes remained fashionable until 1947 or rather, until 1948, were mainly adorned with brooches. Bracelets became important items in summer, when the wrists were left bare, or with evening dresses, or over the tight-fitting long sleeves of chic dresses.

Also the occasion for which jewels were worn was important. Therefore the manufacturers of costume jewelry created different models for daytime wear and for evening wear, and often the same model was made in two versions, a gold-plated or enameled day version and a rhodium-plated and rhinestone version for the evening.

A frequently used definition was "tailored jewelry" that indicated gold-plated metal or sterling jewelry without stones or rhinestones, which was perfect for formal day dresses. This kind of jewelry was featured in the collections of all manufacturers who regularly introduced it in their collections together with the richer lines with enamel motifs, large colored stones, and rhinestones. Only Napier and Monet always prioritized tailored jewelry, making it their signature production, even though such jewelry was sometimes banal. In the costume jewelry industry a major role was played by sports jewels (made of Bakelite, plastic, wood or ceramic), teen jewels, and, in particular, the so-called "novelty pins," which signaled a moving away from traditional classic subjects to the exploiting of an element of novelty. This might mean featuring a curious or funny motif, or mobile components with a trembling effect, or subjects inspired by contemporary events (topical jewelry) and similar items. Of all these lines, the latter produced the best creative items.

A common imperative in fashion and costume jewelry was the need to constantly present the public with new collections, thus achieving large sales volumes. It should not be forgotten that costume jewelry, like clothing, is an industrial product aimed at "emotional consumption," i.e. a desire to purchase beautiful objects that nobody else has. In order to sustain this kind of consumption, it is indispensable to pay attention to the public's taste and constant changes in mood and fashion trends.

Every season costume jewelry manufacturers strove to design new models, made of different materials or material combinations. In this respect *Women's Wear Daily* is a precious source of information, since it regularly published articles commenting on the presentation of new collections, and on the new trends. For example, if the previous season had seen a predominance of flowery motifs, and an abundance of rhinestones, the following season would feature two-tone, gold-plated jewelry or colorful enamel etc.

More important still were the fashion trends, in terms of shapes, materials, and colors of the jewelry, that at a given time found favor with the public, and were consequently adopted by all manufacturers. An example is the size of brooches: in 1938-39 small flat brooches were very fashionable, in 1940 exaggeratedly large, three-dimensional brooches were all the rage, in 1943 large and massive ones, while in 1945-46 there was a revival of small brooches and all manufacturers followed the prevailing trend.

This means that it is impossible to identify the production of a given firm or designer based on precise features that remained unchanged in time. An analysis of Boucher's 1940 production shows that it had little in common with its 1950 production. Similarly, the Du Jay dating from 1935 was characterized by a pavé of minute rhinestones and a large cabochon, while the 1937 collection played on contrasts (between small and large, simple and elaborate), and in 1939 Du Jay presented small figurative enamel brooches practically without any rhinestones, and so on. What remained constant throughout the years was a certain "family feel" created by the designer, whose personal interpretation of the various trends always came through, and by the distinctive manufacturing technique used by the firm. An exception to this rule was sometimes made by Eisenberg, Hobé, and Joseff. Eisenberg always maintained his characteristic use of large crystals entirely covering the jewelry, while changing his figurative subjects. Hobé always remained faithful to the inspiration gained from antique jewelry of which he was a collector, and, finally, Joseff never tired of the exaggerated Hollywood style for which he was famous.

The evolution of costume jewelry always went hand in hand with fashion, where fashion means both haute couture, which dictated the current trends, and ready-to-wear fashion that adjusted these trends to everyday life and to the more modest means of ordinary people. In a way it was this close link between fashion and costume jewelry and the severance of the bond with European fashion during the war, that allowed American costume jewelry to flourish particularly during the war and post-war periods.

In the 1920s and 1930s, Paris was the world capital of fashion. French haute couture strongly influenced American haute couture, the clothing and accessory industry, and the tastes of American women of all social classes who indistinctly wanted to dress smartly a la Parisian style.

Department stores like Lord &Taylor and Bergdorf Goodman, which sold American high fashion using their own label without mentioning the designers' names, stressed their adherence to the dictates of Parisian fashion by suggesting that their creations came from France. Famous tailors like Hattie Carnegie and Nettie Rosenstein drew inspiration from Parisian fashion which they adjusted to the requirements of American women.

The ready-to-wear fashion industry copied Parisian models following two classical methods: either purchasing the designs that illustrated the latest trends in terms of shapes, colors, and fabrics; or directly copying the high fashion models and adjusting them to the requirements of industrial production. The new style launched by Coco Chanel and Jean Patou, characterized by comfortable, practical dresses with a soft line, often inspired by sports or work wear and made of "cheap" fabrics like jersey, or masculine fabrics like tweed, was easy to copy with its simple cut. Moreover, these clothes were cheap due to the small quantity of fabric required. Finally, it was a style perfectly suited to the requirements of both working women and elegant ladies.

In spite of the availability of ready-to-wear items, most medium-low class women still made their own clothes and the most widespread fashion magazines featured clothes that could be made at home, sometimes offering free patterns. In the United States, where

WWD, January 21, 1935: the fashion in the 1930s

many families lived far from the towns or cities, these magazines and mail order catalogues, like the famous Sears, Roebuck & Co. catalogue, were a precious source of information for women who wanted to dress in the latest fashion.

Hollywood followed the latest Paris fashion and sometimes movie costumes were ordered from the great French fashion designers. This practice was abandoned when thousands of feet of film had to be discarded, because Patou had suddenly lengthened hemlines, while the dresses worn in the movie were shorter. From then on, the studios started using their own fashion designers: Adrian, Travis Banton, Walter Plunkett (a friend of Eugene Joseff), and Royer and Edith Head, whose models were similar to the French ones, only more elaborate. Adrian designed a dress with puffed sleeves for Joan Crawford playing the part of Letty Linton in the movie of the same name (1932), a dress which was successfully copied by the clothing industry. This model marked Adrian's coronation as the inventor of padded shoulders even though Schiaparelli and Marcel Rochas had already presented them the year before.

Famous actresses often contributed to the diffusion of fashion trends, as was the case with the famous trench-coat and Basque beret worn by Greta Garbo. In the same way they played an important role in the diffusion of jewelry. However, while as far as clothes were concerned, the public copied those that most characterized an actor's appearance, in the case of jewelry, it was the kind used (brooch, bracelet, etc.) that caught the public's eye more than the actual design which could not be fully appreciated on-screen. Thus, the costume jewelry industry was happy if the Hollywood stars wore jewelry, and lots of it, because this promoted the sales of all costume jewelry, not only of the jewelry worn by movie stars. Famous Parisian fashion designers like Coco Chanel and Elsa Schiaparelli created costly costume jewelry to go with their clothes. This jewelry was aimed at their upper class customers who could afford to wear designer's fakes to go with their clothes and not as substitutes for real jewels.

The fashion of costume jewelry as an art expression and symbol of style began in the 1930s. Artists like Salvador Dalì, Jean Cocteau, Christian Berard, Jean Clement, and particularly Jean Schlumberger, the designer of extraordinary collections, particularly one dedicated to the circus (1938), worked for Schiaparelli. Some of them, particularly Jean Cocteau and Jean Clement, also worked with Chanel, while Etienne de Beaumont, a close collaborator of Chanel, went over to Schiaparelli after leaving Chanel. Paul Iribe, François Hugo, and Fulco Santostefano della Cerda, Duke of Verdura, all worked for Chanel.

Verdura was born in 1899 in Sicily, in Villa Niscemi, and collaborated with Chanel from 1927 to 1934 for whom he designed a famous metal and enamel bracelet ornamented with a Maltese cross set with colored stones. In 1934 he moved to New York where he began to design precious jewelry for Paul Flato, a famous New York-based jewelry designer and manufacturer. In 1939 he established his own company, Verdura Incorporated, with a shop on 712 Fifth Avenue. In the 40s Verdura's designs significantly influenced the work of costume jewelry designers who often drew inspiration from his creations, or even openly imitated them (see for example "Naiad" by Verdura and "Mermaid" by Eisenberg, E26.). Verdura continued to design precious jewelry until his death in 1978.

A less obvious, but equally important influence was Jean Schlumberger's (1907-1987). He had moved to New York in 1940 to design precious jewelry for his jeweler friend Nicolas Bongard. When Bongard died in 1956, Schlumberger started designing jewelry for Tiffany & Co till his death in 1987.

What the clothing industry had done in the 1920s and 1930s for fashion, the American costume jewelry firms did for their products, copying the Paris models and boasting in their ads of their copying skills that allowed them to offer identical copies of Lelong, Chanel, or Schiaparelli models, or items inspired by the work of these designers, at much lower prices.

Authentic bijoux by the great fashion designers were imported and marketed in the States. D. Lisner was a long-standing costume jewelry manufacturer who was also the importer of Lelong and Schiaparelli jewelry.

The jewelry was sold in department stores and through mail order catalogues. With the Wall Street stock exchange crash of 1929, the American market suffered a heavy downfall, which hit luxury goods the hardest, including precious jewelry. Those were the years of what came to be known as the "Great Depression." Living standards went down and the public was forced to turn to cheaper products. Many precious jewelry designers turned to costume jewelry, a growing sector whose uphill trend became apparent in 1936-37, resulting in greater attention to product quality by manufacturers, including the search for new and more original designs. In those years such great firms as Du Jay and Boucher were established, and important fashion designers like Eisenberg created a special department dedicated only to costume jewelry. Many other firms decided to expand their costume jewelry production, to the detriment of other accessories such as combs, compacts, etc.

On 3rd September 1939 war broke out in Europe and from that time until October 1944, the United States remained isolated. In Paris many fashion houses closed down, while others remained open but with a clientele limited to a small number of people connected to the occupation government. This clientele led a brilliant social life that required luxury clothes, in striking contrast with the poverty the majority of the French had to endure. Chanel closed down her maison, which only reopened in 1954. Schiaparelli left France for the United States and resumed her activity only at the end of the war. It was only in 1947, with the presentation on 12th February of Christian Dior's revolutionary "new look" collection, that Paris re-conquered the title of world fashion capital, which culminated in 1949 with the abolition of fabric rationing.

Fashion history books often report that in the period between 1939 and 1947 there was a so-called "war fashion," which was somber and poor, with clothes made with as little fabric as possible, since the use of fabrics was rationed and their value was expressed in "points" that determined the number of ration card coupons required for their purchase. Silk stockings were banned and were replaced by ankle socks, woolen stockings, or even a special paint directly applied to the legs and ironically advertised with the slogan "no more ladders." But it was, above all, a fashion mainly consisting of "making and mending." Women's magazines gave tips on how to adjust old dresses, undo old pullovers to knit new ones, use small fabric pieces to make patchwork clothes. This is the history of Europe during the war.

In the United States, which had entered the conflict on 7th December 1941 and which did not experience the war on their home ground, life went on as usual at first and almost as normal afterwards. The war effort, which peaked in 1943, brought limitations and rationing, although not as strictly as in Europe, and civil production continued, albeit at a much slower pace. In the costume jewelry sector, about 50-70% of equipment was reconverted for war uses, this notwithstanding the fact that demand for costume jewelry remained so high, that non-precious jewels had to be imported from Mexico, where some firms had moved part of their production.

Having lost the source of inspiration provided by Parisian fashion, the United States had to rely solely on the talent of their own designers for the creation of new clothes and jewelry. In this period, many American designers made a name for themselves and had great success with collections that interpreted or created an American style in fashion. One of them was Claire McCardell whose clothes were typical examples of an American style; with jersey dresses and flowing trousers tightened at the waist by a wide belt. She was the first designer to use denim for dresses which featured double rows of contrasting accents and deep pockets that gave the clothes a casual look. Starting in 1940, McCardell designed Townley's collections, a New York ready-to-wear apparel manufacturer. These clothes, which were aimed at a medium market segment, were sold exclusively at Lord & Taylor's.

Many clothes and accessory designs, including shoes and handbags, were patented and this allows for knowledge about the fashion of the time. In 1940, skirts were slightly flared and rather short, with knee-length hemlines as in 1938, fully replacing calf-length skirts. Skirts were worn with short jackets, which were tight at the waist, with padded shoulders and small collars, often with silvery "renard." In 1942, jackets were still tight but longer and skirts, with knee-length hemlines, featured flat pleats or a single deep fold at the front.

Coats were slim, single- or double-breasted, with padded shoulders and large fur collars. Dresses were straight, with open shirt-like collars, buttoned-up bodices and thin belts at the waist.

Samuel Zahn: patent for a jacket
(Jan. 30, 1945 – Des. 140,223).

The summer rage was a dress with an uninterrupted row of buttons up the front, which was worn open over a pair of shorts. Trousers, which had already become a component of women's summer and sports wardrobe in the second half of the 1930s, became an alternative to skirts and were worn with jackets and blouses. Their shape was still the masculine one so loved by Marlene Dietrich. A must-have of American fashion in those years was the "smock-like" dress, a simple printed cotton or mixed cotton-rayon pinafore dress

Nettie Rosenstein: patent for a suit (March 11, 1941 – Des. 125,828).

with a slightly ruffled skirt and flounces on the bib. In the evenings, women wore long important dresses that were sometimes elaborately embroidered and matched with silver fox fur jackets. Fabrics used were mainly mixed, wool or cotton and rayon, rayon satin, acetate and jersey, often in a printed or checked pattern.

In the States, the War Production Board had issued guidelines limiting the amount of fabric that could be used for clothing, although these regulations were less strict than those approved in Europe.

Nettie Rosenstein: patent for a dress (Dec. 21, 1940 – Des. 124,447).

Shoes were rationed items, with the exception of dance shoes. For this reason, fashion designer Claire McCardell advised the shoe-making industry to manufacture dance shoes with sturdy soles and soft uppers. The model was very successful and was worn both with trousers and skirts.

On the other hand, no restrictions had been imposed on hats and accessories such as scarves and foulards (often printed with war subjects), which became very popular. Due to

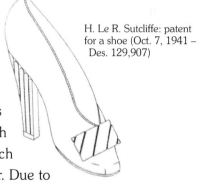

H. Le R. Sutcliffe: patent for a shoe (Oct. 7, 1941 – Des. 129,907)

the difficulty of purchasing new clothes, women tried to revamp their wardrobe with new accessories. Turbans and hairnets became very popular and women chose elaborate wavy hairdos and rather heavy makeup to counteract the forced austerity of their clothes. From that time on, all fashion magazines from *Vogue* to the cheaper *Mademoiselle*, dedicated articles to American fashion designers who were the only real point of reference as designers until 1947-48.

Costume jewelry manufacturers had to rely entirely on the creative spirit of their designers to try and satisfy a taste that, without the examples of European models, was developing independently. As is evident from their surnames, the greatest designers were from Europe and had come to the States with the first wave of immigrants. Their stories will be illustrated in the sections dedicated to individual designers. Some of them had already established their own firms. They came mainly from Italy, France, and Germany and had been educated and trained to be goldsmiths in their countries of origin, before coming to the States in the 1910s and 1920s in search of a better life. Often designers and firm owners shared the same cultural background and origin. They had all been taught an appreciation of beauty influenced by European standards and had fully absorbed the culture and traditional heritage of their countries of origin which they transferred to their artifacts.

Therefore, jewelry designed in this period embodies a perfect fusion of European cultural sophistication and tradition and American style, with all its excesses and contrasts. This jewelry was the perfect complement for clothes that mixed reminiscences of Paris fashion and novelty elements for emancipated women who had become economically independent thanks to their work and who used accessories and jewels as a means for renewing their wardrobe.

The high manufacturing standards of this jewelry were ensured by the manual work of scores of skilled goldsmiths who had a high degree of specialization and were ready to work for low wages. These goldsmiths were highly qualified, sometimes educated and sophisticated artists, who had fled Europe for the States in search of fortune or freedom. The historical and political events of those years had led, after the first massive emigration of 1917 after the Russian October Revolution, to successive immigration waves that peaked in 1938 with the Anschluss, i.e. the annexation of Austria to Nazi Germany. The expansionist policy of Germany with the pretext of expanding its "Lebensraum," the racial laws, the warning signs of imminent war and the actual war thereafter, compelled many Europeans, especially Jews, to flee their own countries. Frequently these émi-grés brought with them a small fortune represented by a bag of stones and crystals that in the States had great value due to the scarcity of these materials because of the impossibility of importing them and the incapacity of American manufacturers to produce equally beautiful and valuable stones and rhinestones. In those years, the costume jewelry industry relied on stones, glass beads, crystals and rhinestones imported from Czechoslovakia (Bohemia), Austria, France, and Italy. These materials were a decisive factor in determining the beauty of jewelry. To understand the importance of jewels in the making of an item of jewelry one need only think of Eisenberg's brooches with their large Swarovski crystals.

Another characteristic of costume jewelry in this period was its high price. For example, Coro's metal brooch "Blazing Lily" of 1941 (C38.) cost $25 and Coro's sterling "Toucan" of 1943 (C91.) cost $30; Eisenberg's "Bowknot" of 1942, made of metal and rhinestones, (E9.) cost $15, while the sterling ballet dancer of 1944 (E22.) cost $30; Trifari's sterling and Lucite "Spider" and "Horse Head" of 1943 and 1944 (JB24. e JB35.) cost $18.50 and $20 respectively; finally, Hobé's "Chessman" of 1944 (H12.) cost $55. To have an understanding of just how high those prices were, it should be remembered that in those days the average weekly wage was about $30, while, in 1942 a wool-rayon two piece suit cost $10.98 dollars, a silver fox fur jacket $229, a coat $50 and a hat $3.

This situation went on until the initial post-war years, with the launch of Dior's new look which in a way marked the slow resurgence of Europe after the disaster of the war. Cultural and commercial relations with the States were revived and the export of stones was resumed.

Dior's new look – characterized by wide skirts that reached almost to the ankle and jackets which were pinched in at the waist and loose at the hips – initially caused an outcry in Europe due to the large quantity of fabric required (over 2 m per item), necessitating a great number of coupons per item. However, in spite of some initial difficulties, the new look was adopted and whenever it was not possible to purchase a new skirt, stripes of fabric were added to old ones. In the States, this new fashion was initially made fun of; its unaffordability for housewives and typists was stressed, in an age when fashion was no longer a privilege of the rich. Nevertheless, in spite of all the dire forecasts, by 1948 the new fashion had already been universally adopted.

Paris was once again the capital of fashion, later joined by London and Milan.

Obviously the new Parisian fashion also had an influence on costume jewelry, which progressively changed to suit the new lines. With the growing use of light fabrics, blouses and low necklines, the importance of brooches decreased. Brooches became smaller and lighter, while the importance of necklaces and bracelets increased. A typical if not absolutely new fashion of the time was represented by "scatter pins," i.e. small pins that were worn in clusters on dresses or blouses. Fantasy subjects were still fashionable but there was also a growing trend in favor of a "real look," a characteristic that, with a few significant exceptions, became even more evident in 1949-50.

ABBREVIATIONS

AC = Accessocraft
AM = Albert Manufacturing
An = Anthony
B = Boucher
C = Coro
Ch = Chanel
BB = Bates & Bacon
Ca = Castlecliff
CLV = Calvaire
DJ = Dujay
DR = De Rosa
E = Eisenberg
EL = Elzac
ES = Ernest Steiner
FB = Fred A. Block
H = Hobé
HA = Hess – Appel
HC = Hattie Carnegie
J = Joseff
JB = Jelly Bellies
Kr = Kreisler
LG = Leo Glass
M = Mazer
MH = Miriam Haskell
Mo = Mosell
Mrl = Marleen
Mrs = Marslieu
NB = Natacha Brooks
NLUM = Nat Levy – Urie Mandle

P = Pennino
PAC = Patriotic Accessocraft
PB = Patriotic Boucher
PC = Patriotic Coro
PCar = Patriotic Cartier
PCh = Patriotic Chanel
PGP = Patriotic Goldstein – Poland
PLG = Patriotic Leo Glass
PR = Patriotic Réja
PRW = Patriotic Rice-Weiner
PSi = Patriotic Silson
PSt = Patriotic Staret
PT = Patriotic Trifari
PU = Patriotic Unsigned
PWL = Patriotic Walter Lampl
R = Réja
Rb = Rebajes
Re = Reinad
RW = Rice-Weiner
S = Sandor
Si = Silson
St = Staret
Sch = Schiaparelli
T = Trifari
U = Unsigned
UM = Urie Mandle
Unc = Uncas
WL = Walter Lampl

MANUFACTURERS

ACCESSOCRAFT

Accessocraft Products Corporation, 389 Fifth Avenue, New York, was probably founded in 1935 by Edgar Roedelheimer and Theodore Steinman, and was still in production until a few years ago. During the relevant period, production included all types of costume jewelry of medium to low quality. Designers for Accessocraft include Theodore Steinman (Des. 124,279, 24th December 1940, and des. 123,654, 19th November 1940 along with Philippe Israel) and Edgar Roedelheimer (Des. 124,392, 31st December 1940, and des. 124,446, 31st December 1940) who also designed an emblem of the US Navy which was produced by Coro (Des. 132,073 of 14th April 1942, *WWD*, July 17th, 1942), Robert R. Appleby, author of the famous "British War Relief" design (PAC37.) and Albert Freedman (AC1.).

Look, December 17, 1940: Vivien Leigh wearing Accessocraft's British War Relief brooch.

AC1. "Superstitious Aloysious," Accessocraft 1941****
Manufacturer Accessocraft Products Corp.
Designer Albert Freedman.
Pat. n° 127,008 Albert Freedman, Brooklyn, N.Y., 6th May 1941, filed on 3rd March 1941.

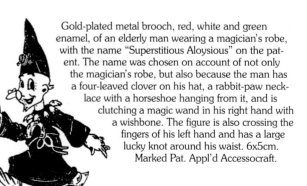

Gold-plated metal brooch, red, white and green enamel, of an elderly man wearing a magician's robe, with the name "Superstitious Aloysious" on the patent. The name was chosen on account of not only the magician's robe, but also because the man has a four-leaved clover on his hat, a rabbit-paw necklace with a horseshoe hanging from it, and is clutching a magic wand in his right hand with a wishbone. The figure is also crossing the fingers of his left hand and has a large lucky knot around his waist. 6x5cm.
Marked Pat. Appl'd Accessocraft.

ALBERT MANUFACTURING COMPANY

The company was founded at the beginning of the 1930s by Albert Weiner. It had a factory in Providence, R.I., and a showroom at 339 Fifth Avenue, New York. From 1935 to 1937 the main designer for the company was Ernest Steiner, a freelance designer as well as the owner of a firm called Ernest Steiner Co., which had its showroom at the same address in New York. In 1935 Steiner designed a collection for Albert Mfg. which was of Indian inspiration, called "Maharaja"and, in 1936, jewelry inspired by the film "Mary of Scotland" starring Katharine Hepburn. The jewelry in the film however was by Joseff. In 1937 Steiner designed the "Floradora Belles" collection.

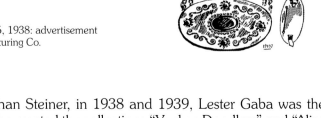

WWD, July 31, 1936: "Mary of Scotland" Jewelry, Ernest Steiner for Albert Manufacturing Co.

Yankee Doodlers

This unusual collection of novelty jewelry has been designed by

LESTER GABA

and is manufactured and sold by

ALBERT MANUFACTURING COMPANY

All necessary steps have been taken to fully protect these "Yankee Doodlers" by trade marks, patents and copyrights. This notice is given to avoid infringement suits against manufacturer and retailer. Albert Manufacturing Company, Showrooms, 339 Fifth Avenue; Factory, Providence, R. I.

WWD, February 25, 1938: advertisement by Albert Manufacturing Co.

Other than Steiner, in 1938 and 1939, Lester Gaba was the designer, who created the collections "Yankee Doodlers" and "Alice in Wonderland," and also worked for Albert Mfg. (AM1. & AM2.)

In 1941 (*WWD* 4ᵗʰ April 1941) Albert Mfg. produced jewelry inspired by the film "That Hamilton Woman," designed by Natacha Brooks along with other accessories on the same subject. The film "That Hamilton Woman," directed by Alexander Korda in 1941, tells the tragic love story of Lady Hamilton, played by Vivian Leigh, and Lord Admiral Nelson, played by Laurence Olivier.

WWD, March 17, 1939: "Alice in Wonderland" Jewelry. Lester Gaba for Albert Manufacturing Co. Advertisement by B. Altman & Co.

ALICE IN WONDERLAND JEWELRY
B. ALTMAN & CO.

WWD, April 4, 1941: accessories inspired by the movie "That Hamilton Woman." Designs by Natacha Brooks. Pin by Albert Manufacturing Co.

Main Floor Promotion

Inspired by Admiral

Above are shown two of the various accessories inspired by Lord Nelson, now becoming familiar to motion picture audiences in his shadow self in "That Hamilton Woman." Natacha Brooks has designed them, and B. Altman is presenting them shortly as an Easter promotion group. They are being produced by a group of manufacturers, includ-ing Albert Mfg. Co, who did the little blue enamel and rhinestone admiral's hat with crossed swords, and Bloch Freres, Inc., who make the blue and red and white printed handkerchief with a similar device. Daniel Hays has done a group of gloves; Schaffer a belt for the coordination, and Jos Cohn has worked out hats.

The company was in business until the 1950s. There is no further information concerning the company from this period onwards.

Albert Mfg. production excelled both in more traditional styles made of metal or silver and in novelty styles, using alternative materials such as wood, and its collections were often cited in *WWD*. The items are not marked, therefore they are not identifiable if patents or documents of the time are not available.

AM1. "Yankee Doodlers Indian," Unsigned 1938****
Manufacturer Albert Manufacturing Company
Designer Lester Gaba
Pat. n° 108,910 Lester Gaba, New York, 22ⁿᵈ March 1938, filed on 15ᵗʰ February 1938, assignor to Albert Weiner, Providence, R.I., doing business as Albert Manufacturing Co.

Gold-plated and rhodium-plated metal brooch, brown enamel, rhinestones, of an Indian Chief who is showing welcome offerings. cm 7x2.
Unmarked

In 1938 Lester Gaba designed the "Yankee Doodlers" collection for Albert Manufacturing Co., which was inspired by subjects from American history. These included a series of eight designs such as (apart from those catalogued,) the Paul Revere on horseback, a Mississippi steamboat, a Conestoga wagon (AM2.), the Moby Dick whale, a Pickaninny, the American Eagle and the Liberty Bell. The name "Yankee Doodlers" is original and comes from an advertisement made by the company in *WWD*, 25ᵗʰ February 1938.

In 1939 Lester Gaba designed another collection for Albert Manufacturing Co. the "Alice in Wonderland" line, advertised in *WWD*, 17ᵗʰ March 1939, and on sale at Altman.

AM2. "Yankee Doodlers Conestoga," Unsigned 1938****
Manufacturer Albert Manufacturing, Company.
Designer Lester Gaba.
Patent n° 108,907 Lester Gaba, New York, 22ⁿᵈ March 1938, filed on 15ᵗʰ February 1938, assignor to Albert Wiener, Providence, R.I., doing business as Albert Manufacturing Co.

Rhodium-plated metal brooch, with black, red and white enamel, baguettes and rhinestones, of a Conestoga wagon driven by a woman. 5.2x3cm.
Unmarked.

The Conestoga wagon takes its name from the Conestoga valley in Lancaster County, Pennsylvania, where, German farmers supposedly invented this wagon. It was one of the main means of transport in the east from 1750 to the advent of railways. Its typical boat shaped wooden body prevented the load from shifting from side to side, and gave the wagon its characteristic appearance. It usually had a vermillion beam, a Prussian blue body and a home-woven white cloth bonnet. It was pulled by four to six horses and had large wheels that prevented it from getting stuck in the mud.

During the great pioneers' migrations to the West, the smaller and lighter version of the original Conestoga was used, the so-called "Prairie Schooner," which was suitable for being hauled very long distances, such as the Oregon Trail, by four or six oxen, or by six to ten mules, which were tougher and less expensive than horses. Among the most important "Prairie Schooner" makers, the Studebaker brothers of South Bend, Indiana, deserve a mention, since they became the most important carriage makers in the world and later, at the start of 1900, changed their trade and became automobile makers.

ANTHONY CREATION INC.
See JB 126.

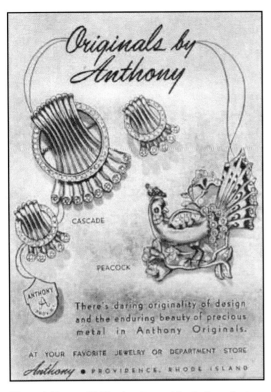

Harper's Bazaar, 1947: advertisement by Anthony featuring the "Cascade" set designed by Antonio Aquilino (Apr. 8 1947, filed May 13, 1946, Des. 146,552).

An1. "Octopus," Anthony 1946****
Manufacturer Anthony Creations, Inc., Providence, R.I.
Designer Antonio Aquilino.
Not patented.
   Gold-plated sterling brooch, with red cabochons and multicolor rhinestones set in the metal, shaped like an octopus. 7x6.5cm.
   Marked Anthony Sterling.
   For information concerning Anthony Creations and Aquilino see JB126.

BATES & BACON INC.

BB1. "Dolphin," Bates & Bacon 1945**
Manufacturer Bates & Bacon Inc., Attleboro, Ms.
Designer Oscar F. Placco.
Patent n° 141,382 Oscar F. Placco, Cranston, R.I., 29th May 1945, filed on 10th March 1945.

Gold-plated sterling brooch, with red cabochons and rhinestones, of a dolphin. 5.2x2.9cm.
   Marked BB Sterling.
   Very little information is available about Bates & Bacon of Attleboro, Ms., a company set up in 1856 by George M. Bacon and J. M. Bates. In addition to jewelry, the company also manufactured chains, pencils and knives.
   Oscar F. Placco worked constantly for Coro from 1938 to the mid 1940s.

BB2. "Stork," Bates & Bacon 1945**
Manufacturer Bates & Bacon Inc., Attleboro, Ms.
Designer Oscar F. Placco.
Patent n° 141,384 Oscar F. Placco, Cranston, R.I., 9th May 1945, filed on 10th March 1945.

Gold-plated sterling brooch, with green faceted stone and rhinestones, of a stork. 7x2.8cm.
   Marked Design Pat. 141384, Sterling B&B on an applied oval plaque.
   A third design of a spider was patented with n° 141,383.

FRED A. BLOCK

Fred A. Block, Inc., was a Chicago-based company, producing ladies' pret-à-porter, which during the period of matching jewelry-clothing fashion, marketed costume jewelry, creating a new division known as the Fred A. Block Jewelry, Inc. The earliest definite information is from January 1940 (an advertisement in *WWD*), which stated that the company was opening a showroom and offices at the Merchandise Mart in Chicago, where it remained.

Partial view (looking toward stage) of our newly opened luxurious and practical Sales Salon in The Merchandise Mart.

FRED A. BLOCK
INCORPORATED

Announces

The Opening of Their Sales Salon and General Offices in

THE NEW READY-TO-WEAR CENTER

On the Second Floor of

THE MERCHANDISE MART

Buyers attending The Merchandise Mart Apparel Markets, January 29th to February 10th, are cordially invited to inspect our Spring Showing.

Fred A. Block originals

MANUFACTURERS OF BETTER
COSTUME ENSEMBLES • DRESSES • GOWNS
ROOM 265 THE MERCHANDISE MART CHICAGO

WWD, January 19, 1940: Fred A. Block's advertisement announcing the opening of their Sales Salon.

FB1. "Aztec Mask," Fred A. Block 1942****
Manufacturer Sandor Goldberger, New York, for Fred A. Block Jewelry, Inc., Chicago.
Designer Sandor Goldberger.
   White metal pin clip, carved citrine lucite, green cabochons, depicting an Aztec mask. 7.7x5cm.
   Marked Fred A. Block Originals.
   This item too confirms the relation between Fred A. Block and Sandor. Indeed *WWD* of February 8th 1942, in its presentation of the Sandor Collection, wrote: "Growing interest in Mexican-style jewelry is reported at this house where designs combining white metal with carved wooden or tinted lucite masks have been enlarged for springtime selling".

   Its costume jewelry production most probably started at the end of the 30s with the aim of helping the development of the reputed clothing brand-name. The company was still in production in December 1949 when Sidney A. Block left Fred A. Block, Inc., where he was vice-president, in order to fully dedicate his time to Fred A. Block Jewelry.

   The identity of Fred A. Block Jewelry items, with pieces by Sandor (see "Pond Lily" JB98., "Snowman" JB99., Sandor's "Sunburst" S5., almost the same as that advertised by Fred A. Block in *Vogue*, 1st December 1946) leads to the conclusion that Fred A. Block had its jewelry designed and produced either in part or entirely, by Sandor Goldberger.

   The items are marked Fred A. Block – in block letters – sometimes with the addition of Originals, Jewelry, or Sterling (when it was used). The designs are not patented and the few items available on the market today are all very beautiful.

FB2. "Topaz Pin," Fred A. Block 1944***
Manufacturer Sandor Goldberger, New York, for Fred A. Block Jewelry, Inc., Chicago.
Designer Sandor Goldberger.
Gold-plated sterling pin clip in square shape, with big central topaz surrounded by white crystals in marquise and rosette cut. 4.8x5cm.
   Marked Fred A. Block Sterling.
   The company mark is on an applied oval plate, the Sterling pusher hallmark on an applied rectangular plate.

MARCEL BOUCHER

WWD, January 21, 1949: Marcel Boucher.

Marcel Boucher was born in Paris in 1899. After obtaining his final diploma from the Bernard Palissy school of applied arts, he worked for Cartier initially in Paris and then in New York where he moved in 1925. In 1930 he was hired by Mazer Bros. where he remained until 1937. Boucher, who was living in Eltingville, Staten Island, New York, patented two mechanisms for Mazer, which permitted two separate clips to be joined, thus forming a single brooch (des. n° 2,032,907, 3rd March 1936 and des. n° 2,032,908) and the design of a brooch (des. n° 103,385, 2nd March 1937). During the years he spent at Mazer, Boucher patented (this time in his name only) two designs of a "Watch clip that allowed for the assembling of a watch movement to a clip that could be easily attached to every suitable dress part" (des. n° 1,952,307 and n° 1,965,095 of 1934, filed in 1931) as well as four other mechanisms for the assembly of two clips (des. n° 2,034,128 and 2,034,129 of 17th March 1936; n° 2,072,080 of 2nd March 1937; n° 2,143,538 of 10th January 1939, filed on 10th October 1935).

In March 1937, together with his wife Jeanne and Arthur Halberstadt, Boucher established his own firm, Marcel Boucher Ltd. Novelty Jewelry, with a registered office in New York, 29 West 35th Street.

Arthur Halberstadt, who had been a salesman for Trifari from 1925 to 1935 and Mazer Bros. from 1st January 1936, was the company president and was responsible for the commercial sector.

The first collection was presented in July 1937. For its preparation, Marcel Boucher had traveled to Paris for inspiration. According to *WWD*, 23rd July 1937, the designer had drawn inspiration from ribbons and draped fabrics for his bow-shaped brooches with stones that emphasized the folds of the ribbons and metal parts suggesting the rippling of the bow ends, while the clips with relief patterns imitated the draping of fabrics. *WWD* always paid attention to Boucher's activity and collections, even though the firm did not regularly advertise its products. For example, in January 1940 it presented

"Punchinello," a wonderful rhodium-plated and enamel brooch (B10.), and in August of the same year it published an article on its fall collection, and also gave precious information on the previous spring collection. The spring collection featured colored enamel and rhinestone items, while for the fall collection Boucher had used only white crystals – rhinestone pavés, baguettes and square stones – sometimes in combination with pearls, for an iced effect. The motifs included natural subjects – fish ("Swordfish," B24 and "Paradise fish"), birds ("Hummingbird," "Paradise Bird," "Lovebirds Over The Nest"), flowers ("Thistle Lily," "Columbine," B5, "Tiger Lily," "Cyclamen," B7, bell flowers, roses, orchids,) an oak leaf with acorns made of pearls, B52, chestnuts in their husks with pearls, a hen with rhinestone wings and a pearl for the head, vines, grapes, feathers, seashells and an eagle – together with a series of knots made of rhinestones and square stones with iridescent enamel borders. Some designs were patented, others were reproduced in advertisements.

In March 1944 the firm changed its name to Marcel Boucher & Cie, without however changing its corporate composition. In addition to the New York showroom (from 1941 at 383 Fifth Avenue), the firm had a sales office in Los Angeles, 667 South Hill Street. In 1949 the New York showroom address was 347 Fifth Avenue.

During the war the manufacturing plant, located in New York, 304-10 East 23rd Street, was partially used for war production; however costume jewelry production continued with excellent sterling items made on the basis of very fine designs, some of which were patented. Part of the production structure had relocated to Mexico.

The original partnership lasted until 1949, when (*WWD*, 22nd January) it was announced that from 19th February Mr. and Mrs. Marcel and Jeanne Boucher would be the only owners of Marcel Boucher & Cie and that the company would maintain the same style, design, and production characteristics and the same quality standards that had won it its good reputation. The company dissolution did not cause any leadership changes apart from the change of commercial director: responsibility of this sector, originally entrusted to Halberstadt, passed to Milton Ledner, who had been with the firm for seven years.

In the same year "Sandra" Raymonde Semensohn joined the firm as assistant designer: her collaboration was discontinuous – from 1949 to 1958, when Semensohn went to work for Tiffany, and again from 1961 – and of small importance for the period being reviewed.

On 22nd January 1965 Boucher, who shortly before, probably in 1964, had divorced Jeanne and married Semensohn, suddenly died at 66 and, in March of the same year, Mrs. Semensohn became president of the company. In *WWD* of 28th January, an obituary in his memory was written by Jeanne Boucher who, together with daughter Micheline Sokol, wrote about Marcel as if he had still been her husband.

In 1972 the company was sold to Davorn Industries, a watch manufacturer with which Mrs. Semensohn collaborated until September 1975.

The last known information about the Marcel Boucher firm is dated from 1977 (*WWD*, 18th August 1977) when the company, owned at the time by Stutz Fashion Designs Ltd., presented its watch collection.

Boucher was a small company – in 1956 it had about 70 employees – with moderate production volumes for the size of the American market and also the Canadian market on which it operated at the end of 1950 by virtue of a cooperation agreement with Avon Jewelry Ltd., Belleville (Ontario), whose name appeared together with Boucher's in advertisements. Its products belonged to the medium-high price range and were sold in the best department stores and boutiques.

The designs were all by Marcel Boucher – except for the later production designed by Mrs. Semensohn – and were continuously if not systematically patented, with an indication of the patents in the advertisements as a guarantee of the items' originality. "Signal man" (B2.) was the first patented design.

Marcel Boucher was an inventive, sophisticated designer, who could translate a subject of fantasy into an item of jewelry and a "real look" theme into a bijou. He was said to be a master in the imitation style of jewelry, and while this is certainly true, the best part of his production, the part most appreciated by collectors, was the one in which his creative imagination prevailed over his imitation technique, which was in itself excellent. Almost all the production of the period under review, deserves to be mentioned, although the best collections belong to the pre-war years – from 1939 to 1942. They were made of rhodium or gold-plated metal, with enamel and rhinestone pavés and portrayed fantasy subjects with exceptional dimensions or, as in the fall of 1939, delicate designs of enamel, rhinestone and pearl bows.

The "mythical" collection of three-dimensional birds – twelve in all – which, according to current thesis, had been purchased by Saks Fifth Avenue, marking the start of Boucher's activity, actually dates from the fall of 1941. Therefore, it was not decisive for Boucher's initial choices, but came after the above mentioned important 1940 collections, after the "movables," and after the 1941 collection that included some extraordinary enamel or rhinestone pieces with animal, floral, or vegetable subjects. The same collection also features the Chinese and the Mexican series. However, mention should also be made of the bird series, characterized by the three-dimensionality of the subjects, which was a great commercial success, determining the fame of the manufacturer. The metal-enamel combination was also maintained in the spring 1942 collection.

The production of the war years was made of sterling. The best collections were those of Cubist style ballerinas and animals (fish and birds) with large central stones, dating from the end of 1944, and the animal series made of heavy gold-plated sterling and colored carré stones of 1945.

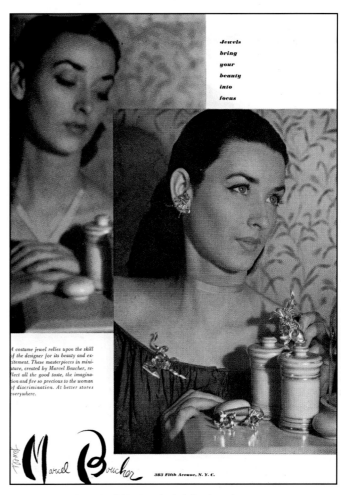

Vogue, November 15, 1944. Boucher's full color advertisement.

Ballet dancers were a congenial subject for Boucher, who returned to them several times during his career, with some alterations to suit the fashion of the time, but always with excellent results. In 1946 he made a series of ballet dancers, also in Cubist style, made of gold-plated sterling, characterized by tutus studded with small multicolor navettes, while in 1949-50 he designed "Ballet of Jewels" (B78., B80., B81.), a series of eight small brooches made of two-color metal and rhinestones that could be worn in couples.

Use of sterling continued throughout 1947 when use of metal alloys was resumed. The ethnic figures made of enamel and colored stones and the feminine figures symbolizing the four seasons are worthy of mention. The "real look" themes were less intriguing, although some of them, such as "Night and Day," became famous. In the fall of 1948, Boucher developed a design of a flower with mobile petals that closed and opened to reveal rhinestone pistils inside. Between the end of the 40s and the beginning of the 50s, brooches became less fashionable, while production of necklaces, bracelets and earrings in purely "real look" styles increased. Sales prices dropped to $5-15, prices equal to or even lower than those of 1940-41, confirming that marketing requirements had partly prevailed over quality and that, perhaps, in spite of the official statements, the dissolution of the partnership with Halberstadt had had a negative influence on the sales network and on the relationship with the clientele.

In 1945, in the manner of great jewelers, the company started punching on each item Boucher's in-house design catalog number referring to the design of the jewel. This catalog probably included designs dating from the beginning of Boucher's activity, which would explain the four digit numbers, exceeding the two-thousand figure, marked on the first 1945 items. These numbers, beginning with those punched on the patented items, allow for dating with almost absolute certainty the non-patented, numbered pieces. The numbers from 2,300 to 2,350 date from 1945, the numbers from 2,351 to 2,450 date from 1946, the numbers from 2,450 to 2,550 date from 1947, the numbers from 2,550 to 2,750 date from 1948, the numbers from 2,750 to 3,000 date from 1949 and the numbers from 3,000 to 3,500 from 1950.

Two markings were used: "MB" and "BOUCHER." The mark MB was topped by a Phrygian cap with a tri-colored rosette – and not by the head of a hawk, cock, or any other stylized bird as is often believed – the emblem of the French revolution and France (it should be pointed out that "Marianne," the female figure symbolizing France, always wears the Phrygian cap of the "Sancoulottes" perhaps because, especially in ancient Rome, this cap was worn by liberated slaves). France was Boucher's country of origin and he played on this fact in his advertisements, in which he called himself a "Parisian." The trademark was registered on 19th October 1944 and was used from the beginning of the firm's activity to the end of 1949 and also, rarely, thereafter, until about 1955, particularly on necklaces, earrings and bracelets, where, for lack of space, it was difficult to stamp the trade name "BOUCHER." The latter trademark was used between 1950 and 1955, when the trademark "BOUCHER©" was adopted. Boucher was one of the most passionate supporters of the protection of design property rights against copycat, both through patents and through the numbering of pieces. He fought and won some cases of patent infringement and enthusiastically adopted the practice of copyright, especially after Trifari's legal victory. In addition to "BOUCHER," the pieces bore a catalog number which, together with the copyright, allows for dating with close approximation the pieces manufactured after 1954. It should be noted that, although the symbol © appears on all pieces, not all designs were actually copyrighted. Moreover, from the year 1960 (numbers from 7,500), the pieces also bore a letter: B for bracelet, E for earrings (and DE for dangling earrings), N for necklace and P for pin. Boucher was used to protecting his designs throughout the world, which accounts for the "DEPOSÉ" mark found on some pieces that had obviously been made in France.

He registered two other trade names which he used for communication purposes, but not for stamping the jewelry: *m*B topped by the Phrygian cap, registered in 1949 and used in advertisements from the second half of 1949 and *Marcel Boucher,* registered on 20th April 1949 and again on 23rd July 1956, written in italics as was Boucher's own signature in the patents, and used as a logo in advertisements. The trademark MARBOUX, registered by Marcel Boucher Ltd., New York, on 1st May 1937, in 1949 was used only as the cable address of the company. The trade name *Marboux,* written in italics and preceded by a star, was registered in 1953 as the name of a new low priced line (from $1 to $5) of tailored jewelry. Boucher also registered some trademarks corresponding to the names of lines of jewelry, such as "Earrite" of 23rd October 1950.

B1. "Bowknot," Boucher 1939****
Manufacturer Marcel Boucher Ltd.
Designer Marcel Boucher.
Patent n° 116,472 Marcel Boucher, New York, 5th September 1939, filed on 31st July 1939.

Rhodium-plated metal brooch shaped like a bowknot with pale green enamel, rhinestones and a large white pearl in the middle. 7.8x6.8cm.
  Marked MB Pat. Pend.
  There are several design and color variants of this brooch.
  In the fall of 1939 Boucher patented only two brooch designs, both of bowknots.

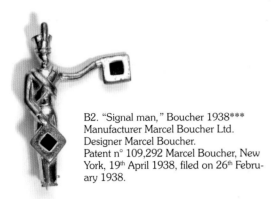

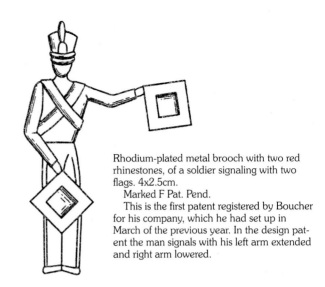

B2. "Signal man," Boucher 1938***
Manufacturer Marcel Boucher Ltd.
Designer Marcel Boucher.
Patent n° 109,292 Marcel Boucher, New York, 19th April 1938, filed on 26th February 1938.

Rhodium-plated metal brooch with two red rhinestones, of a soldier signaling with two flags. 4x2.5cm.
  Marked F Pat. Pend.
  This is the first patent registered by Boucher for his company, which he had set up in March of the previous year. In the design patent the man signals with his left arm extended and right arm lowered.

B3. "Victorian Bow," Boucher 1940***
Manufacturer Marcel Boucher Ltd.
Designer Marcel Boucher.
Patent n° 120,611 Marcel Boucher, New York, 21st May 1940, filed on 11th April 1940.

Rhodium-plated metal brooch, black enamel and rhinestones, in the shape of a bow. 5.5x5cm.
Marked MB Pat. Pend. "I".
  The name "Victorian Bow" comes from an advertisement in *Vogue*, February 1st 1940, advertising "Punchinello" as well as "Victorian Bows," as a part of the spring collection 1940.

B4. "Victorian Bow," Boucher 1940***
Manufacturer Marcel Boucher Ltd.
Designer Marcel Boucher.
Patent n° 120,612 Marcel Boucher, New York, 21st May 1940, filed on 11th April 1941.

Rhodium-plated metal brooch, azure enamel and rhinestones, in the shape of a bow. 7.2x3.7cm.
  Marked MB Pat. Pend.
  For the name see B3.

B5: "Columbine," Boucher
1940****
Manufacturer Marcel
Boucher Ltd.
Designer Marcel Boucher.
Not patented.

"Columbine"
PAT. PENDING

fragile loveliness forever
crystalized in rhinestones by

MARCEL
BOUCHER

This exquisite pin, sparkling with a multitude of tiny gems and
baguettes, actually rivals in beauty the dainty flower which
inspired its design . . . . About $17.00
AT ALL LEADING STORES

Other Marcel Boucher exclusive creations priced from $3.00.

MARCEL BOUCHER, Ltd., 29 W. 35 St., N.Y.C.

Vogue, September 15, 1940: "Columbine" by Boucher.

Rhodium-plated metal brooch with rhinestone pavé, baguettes and small
white pearls, of a columbine. 9.5x5cm.
Marked MB Pat. Pend. "B".
The name "Columbine" is the original name of the brooch and was
taken from an advertisement for the brooch published in *Vogue*, 15th
September 1940. The sales price of $17 is stated in the advertise-
ment, along with the slogan: "fragile loveliness forever
crystallized in rhinestones by Marcel Boucher." The
design was described as Pat. Pending both in the
advertisement and in the marking, however the patent was never issued. Indeed, no item from the fall
1940 collection was patented.
Staret manufactured a rhodium-plated metal brooch
with rhinestone pavé similar to the Boucher one, only
larger and with a less delicate line (St2.)

B6. "Sweet Peapod," Boucher 1940****
Manufacturer Marcel Boucher Ltd.
Designer Marcel Boucher.
Not Patented.
   Large rhodium-plated metal brooch of a pea plant in
bloom. The trunk is made of rhodium-plated metal, the
leaves are studded with rhinestones. The two flowers
have two-toned pastel pink enamel petals with rhinestone
veins. Two pale green enamel pods hang from the plant,
one small and closed, the other larger and open, with the
peas, made of white pearls, showing. 11.5x6cm.
   Marked MB "X" (stone setter reference).

B7. "Cyclamen," Boucher 1940****
Manufacturer Marcel Boucher Ltd.
Designer Marcel Boucher.
Not Patented.
   Rhodium-plated metal brooch of a rhinestone and baguette
studded cyclamen. 10.2x6.3cm.
   Marked MB "Y".
   This item belonged to the fall 1940 collection. In 1950 Boucher
designed and patented another cyclamen shaped brooch made of
gold-plated metal with a light fretwork execution and rhinestone
accents (B77.)

B8. "Flower," Boucher 1941****
Manufacturer Marcel Boucher Ltd.
Designer Marcel Boucher.
Patent n° 127,014 Marcel Boucher, New
York, 6th May 1941, filed on 8th April 1941.

Rhodium-plated metal and enamel brooch of a flower with lilac enamel
petals, and green enamel stalk and leaves with rhinestone accents.
7.9x6cm.
    Marked MB Des. Pat'd.
    Another version of this model was made of two-color rhodium- and
gold-plated metal. The double version, with enamel and two-toned metal,
was typical of the 1941 collections. Also typical was the "lozenge" manufacture, in which small segments of metal were treated in different ways, or
coated with different color enamel. Lozenges were also created by alternating rhodium- and gold-plated metal.

B9. "Ear," Boucher 1940****
Manufacturer Marcel Boucher Ltd.
Designer Marcel Boucher.
Not patented.
    Rhodium-plated metal brooch, rhinestones pavé,
of an ear of wheat. 11x5.5cm.
    Marked MB "H".
    Forms part of the fall 1940 collection (WWD, 2nd
August 1940).

B10. "Punchinello," Boucher 1940*****
Manufacturer Marcel Boucher Ltd.
Designer Marcel Boucher.
Patent n° 119,649 Marcel Boucher, New
York, 26th March 1940, filed on 6th Janu-
ary 1940.

Rhodium-plated metal pin clip, yellow, black and red
enamel, sky blue moonstone and rhinestones, of a
Punchinello with arms and legs that can be moved by
pulling on the small dangling chain. 7.3x5.5cm.
    Marked MB Pat.Pend. "I".
    The name "Punchinello" appeared in an advertisement
in Vogue, 1st February 1940. The item on sale was $ 10
plus tax. A description and picture of "Punchinello" was
also published in WWD, in the issues of the 19th and 26th
January 1940, and Glamour, July 1940.
    "Punchinello," "Clown" (B11.), "Cambodian" (B12.),
"Jester" (B13.), "Buddha" (B14.), "Hungry Pelican"
(B15.) and "Cuckoo" (B16.) are part of the extraordinary
series of "movables" produced in 1940.

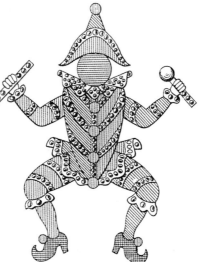

B11. "Clown," Boucher 1940*****
Manufacturer Marcel Boucher.
Designer Marcel Boucher.
Not patented.

Glamour, July 1940: "Movable Clown".

Rhodium-plated metal pin clip, white, pink, red, sky-blue and black enamel, rhinestones, depicting a clown. Its mouth can be opened and closed by pulling on a little dangling chain. 9.5x4.5cm.
    Unmarked
    The pin clip was published in an advertisement in *Glamour,* July 1940 with "Punchinello" and other items.
    The existence of pieces marked MB, along with trademark style, design and construction, confirm attribution to Boucher.

B12. "Cambodian," Boucher 1940*****
Manufacturer Marcel Boucher Ltd.
    Designer Marcel Boucher.
    Patent n° 120,027 Marcel Boucher, New York, 16th April 1940, filed on 5th February 1940.

Rhodium- and gold-plated metal pin clip, sky-blue, blue and burgundy enamel, red, green and blue stones and rhinestones, of a Cambodian dancer whose arms and legs can be moved by pulling on the small dangling chain. 8x5cm.
    Marked MB Pat. Pend.
    The name "Cambodian" appeared in an advertisement for the item in *Vogue,* 1st March 1940. The item was on sale for $10.

B13. *"Jester,"* Boucher 1940*****
Manufacturer Marcel Boucher Ltd.
Designer Marcel Boucher.
Patent n° 120,028 Marcel Boucher,
New York, 16th April 1940, filed 5th
February 1940.

Rhodium-plated metal pin clip, black, yellow, pink, white and red enamel, rhinestones, of a jolly little man with movable head, wearing a jester costume. 6.5x4.5cm.
Marked MB Pat. Pend.
The item was published under the name "Jester" in an advertisement in *Mademoiselle,* March 1940, and was on sale for $10. On the back of this piece the inscription *"Tzcepa"* is engraved, most probably a dedication.

B14. *"Buddha,"* Boucher 1940*****
Manufacturer Marcel Boucher Ltd.
Designer Marcel Boucher.
Not patented.
Gold- and rhodium-plated metal pin clip, white, blue and red enamel, rhinestones, of a sitting Buddha with movable head. 6.5x4cm.
Marked MB Pat. Pend.
Despite the mark "Pat. Pend." the item is not patented.

B15. "Hungry Pelican," Boucher 1940*****
Manufacturer Marcel Boucher Ltd.
Designer Marcel Boucher.
Not patented.
Rhodium-plated metal brooch with yellow, pink and black enamel and rhinestones. The brooch is of a pelican. When the hanging chain is pulled, the pelican's beak opens to reveal a rhodium-plated metal and pink enamel fish inside. This brooch belongs to the 1940 "movables" series. 8.6x6cm.
Marked MB "X".

B16. "Cuckoo," Boucher 1940*****
Manufacturer Marcel Boucher Ltd.
Designer Marcel Boucher.
Not patented.

Vogue, February 15, 1941: "Musts" by Boucher.

Rhodium-plated metal pin clip with pale green enamel and rhinestones.
The pin is of a cuckoo clock. When the hanging chain is pulled, the house
door opens showing a rhodium-plated metal bird. The bird is coated with
yellow and mother-of-pearl enamel. It holds a small metal bar with the word
"cuckoo" on it in its beak. 5.5x4.5cm.
    Marked MB Pat. Pend. In spite of the mark Pat. Pend. this item was
never patented.
    It belonged to the 1940 "movables" series and was reproduced in an
advertisement published in *Vogue*, on 15th February 1941, in which the
pin was described as being an absolute "Must," available in four enamel
colors and on sale for $ 10.
    In the same advertisement another "Must" was featured. It was called
"Fashuntext," and was a series of twenty-four gold-plated metal brooches
with rhinestones shaped in the letters of the alphabet. The advertisement
displayed the letters M and B, the trademark of the company.

B17. "Jay," Boucher 1940***
Manufacturer Marcel Boucher Ltd.
Designer Marcel Boucher.
Not patented.
    Rhodium-plated metal brooch of a jay
perched on a branch. The jay has a yellow
enamel head and rhinestone pavé crest, yellow
and pale green enamel lozenges for its body with
rhinestone accents on the breast, a long green
enamel tail with rhinestones at the tip of the tail
feathers. 9.8x3.5cm.
    Marked MB.

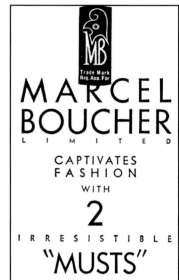

MARCEL
BOUCHER
L I M I T E D

CAPTIVATES
FASHION
WITH

2

I R R E S I S T I B L E

"MUSTS"

C U C K O O

An exciting   conceit—Cuckoo—and a
MUST—definitely. As you pull the slender,
pearl-pendanted chain, the little door opens
and you say, "Cuckoo to you!" Fun? Barrels
of it! Choice of four charming, iridescent
pastel shades. Solidly paved with sparkling
rhinestones—about $10 at the finer stores.

FASHUNTEXT

Irresistibly lovely initials—modern MUSTS.
These two are typical. The other 24—oh! but
you must see them on your own frock. Available at better stores everywhere. Beautifully
worked in heavy gold plate and brilliantly
studded with rhinestones. Each initial, $3.

MARCEL BOUCHER
L I M I T E D

383 FIFTH AVENUE, NEW YORK

MARCEL BOUCHER *jeweled* CREATIONS
AVAILABLE AT LEADING STORES EVERYWHERE

B18. "Phœnix," Boucher 1941****
Manufacturer Marcel Boucher Ltd.
Designer Marcel Boucher.
Not patented.
   Rhodium-plated metal brooch,
yellow and orange enamel,
rhinestones, of a phoenix bird.
7x7cm.
   Marked MB "Y".

B19. "Blue Bird," Boucher 1940****
Manufacturer Marcel Boucher Ltd.
Designer Marcel Boucher.
   Patent n° 120,539 Marcel Boucher, New
   York, 14th May 1940, filed on 15th Febru-
   ary 1940.

Rhodium-plated metal brooch, blue
and sky-blue enamel, rhinestones,
of a long-tailed bird perched on a
branch. 10x4.5cm.
   Marked MB Pat. Pend.
   Birds were one of Boucher's favorite subjects and he produced a great
deal of them.

B20. "Lovebirds on the Nest," Boucher 1940*****
Manufacturer Marcel Boucher Ltd.
Designer Marcel Boucher.
No Patented.
   Rhodium-plated metal brooch, green and red enamel, small white
pearls and rhinestones, of two lovebirds in a nest with small pearl eggs.
8x11cm.
   Marked MB "0".
   There are smaller versions of this item in enamel and rhinestones.
The smaller rhinestone version was described by *WWD*, 2nd August
1940, as being part of the Boucher fall collection, which featured
rhinestones and baguettes.

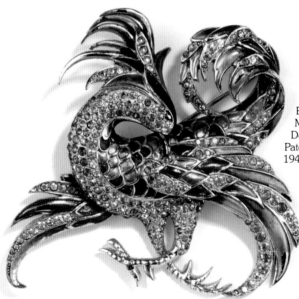

B21. "Gryphon," Boucher 1941*****
Manufacturer Marcel Boucher Ltd.
Designer Marcel Boucher.
Patent n° 129,843 Marcel Boucher, New York, 7th October
1941, filed on 6th September 1941.

Rhodium-plated metal brooch, with red and aqua enamel and rhinestones, of a magpie with ruffled tail, wings and crest. Its head, breast
and feet are covered with rhinestone pavé; while its wings, tail and
crest are coated with shaded red and aqua enamel in small lozenges.
The elaborate manufacture, pose and use of colors give the subject
the appearance of a bird of fantasy and make it look like a gryphon.
7.5x10cm.
   Marked MB Des. Pat'd.
   The patent refers to the gold-plated metal brooch with rhinestones of
the second version of the design.
   There are several contemporary copies of this model, which
are unmarked and of poor quality, made of raw white metal and
pastel enamel. Reinad also made an identical gold-plated metal
and rhinestone brooch, of good quality, marked Reinad.

B22. "Pheasant," Boucher 1940****
Manufacturer Marcel Boucher Ltd.
Designer Marcel Boucher.
Not patented.
    Gold-plated metal brooch, green, blue and red
enamel, rhinestones, of a pheasant. 6x8cm.
Marked MB.

Rhodium-plated metal brooch, green, blue and
black enamel, pearls and rhinestones, of two birds
perched opposite each other on a branch. 5x9.5cm.
Marked MB Pat. Pend.

B23. "Lovebirds," Boucher 1940*****
Manufacturer Marcel Boucher Ltd.
Designer Marcel Boucher
Patent n° 120,540 Marcel Boucher, New York, 14th May 1940, filed on 15th
February 1940

B24. "Swordfish," Boucher 1940*****
Manufacturer Marcel Boucher Ltd.
Designer Marcel Boucher.
Not patented.
    Rhodium-plated metal brooch shaped like a swordfish with rhinestone pavé
and baguettes. 8.9x9cm.
    Marked MB "F".
    There is also an enamel version of this item.
    This item belonged to the fall 1940 collection which featured, according to
WWD, 2nd August 1940, a combination of rhinestones and baguettes and an
almost total absence of enamel. According to *WWD*, one of the most significant
designs was "Swordfish" which it described in detail. The line included animal
subjects– rhinestone lovebirds in a small rhinestone nest with eggs made of
pearls; a rhinestone-winged hen with baguette feathers and tail and a pearl
for its head; various fish, including a "paradise fish"; a hummingbird sucking
nectar from a flower bud; a seashell; a feather; an eagle – floral and plant
subjects – roses; an orchid; "Columbine" (B5.); vines; grapes; leaves
including a rhinestone oak leaf with large acorns with pearls ("Oak
leaf with Acorns" B52.); tiger lily; bluebells; chestnuts made of pearls
in their husk; a thistle lily. The collection includes also a series of
bowknots with iridescent enamel borders, set with rhinestones,
baguettes and square stones.

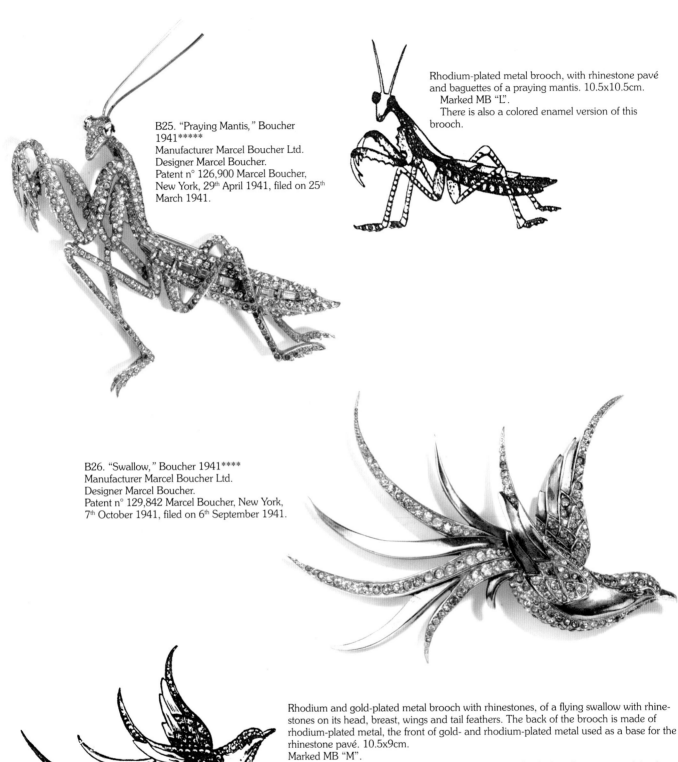

B25. *"Praying Mantis,"* Boucher 1941*****
Manufacturer Marcel Boucher Ltd.
Designer Marcel Boucher.
Patent n° 126,900 Marcel Boucher, New York, 29th April 1941, filed on 25th March 1941.

Rhodium-plated metal brooch, with rhinestone pavé and baguettes of a praying mantis. 10.5x10.5cm.
Marked MB "L".
There is also a colored enamel version of this brooch.

B26. *"Swallow,"* Boucher 1941****
Manufacturer Marcel Boucher Ltd.
Designer Marcel Boucher.
Patent n° 129,842 Marcel Boucher, New York, 7th October 1941, filed on 6th September 1941.

Rhodium and gold-plated metal brooch with rhinestones, of a flying swallow with rhinestones on its head, breast, wings and tail feathers. The back of the brooch is made of rhodium-plated metal, the front of gold- and rhodium-plated metal used as a base for the rhinestone pavé. 10.5x9cm.
Marked MB "M".

There is also a colored enamel version of this brooch which is the negative of the design: the rhinestone studded parts are enameled, while the metal parts are rhinestone-studded. The patent refers to the gold-plated rhinestone version.

This was probably the first of an extraordinary series of three-dimensional birds made for Saks which marked Boucher's definitive coronation as one of the best designers and manufacturers of costume jewelry. Only two designs – "Swallow" and "Gryphon" (B21.) were patented. The series also includes an ibis, "Heron" (B28.), "Phoenix" (B18), "Jack to Marta" (B27.) and other birds. The items were manufactured in two versions with enamel and gold- and rhodium-plated metal.

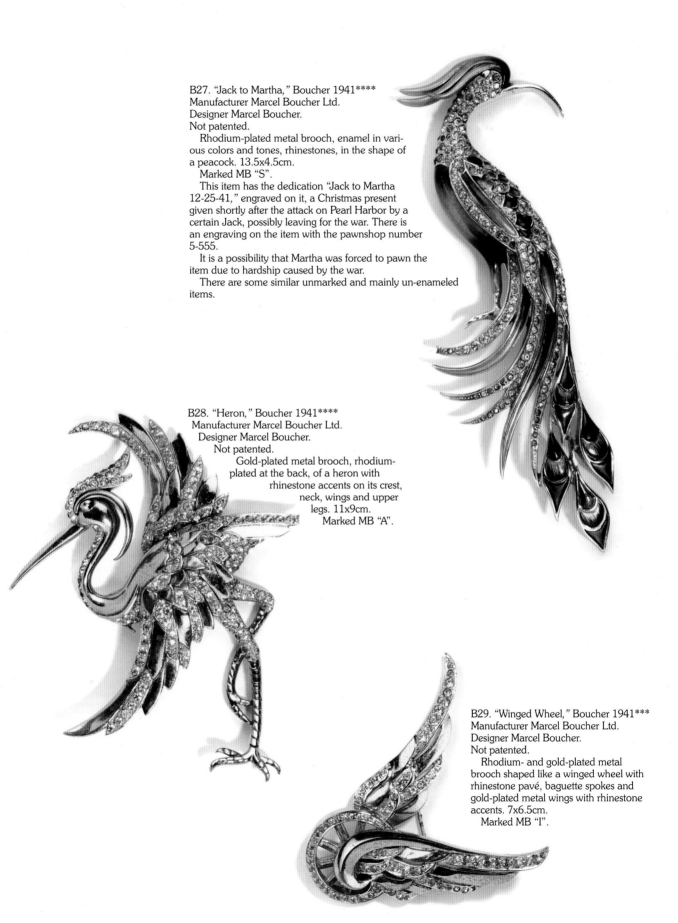

B27. "Jack to Martha," Boucher 1941****
Manufacturer Marcel Boucher Ltd.
Designer Marcel Boucher.
Not patented.
   Rhodium-plated metal brooch, enamel in various colors and tones, rhinestones, in the shape of a peacock. 13.5x4.5cm.
   Marked MB "S".
   This item has the dedication "Jack to Martha 12-25-41," engraved on it, a Christmas present given shortly after the attack on Pearl Harbor by a certain Jack, possibly leaving for the war. There is an engraving on the item with the pawnshop number 5-555.
   It is a possibility that Martha was forced to pawn the item due to hardship caused by the war.
   There are some similar unmarked and mainly un-enameled items.

B28. "Heron," Boucher 1941****
Manufacturer Marcel Boucher Ltd.
Designer Marcel Boucher.
   Not patented.
   Gold-plated metal brooch, rhodium-plated at the back, of a heron with rhinestone accents on its crest, neck, wings and upper legs. 11x9cm.
   Marked MB "A".

B29. "Winged Wheel," Boucher 1941***
Manufacturer Marcel Boucher Ltd.
Designer Marcel Boucher.
Not patented.
   Rhodium- and gold-plated metal brooch shaped like a winged wheel with rhinestone pavé, baguette spokes and gold-plated metal wings with rhinestone accents. 7x6.5cm.
   Marked MB "I".

B30. "Cob," Boucher 1941*****
Manufacturer Marcel Boucher Ltd.
Designer Marcel Boucher.
Patent n° 128,104 Marcel Boucher, New York,
8th July 1941, filed on 8th April 1941.

Rhodium-plated metal brooch
with enamel and rhinestones, in
the shape of corncobs. The cobs
are made of yellow enamel
with green enamel leaves and
rhinestone accents. 9.5x9cm.
Marked MB Des. Pat'd.

Rhodium-plated metal brooch, with green
and yellow-gold enamel and rhinestones,
of a pineapple. The fruit is made of yellow-
gold enamel with green enamel leaves with
rhinestones at the tips. 8x7.3cm.
Marked MB Des. Pat'd.

B31. "Pineapple," Boucher 1941****
Manufacturer Marcel Boucher Ltd.
Designer Marcel Boucher.
Patent n° 128,324 Marcel Boucher, New
York, 15th July 1941, filed on 8th April
1941.

B32. "Peppers," Boucher 1941****
Manufacturer Marcel Boucher Ltd.
Designer Marcel Boucher
Not patented
    Rhodium-plated metal brooch, red and green enamel, rhinestones, of three red chilli peppers. 7x7cm.
    Marked MB Des. Pat'D.
    Despite reference to a patent, the design is not patented. However the 1941 patents are similar for single parts or in general terms.

Rhodium-plated metal and enamel brooch of a grasshopper on a branch with rhinestone ornamented leaves. 4x9.8cm.
    Marked MB Des. Pat'd.

B33. "Grasshopper," Boucher 1941*****
Manufacturer Marcel Boucher Ltd.
Designer Marcel Boucher.
Patent n° 127,015 Marcel Boucher, New York, 6th May 1941, filed on 8th April 1941.

B34. "Radishes," Boucher 1941****
Manufacturer Marcel Boucher Ltd.
Designer Marcel Boucher.
Not patented.
    Rhodium-plated metal brooch, red and green enamel, rhinestones, of three radishes. 7.5x6.2cm.
    Marked MB.

B35. "Cherries," Boucher 1941****
Manufacturer Marcel Boucher Ltd.
Designer Marcel Boucher.
Not patented.
    Rhodium-plated metal brooch, red, yellow and green enamel, rhinestones, of a cherry-tree branch. 6x5.5cm.
    Marked MB Des. Pat'D.
    Once again this item is not patented.

B36. "Currant," Boucher 1941****
Manufacturer Marcel Boucher Ltd.
Designer Marcel Boucher.
Not patented.
   Rhodium-plated metal brooch, with green and lilac enamel and rhinestones, of a currant branch. 6x4.8cm.
   Marked MB DES. PAT'D "U". This design was also not patented.

B37. "Strawberries," Boucher 1941*****
Manufacturer Marcel Boucher Ltd.
Designer Marcel Boucher.
Not patented.
   Rhodium-plated metal brooch, with pink, green and yellow enamel and rhinestones, of a strawberry plant with six strawberries and a flower. 9x4.5cm.
   Marked MB 5.
   There is also a smaller version with four strawberries instead of six.

B38. "Original Sin," Boucher 1941*****
Manufacturer Marcel Boucher Ltd.
Designer Marcel Boucher.
Not patented.
   Rhodium-plated metal brooch, red and yellow enamel, rhinestones, of a snake wrapped around a branch, which is about to seize an apple. 4x9.3cm.
   Marked MB "F".

B39. "Fuchsia," Boucher 1941****
Manufacturer Marcel Boucher Ltd.
Designer Marcel Boucher.
Not patented.
   Rhodium-plated metal brooch, pink and pale green enamel, rhinestones and baguettes, in the shape of a fuchsia flower. 9.5x6.3cm.
   Marked MB "W".
   Other well known designs of plants and flowers, often in two sizes: one bigger, one smaller include: "Raspberries," "Carnation," "Gourd," "Hyacinth" and "Lily".

B40. "Chinese Couple," Boucher 1941*****
Manufacturer Marcel Boucher Ltd.
Designer Marcel Boucher.
Not patented.
   Rhodium- and gold-plated metal pin clips, yellow, pink and black enamel, rhinestones, of a Chinese couple. Both 5.8x2.8cm.
   Marked boy MB Pat. Pend., girl MB Pat. Pend. "R".

B41. "Dwarf Tree," Boucher 1941*****
Manufacturer Marcel Boucher Ltd.
Designer Marcel Boucher.
Not patented.
   Rhodium- and gold-plated metal brooch, yellow, and red and blue enamel, rhinestones, of a dwarf conifer. 10.5x8cm.
   Marked MB.

B42. "Dragon," Boucher 1941*****
Manufacturer Marcel Boucher Ltd.
   Designer Marcel Boucher.
   Patent n° 126,944 Marcel Boucher, New York, 29th April 1941, filed on 25th March 1941.

Rhodium-plated metal brooch, green, red, orange and black enamel, rhinestones, of a Chinese dragon. 6x9.5cm.
   Marked MB Pat. Pend.
   This is the only patented item from the extraordinary series of Chinese-inspired designs presented here.

B43. "Mandarin," Boucher
1941*****
Manufacturer Marcel Boucher Ltd.
Designer Marcel Boucher.
Not patented.
    Rhodium- and gold-plated
metal pin clip, ivory, pink and blue
enamel, rhinestones, of a mandarin. 6.5x4.3cm.
    Marked MB.

B44. "Junk," Boucher 1941*****
Manufacturer Marcel Boucher Ltd.
Designer Marcel Boucher.
Not patented.
    Rhodium-plated metal brooch, yellow and red
enamel, rhinestones, of a sailing junk. 7.2x6cm.
Marked MB.

B45. "Mexican Head," Boucher 1941*****
Manufacturer Marcel Boucher Ltd.
Designer Marcel Boucher.
Not patented.
    Two-toned, rhodium- and gold-plated metal
brooch of a Mexican woman's head wearing
an earring and a sombrero with six green, azure
and blue faceted rectangular stones on the brim.
7.5x8cm.
    Marked MB DES. PAT D. In spite of the marking, like other
contemporary items, the design was not patented.

B46. "Standing Mexican", Boucher
1947***
Manufacturer Marcel Boucher & Cie, Inc.
Designer Marcel Boucher.
Patent n° 147,954 Marcel Boucher, New
York, 25th November 1947, filed on 11th
February 1947.

Gold-plated metal pin clip, yellow,
red and blue enamel, rhinestones, of a
Mexican standing up, wearing a poncho
and sombrero. 4.5x2cm.
Marked Pat. Pend. 2510.
The number refers to the Boucher internal catalog. These numbers first appeared
on items in January 1945.

B47. "Mexican," Boucher 1941*****
Manufacturer Marcel Boucher Ltd.
Designer Marcel Boucher.
Not patented.
Rhodium-plated metal pin clip, enamel and rhine-
stones in various colors, of a Mexican wearing a poncho
and sombrero. 8.5x5cm.
Marked MB Pat. Pend.
Despite the mark "Patent Pending" the design was not
patented, but see the very similar design of the patented
"Sleeping Mexican" (B50.)

B48. "Mexican on a Chariot," Boucher 1941****
Manufacturer Marcel Boucher Ltd.
Designer Marcel Boucher.
Patent n° 126,902 Marcel Boucher, New York,
29th April 1941, filed on 25th March 1941.

Rhodium-plated metal brooch, enamel and
rhinestones in various colors, of a sleeping
Mexican leaning against a cart pulled by a
donkey which is also asleep. The cart's wheel
can turn. 4x6cm.
Marked MB Pat.Pend.

B49. "Mexican earrings," Boucher
1941*****
Manufacturer Marcel Boucher Ltd.
Designer Marcel Boucher.
Not patented, but see patents of
B48. and B50.

Rhodium-plated metal screw earrings with pale
green, red and yellow enamel and rhinestones,
of a cactus with a jar at the base. 2.5x2cm.
    Marked MB Pat. 1649187.
    The patent refers to the screw mechanism,
which is particularly complex and was assigned
to Philip Reiter, New York, on 15th November
1927, in response to an application filed on
22nd October 1926.
    The earrings can be worn as part
of a set both with the "Mexican on
a Chariot" (B48.), and with the
"Sleeping Mexican" (B50.)

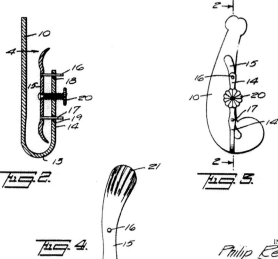

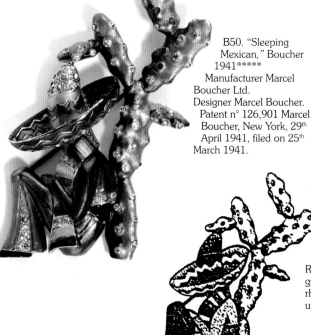

B50. "Sleeping
Mexican," Boucher
1941*****
Manufacturer Marcel
Boucher Ltd.
Designer Marcel Boucher.
Patent n° 126,901 Marcel
Boucher, New York, 29th
April 1941, filed on 25th
March 1941.

Rhodium-plated metal brooch, pale
green, red, yellow and black enamel,
rhinestones, of a Mexican sleeping
under a cactus plant. 7.8x5cm.
    Marked MB "z".

Gold- and rhodium-plated metal pin with dark
red enamel and rhinestones, of a dancing Hussar
with a rhinestone pavé fur hat, a tunic with buttons
and lining in red enamel with rhinestone borders,
pockets with red baguettes, rhodium-plated metal
trousers and bright red enamel boots. His face is a
white pearl. 7x7cm.
    Marked MB Des. Pat'd "C".

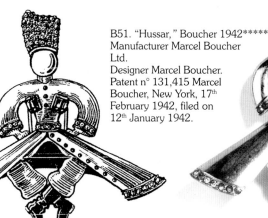

B51. "Hussar," Boucher 1942*****
Manufacturer Marcel Boucher
Ltd.
Designer Marcel Boucher.
Patent n° 131,415 Marcel
Boucher, New York, 17th
February 1942, filed on
12th January 1942.

B52. "Oak Leaf with Acorns," Boucher 1940*****
Manufacturer Marcel Boucher Ltd.
Designer Marcel Boucher.
Not patented.
   Rhodium-plated metal brooch, with pale green and black enamel, pearls and rhinestones, of an oak leaf with acorns. 6.5x6cm.
   Marked MB.
   The item was featured with this name in *WWD*, 2nd August 1940, in the fall 1940 collection, which, however, was generally characterized by an almost complete absence of enamel. Therefore, this enamel version may refer to the spring 1941 collection, which was made up of mainly floral and plant subjects in various enamel colors and shades.

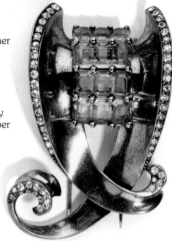

B55. "Crossed Pin," Boucher 1946****
Manufacturer Marcel Boucher & Cie, Inc.
Designer Marcel Boucher.
Patent n° 145,151 Marcel Boucher, New York, 9th July 1946, filed on 27th December 1945.

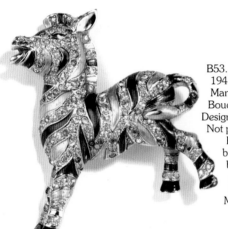

B53. "Zebra," Boucher 1941****
   Manufacturer Marcel Boucher Ltd.
Designer Marcel Boucher.
Not patented.
   Rhodium-plated metal brooch, yellow, red and black enamel, rhinestones, in the shape of a zebra. 6.2x5.3cm.
Marked MB.

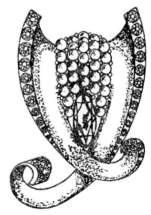

Gold-plated sterling pin clip, sky blue stones and rhinestones. 6.3x2.4cm.
   Marked MB Sterling.
   Some examples have also the internal catalog number 2355.

B54. "Hummingbird," Boucher 1945***
Manufacturer Marcel Boucher & Cie, Inc.
Designer Marcel Boucher.
Not patented.
   Gold-plated sterling brooch of a humming bird with rhinestone pavé crest and rectangular amethyst wings, one of which is bordered with rhinestones. 8x5.5cm.
   Marked MB Sterling 2307.
   There is also a smaller version.

B56. "Cockatoo," Boucher 1944***
Manufacturer Marcel Boucher & Cie, Inc.
Designer Marcel Boucher.
Not patented.
   Gold-plated sterling brooch of a cockatoo
with large faceted azure crystal in the middle of
its body and rhinestones at the center of a wing.
9.8x4cm.
   Marked MB Sterling.

B57. "Lovebirds," Boucher 1944****
Manufacturer Marcel Boucher & Cie.
Designer Marcel Boucher.
Not patented.
   Pair of rhodium- and gold-plated sterling brooches
with pink rectangular amethysts and rhinestones, of a
couple of parakeets facing each other. 6.4x3.8cm.
Marked MB Sterling.

B58. "Swan," Boucher 1945***
Manufacturer Marcel Boucher & Cie, Inc.
Designer Marcel Boucher.
Not patented.
   Gold-plated sterling brooch of a flying swan with a rhodium-
plated bill, a rhinestone pavé crest and rhinestone-bordered
wings with rectangular topazes. 6x9.5cm.
Marked MB sterling 2308.

B59. "Sea Horse," Boucher 1944***
Manufacturer Marcel Boucher & Cie, Inc.
Designer Marcel Boucher.
Not patented.
   Gold-plated sterling brooch, amethyst-color crystal in
the center, rhinestones, of a sea horse. 8x3.5cm.
Marked MB Sterling.

B60. "Fox," Boucher 1945*****
Manufacturer Marcel Boucher & Cie, Inc.
Designer Marcel Boucher.
Not patented.
   Large gold-plated sterling brooch of a fox's head whose muzzle and ears
have rhinestone accents and with five rectangular topazes on its head. The
item consists of two separate parts joined by a small screw. Through clever
alternation of fullness and emptiness, and through a skilful use of borders,
the subject acquires tri-dimensionality and expressiveness. 8.5x6.5cm.
   Marked MB Sterling 2305.
   This item belongs to an extraordinary series of brooches (*WWD*, 18ᵗʰ January
1945) of gold-plated sterling animals with rhinestones and rectangular stones
(topazes, amethysts, rubies, etc.) that, on the basis of the in-house catalog's progressive numbers, can be dated from 1945. The same series includes the "Hummingbird" (B54.), the "Lovebirds" (B57.), the "Swan" (B58) and the "Elephant
Head" (B61.). Other subjects include: a horse's head, a dolphin, a rabbit.

B61. "Elephant Head," Boucher 1945****
Manufacturer Marcel Boucher & Cie, Inc.
Designer Marcel Boucher.
Not patented.
   Gold-plated sterling pin of an elephant
head with a rhinestone on top of the head,
rhinestones at the tips of its rhodium-plated
sterling tusks, a large drop-shaped rhinestone
in its trunk and rectangular rubies on its ears.
6.8x5.8cm.
Marked MB Sterling 2312.

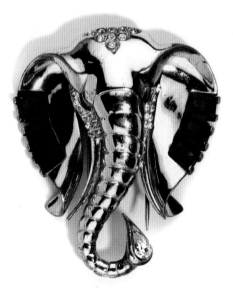

B62. "Skater," Boucher 1944***
Manufacturer Marcel Boucher & Cie, Inc.
Designer Marcel Boucher.
Patent n° 139,675 Marcel Boucher, New York, 12th December
1944, filed on 30th October 1944.

Gold-plated sterling pin clip with rhinestones, of a skater whose bust is made
of a sky-blue crystal. 6x7cm.
Marked MB Sterling.
There are also patented
matching earrings (Des n°
139,678).
The brooch was featured
in an advertisement in
Vogue November
15th 1944.

B63. "Cubist Ballerina," Boucher
1944***
Manufacturer Marcel Boucher &
Cie, Inc.
Designer Marcel Boucher.
Patent n° 139,676 Marcel
Boucher, New York, 12th
December 1944, filed on
30th October 1944.

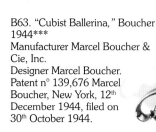

Gold-plated sterling brooch of a curtseying ballerina whose body is made of an azure crystal
and who has rhinestones on her gown and
neck. 7x5cm.
Marked MB Sterling.
In October-December 1944 Boucher designed a series of rather light sterling brooches
with a cubist design, of animal and figurative
subjects. These brooches featured a large faceted
stone in the middle of the body. The patented designs are of
a fish, a skater with matching earrings, (B62.) and two ballet
dancers, one curtseying and the other doing the splits (B64.).
Among the animal subjects of the same series the "Cockatoo"
(B56.) and the "Sea Horse" (B59.) are worthy of mention.

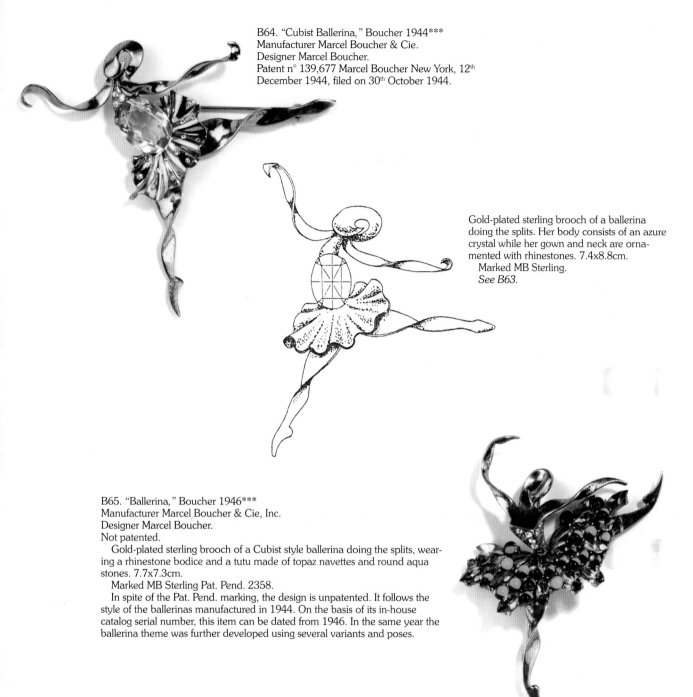

B64. "Cubist Ballerina," Boucher 1944***
Manufacturer Marcel Boucher & Cie.
Designer Marcel Boucher.
Patent n° 139,677 Marcel Boucher New York, 12th
December 1944, filed on 30th October 1944.

Gold-plated sterling brooch of a ballerina doing the splits. Her body consists of an azure crystal while her gown and neck are ornamented with rhinestones. 7.4x8.8cm.
   Marked MB Sterling.
   See B63.

B65. "Ballerina," Boucher 1946***
Manufacturer Marcel Boucher & Cie, Inc.
Designer Marcel Boucher.
Not patented.
   Gold-plated sterling brooch of a Cubist style ballerina doing the splits, wearing a rhinestone bodice and a tutu made of topaz navettes and round aqua stones. 7.7x7.3cm.
   Marked MB Sterling Pat. Pend. 2358.
   In spite of the Pat. Pend. marking, the design is unpatented. It follows the style of the ballerinas manufactured in 1944. On the basis of its in-house catalog serial number, this item can be dated from 1946. In the same year the ballerina theme was further developed using several variants and poses.

B66. "Winter," Boucher 1947****
Manufacturer Marcel Boucher & Cie, Inc.
Designer Marcel Boucher.
 Not patented.
   Gold-plated metal brooch with rhinestones, of a woman wearing a fur coat, muff, Cossack hat and boots. 5.3x3.8cm.
   Marked MB 2450.
      According to *WWD*, 7th March 1947, this is one of the four seasons: "Marcel Boucher bejeweled little ladies that suggest winter, spring (B67.), summer (B68.) and fall by their filigree costume. Stone details trim the skirts".

Gold-plated metal pin clip, sky-blue and pink enamel, rhinestones, of a woman in costume. 5x3cm.
Marked MB Pat. Pend. 2509.
The woman is one of the afore-mentioned four seasons and represents spring (s. B66. and B68.).

B67. "Spring," Boucher 1947****
Manufacturer Marcel Boucher & Cie, Inc.
Designer Marcel Boucher.
Patent n° 147,952 Marcel Boucher, New York, 25th November 1947, filed on 11th February 1947.

B68. "Summer," Boucher 1947****
Manufacturer Marcel Boucher & Cie.
Designer Marcel Boucher.
Patent n° 142,953 Marcel Boucher, New York, 25th November 1947, filed on 11th February 1947.

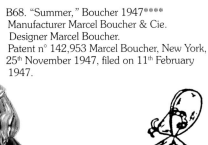

Gold-plated metal brooch with green and pink enamel, faceted oval aquamarines and rhinestones, of a woman wearing a costume. 5x3.4cm.
Marked MB PAT. PEND. 2509.
This is one of the four seasons, most probably summer, see B66 and B67

Couple of gold-plated sterling brooches, with blue, green and yellow enamels, red and blue stones and rhinestones, of a Cambodian water bearer in traditional costume, carrying two buckets made of large blue stones. 4.8x3.8cm.
Marked MB Sterling 2472.
The name is original and was reported in *WWD*, 21st February 1947.

B69. "Cambodian Water Boy," Boucher 1947****
Manufacturer Marcel Boucher & Cie, Inc.
Design Marcel Boucher.
Patent n° 147,951 Marcel Boucher, New York, 25th November 1947, filed on 11th February 1947.

MARCEL BOUCHER

B70. "Bejeweled Sultan," Boucher 1947****
Manufacturer Marcel Boucher & Cie, Inc.
Designer Marcel Boucher.
Not patented.
    Gold-plated and white sterling pin clip, blue, sky-blue and white enamel, amethyst-color crystal, red stones and rhinestones, of a seated sultan. 5x3cm.
    Marked MB Sterling.
    This item was named "Bejeweled sultan" by *WWD,* 21st February 1947 which in the same issue also mentioned the "Indian Boy" (B71.) and "Cambodian Water Boy" (B.69).

B71. "Indian Boy," Boucher 1947***
Manufacturer Marcel Boucher & Cie, Inc.
Designer Marcel Boucher.
Patent n° 147,399 Marcel Boucher, New York, 2nd September 1947, filed on 11th February 1947.

Small gold-plated sterling pin clip with enamel, of a boy with richly ornamented enameled clothes and a flabellum with small amethysts and rhinestones. 6.5x2.2cm.
    Marked MB Sterling 2470.
    The model was described, with this name, in an article published in *Women's Wear Daily* on 21st February 1947. This is the first of a series of patented sterling and enamel brooches with figurative subjects, including the "Cambodian Water Boy" (B69.), two feminine figures representing two of the four seasons (B67., B68.) – the other two are unpatented (see B66.) – and a standing Mexican (B46.). Another unpatented design is of a bejeweled sultan (B70.).
    The serial number 2470 refers to Boucher's in-house design catalog. This numbering procedure came in use in 1945, therefore, taking the patented numbered items as a reference point, it is also possible to date unpatented numbered items quite accurately.

B72. "Angel Fish," Boucher 1948***
Manufacturer Marcel Boucher & Cie, Inc.
Designer Marcel Boucher.
Not patented.
    Gold- and rhodium-plated metal brooch of a fish with rhinestone pavé snout, fretwork fins and tail with rhinestone borders and a body studded with red oval stones 7x5cm.
    Marked MB 2592.

B73. "Squirrel," Boucher 1948***
Manufacturer Marcel Boucher & Cie, Inc.
Designer Marcel Boucher.
Patent n° 151,503 Marcel Boucher, New York, 26th
October 1948, filed on 14th February 1948.

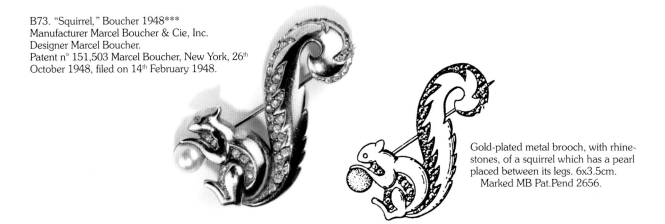

Gold-plated metal brooch, with rhinestones, of a squirrel which has a pearl
placed between its legs. 6x3.5cm.
Marked MB Pat.Pend 2656.

B74. "Sea Horse," Boucher 1948****
Manufacturer Marcel Boucher & Cie.
Designer Marcel Boucher.
Not patented.
    Two-toned gold- and rhodium-plated brooch, with
rhinestones and small red cabochon, of a seahorse and
seaweed. 7.2x5cm.
    Marked MB PAT. PEND. 2676. In spite of its mark-
ing, the design is unpatented but can be accurately
dated to 1948 thanks to its catalog number.

B75. "Lyrebird," Boucher 1948*****
Manufacturer Marcel Boucher & Cie, Inc.
Designer Marcel Boucher.
Patent n° 151,500 Marcel Boucher, New York, 26th
October 1948, filed on 14th February 1948.

Gold- and rhodium-plated metal brooch,
pearls and rhinestones, of a lyrebird
perched on a branch and holding a pearl in
its beak. 9.5x8.5cm.
    Marked MB Pat. Pend. 2633.

B76. "Necklace and Clip," Boucher 1948****
Manufacturer Marcel Boucher & Cie.
Designer Marcel Boucher.
Not patented.
　　Gold-plated metal snake-chain, with rhodium-plated metal clasp with rhinestones and baguettes, three rhinestone pendants and a rhodium-plated clip that can be detached and worn separately. Necklace and pendants are 27.5cm long. Clip size: 4.5x3cm.
　　Marked MB (Clip).
　　A few patented items made with the same materials (snake-chain and pendants), allow for an accurate dating of this item to 1948.

B77. "Gilded Cyclamen," Boucher 1950***
Manufacturer Marcel Boucher & Cie, Inc.
Designer Marcel Boucher.
Patent n° 159,591 Marcel Boucher, New York, 8th August 1950, filed on 1st February 1950.

Gold-plated metal brooch in the shape of a cyclamen with fretwork petals, a small pearl in the middle and rhinestone accents. 7x5.5cm.
　　Marked Boucher Pat. Pend. 3176.
　　A comparison between the cyclamen of 1940 (B7.) and this one shows the inaccurateness of the thesis according to which designs were reproduced unchanged over long periods of time. In this case it is obvious that this is the same subject designed by the same author, however at in two different periods and displaying features suited to the fashion and taste of the time.
　　The brooch also has matching earrings patented with n° 159,594 at the same time as the brooch. The earrings have the same, albeit smaller, design as the brooch.

B78. "Ballet of Jewels": "Prima Ballerina,"
Boucher 1950*
Manufacturer Marcel Boucher & Cie.
Designer Marcel Boucher.
Patent n° 159,586 Marcel Boucher, New York, 8th
August 1950, filed on 5th November 1949.

Gold- and rhodium-plated
metal brooch with rhine-
stones of a ballerina wearing
a fretwork gown with flounces
bordered with rhinestones and a rhinestone pavé bodice. 4.5x5cm.
Marked Boucher Pat. Pend. 3053.
In *Women's Wear Daily,* 8th July
1949, Marcel Boucher publicized an
invitation to the presentation in his
showroom in 347 Fifth Ave. of the fall
collection inspired by the city of Paris,
which included the lines "Ballet of Jewels,"
"Louvain Lace" and "Vendôme".

B79. "Swirl Necklace," Boucher 1950****
Manufacturer Marcel Boucher & Cie.
Designer Marcel Boucher.
Not patented.
   Rhodium-plated metal swirl necklace,
with rhinestones and baguettes. Part of the
necklace is detachable, thus transforming it into a choker. The central motif
measures 13cm.
   Marked Boucher 3312.
   Thanks to the in-house catalog number, the item can be accurately dated
to 1950.

❧ MARCEL BOUCHER ❧

B80. "Ballet of Jewels": "Carnival," Boucher 1950**
Manufacturer Marcel Boucher & Cie, Inc.
Designer Marcel Boucher.
Patents: Ballerina – Columbine n° 159,583, Dancer –
Harlequin n° 159,584 Marcel Boucher, New York, 8th
August 1950, filed on 5th November 1949.

Pair of gold- and rhodium-plated metal brooches of a ballerina
with a fretwork bodice and gown hem studded with rhinestones
and a male dancer with rhinestone pavé vest and lozenge
trousers, with green, red and blue stones. The pose of the two
figurines allows the male dancer to stand arm in arm with the ballerina. Ballerina 5x3.6cm; Male dancer 5.5x2.8cm.
   Marked Ballerina Boucher Pat. Pend. 3047. Dancer Boucher
3048.
   The third brooch of this group is of a dancing Pierrot kneeling
towards the couple, while imploring his Columbine.

B81. "Ballet of Jewels": "Peter and Sonia," Boucher
1949**
Manufacturer Marcel Boucher & Cie, Inc.
Designer Marcel Boucher.
Patents Sonia n° 154,095, Peter n° 154,096 Marcel
Boucher, New York, 14th June 1949, filed on 23rd
February 1949 Sonia and Peter 3rd March 1949.

Pair of gold- and rhodium-plated metal brooches with rhinestones, of a
couple of dancers doing the splits. Sonia 5x4.8cm; Peter 5.3x4.6cm.
   Marked Sonia MB 2977 Pat. 154095. Marked Peter MB 2977 "M".
   The pair of brooches appeared in an advertisement in *Vogue*, 1st April
1949, with the names Peter and Sonia, and were on sale for $5 and $7.50,
respectively. The same subject appeared in another advertisement for the
"Ballet of Jewels" series, in *Vogue*, 1st December 1949. Besides "Peter and
Sonia," this series included; "Carnival" composed of three items, "Sleeping Beauty" made up of two items and "Prima Ballerina". While "Peter and
Sonia" are still marked MB, the other items in the series are marked Boucher
and in effect they date from the period in which the company was in the
process of changing its mark. In November 1949, in order to safeguard these
two patents, Boucher brought three different suits against Roxee Corporation, Koslo Costume Jewelry, Co. and Mandel Bead Co., Inc.

NATACHA BROOKS

The Saturday Evening Post, May 31, 1947: Natacha Brooks.

Natacha Brooks was a well-known freelance designer of accessories who had worked for various producers of jewelry such as Albert Manufacturing Co. She started up her own company in 1944; the Natacha Brooks Co., which produced high-quality and expensive jewelry. Brooks still continued to work for other companies as well, such as Rice-Weiner with a line called "Jeray" in 1947. In 1949, Brooks entered into partnership with Michael Paul, who was already a designer for Hattie Carnegie, and had started-up his own company called Michael Paul, Inc.

Jewelry with the Natacha Brooks mark is very rare and none of the designs are patented.

WWD presented the first collection "Scheherazade" in the fall of 1944, a collection of Russian inspiration for spring 1946 and the "Romance" line which was inspired by old French motifs in the fall of 1946.

NB1. "Scheherazade," Natacha Brooks 1944*****
Manufacturer Natacha Brooks Co.
Designer Natacha Brooks.
Not patented.
  Gold-plated and rhodium-plated sterling brooch and earrings, yellow, red and black enamel, depicting the face of an Oriental figure with a feather turban and large hoop-earrings. Brooch 10x4.5cm, earrings 3.8x1.5cm.
  Marked Natacha Brooks Sterling (both).
  This brooch is part of the first collection designed by Natacha Brooks for her own company and was inspired by the "Scheherazade" ballet (*WWD*, 15th September 1944).

WWD, February 8, 1946: "Russian Collection" by Natacha Brooks.

CALVAIRE

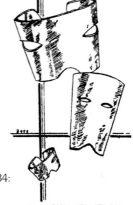

WWD, January 1930: advertisement by Calvaire.

WWD, March 3, 1934: "Mask Jewelry" by Calvaire.

"MASK" JEWELRY
The "Mask" ensemble done in silver metal, with little almond shaped "eye-holes," includes cuff bracelet, huge clip, and a ring It comes also in gold.
Calvaire.

CLV1. *"Debutante,"* Calvaire 1941****
Manufacturer Calvaire, Inc.
   Gold-plated metal pin clip, pink and red enamel, green cabochons, blue and white rhinestones, of a girl wearing an evening dress. 8x6cm.
   Marked Calvaire.
   Calvaire, Inc., of New York, was founded in the early 1920's by Ray Calish, who ran the firm with his wife, and was both an importer and manufacturer of costume jewelry. Information about the company is scarce but it was well known at the time and its collections were sometimes cited in "WWD." For example, mention was made of the "Calvaire pearl" (also a registered trademark), (*WWD*, 26th August, 1924), and the "Mask Jewelry" (*WWD*, 2nd March, 1934). During World War II, Calvaire also produced sterling jewelry. *WWD*, 22nd January 1943, reported: "Calvaire, Inc., specializing in gold-plated sterling silver is featuring a collection of butterflies, flowers, leaves and bowknots in pins and clips, studded with various sized multicolored stones." No further information is available and the company probably folded in 1950. The pieces are marked Calvaire with the "C" including part of the other letters.

HATTIE CARNEGIE

Hattie Carnegie (Henrietta Kanengeiser 1886-1956)

Henrietta Kanengeiser was born in Vienna in 1886. When she was six, her family moved to New York. In 1904 she started work as a messenger at R.H. Macy's. Within five years she changed her name choosing that of the richest man in the country, Andrew Carnegie, and opened a small custom made clothes shop on East 10th Street, soon successful enough to move up to West 86th Street. In 1923 Hattie Carnegie moved her business again to a noble town house on East 49th Street, off Park Avenue.

Like Coco Chanel, she modelled her designs herself by wearing them to fashionable restaurants and her clothes soon became famous. In addition to her custom made fashions she introduced ready-to-wear labels "Hattie Carnegie Originals" and spectator sports. Besides the stylish – almost businesslike – yet feminine "little Carnegie suit" for the day, her elegant evening dresses influenced the look of a generation.

According to *WWD*, August 11th, 1939, in the fall of that year Hattie Carnegie announced that for the first time a wholesale collection of costume jewelry would be presented to specialized shops throughout the country. The first wholesale group numbered about 35 pieces.

The firm stated that in this and future collections it planned to work closely with French couture. All the items in the line carry a seal with the Hattie Carnegie name.

So costume jewelry production by Hattie Carnegie started in 1939 and the items were marked at least until the end of 1940s with HC within a lozenge.

The identicalness of the two "Oriental Princesses" shows (s. Re1. and HC1.) Reinad also worked for Hattie Carnegie.

The only jewelry designer, known on the basis of documentation of the time, was Michael Paul who worked for Hattie Carnegie during the 1940s until 1949. Some designs of jewelry items are even attributed to clothes designers who worked for the company, however there is no confirmation of this.

A brooch in the shape of a ship lamp, marked HC, was made from a design patented by Irving Apisdorf on September 22nd, 1941 n° 129,828. Apisdorf is quoted with Michael Paul in an article of *WWD*, March 1st, 1946, concerning the spring collection.

Brooches with the signs of the Zodiac also went under the Hattie Carnegie mark, apparently made from designs by Hugo De Alteriis, New York, some of which were patented in November 1944. These pieces are in metal, while the date of the designs refers to a year when only sterling silver was used and are marked Hattie Carnegie, instead of HC, then the company mark.

The items marked HC are rare and not always of valuable design.

Hattie Carnegie died in 1956 and the company continued its activity until the 1980s.

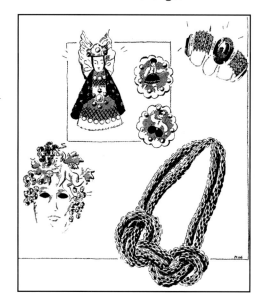

WWD, June 18, 1943: Hattie Carnegie Jewelry.

HC1. "Oriental Princess," Hattie Carnegie 1940****
Manufacturer Hattie Carnegie, Inc.
   Gold-plated metal pin clip, amethyst stones, rhinestones, of a bust of an Oriental princess with a mobile necklace. 9.5x6.8cm.
   Marked HC in a lozenge.
   The fact that this and the item Re1 are almost identical is proof that Reinad also worked for Hattie Carnegie.

CASTLECLIFF

Castlecliff Co., Inc., of New York was founded in 1918 by Clifford Furst (1898-1958) and Joseph A. Bobley. From this time on Castlecliff became one of the most important producers of costume jewelry and its founder, Furst, one of the most well-known businessmen in the sector, often consulted and interviewed by specialized press editors on the fashion trends and problems in the jewelry industry. Among the most important collections is the "Marqueterie" of 1929 advertised in *WWD* 21st March of the same year with the slogan "Once again we are the first."

WWD, March 9, 1934: Castlecliff "Mattress Ticking" Collection.

WWD, March 14, 1929: advertisement by Castlecliff Co.

The Head Office was and stayed in New York, 358-366 Fifth Avenue.

In 1940 Willard Markle joined the company as head designer. Markle, born in Palestine, Texas, had studied architecture at the University of Texas and in France at the Ecole des Beaux-Arts at Fontainebleau and had worked for various years as an architect in New York. In 1946 Markle became treasurer and Board secretary of the company.

WWD, April 26, 1946: Willard Markle's portrait of Rose Bampton with a Castlecliff jewel. Rose Bampton was a famous soprano of the Metropolitan Opera House.

In 1958, at the age of 60, Clifford Furst died of lung cancer and, in the same month, Willard Markle became president of the company.

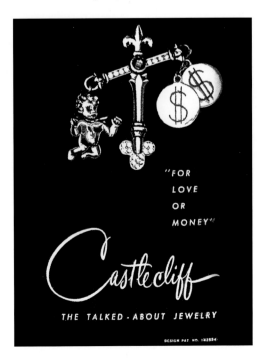

Vogue, December 1, 1945: Castlecliff advertisement of "For Love or Money," brooch designed by Clifford Furst.

Apart from Willard Markle, Elizabeth Hawes (*WWD*, 2nd March 1934), Clifford Furst and, in the 1950s, Joanne Moonan who was already at Authentics Inc., and Anne Dogarthy, all designed for Castlecliff.

Towards the end of the 1960s Castlecliff was taken over by Lucien Piccard Industries which also had Lucien Piccard and Pierre Cardin as part of the group.

According to *WWD* 7th January 1977 Castlecliff, then based at 417 Fifth Avenue, was part of the Carnegie Industries Co., as Hattie Carnegie (437 Fifth Avenue).

There is no further information about Castlecliff after this date.

Ca1. "Clock," Castlecliff 1940***
Manufacturer Castlecliff Co., Inc.
Designer Willard Markle.
Patent n° 122,218 Willard Markle, New York,
August 27th 1940, filed July 27th 1940.

Gold-plated metal brooch, with rhinestone pavé and red cabochon, of a tower clock with the hours written in ancient Roman numbers and with mobile hands. The clock is attached to a metal bowknot with rhinestone pavé. 7x5.5cm.
Marked Des. Pat. 122218.

According to an article headed *Merchant of Glitter* by Elsie McCormick, published in the *Saturday Evening Post*, 31st May 1947, a few years earlier a designer from Castlecliff, whose name is not mentioned, had made a brooch with mobile hands for a young lady friend who was always late, so that she could put the hands to the time of their date as a reminder. The brooch was very successful, especially among men, and was also copied by Coro which produced a similar design patented by Adolph Katz on 31st March 1942 Des. 131,811, filed on 19th January 1942.

Gold-plated metal brooch, rhinestone pavé and green enamel, of a grasshopper playing a fiddle. The legs and the fiddle are *en tremblant*. 7x5cm.
Unmarked.

WWD, 21st March 1941, stated that: "The Castlecliff Co. has filed suit in the U.S District Court (New York), alleging infringement of design patent number 125,693, a design for a pin, by Brier Mfg. Co., Inc., F.W. Woolworth & Co. and Crystal Novelty Co., Inc." The suit was then transferred to Providence where: "a consent decree in an infringement action brought by Clifford Furst and Joseph A. Bobley, co-partners using the trade name of Castlecliff Co., of New York, against the Brier Mfg. Co., has been filed in the U.S. District Court here. The decree signed by Judge John P. Hartigan grants a perpetual injunction against the Brier concern, restraining it and its officers from infringing on an ornamental brooch pin design. The plaintiffs, according to the decree, are the sole owners of the design patent 125,693 which covers the brooch in question." (*WWD*, May 16th 1941). This lawsuit is one of the rare examples of a victory in defense of a patented design. After this episode, Castlecliff started to mark its own jewelry.

The brooch was published in *Town & Country*, December 1940, in an advertisement for Bergdorf Goodman where it was on sale for $10.

Ca2. "Fiddling Grasshopper," Castlecliff 1941*****
Manufacturer Castlecliff Co., Inc.
Designer Willard Markle.
Pat. n° 125,693 Willard Markle, New York, 4th March 1941, filed on 28th January 1941.

Ca3. "For Love or Money," Castlecliff 1945***
Manufacturer Castlecliff Co., Inc.
Designer Clifford A. Furst.
Pat. n° 142,554 Clifford A. Furst, New York, 16th October 1945, filed on 16th June 1945.

Gold-plated sterling brooch, citrine-colored cabochon and rhinestones, depicting scales with some dollars on the left side and winged Cupid on the right which, being heavier, makes the scales hang to the side of love. 5.5x4.5cm.
Marked Castlecliff Sterling.
The item was published under the name "For Love or Money" in an advertisement for Castlecliff - "The talked-about jewelry" - in *Vogue*, December 1st 1945.

Ca4. "Crown Jewel," Castlecliff 1943***
Manufacturer Castlecliff Co., Inc.
Designer Clifford A. Furst.
Not patented.

"Easter Bells"—"Crown Jewels"
New Jewelry Stresses Design

WWD, February 19, 1943: "Crown Jewels" and "Pierced Heart" (Ca5) by Castlecliff.

Gold-plated sterling brooch, white pearls and rhinestones, in the shape of a crown. 5x4.7cm.
Marked Castlecliff Sterling.
The crown, along with the matching earrings, was published in *WWD*, 19th February 1943, under the name of "Crown Jewel".

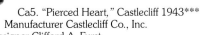

Ca5. "Pierced Heart," Castlecliff 1943***
Manufacturer Castlecliff Co., Inc.
Designer Clifford A. Furst.
Not patented.
Gold-plated sterling brooch with large central topaz crystal, of a heart pierced by an arrow. 6.5cm (arrow), 3.7x3.6cm (hearth).
Marked Castlecliff Sterling.
The brooch was reproduced, together with the "Crown Jewel," in *WWD*, 19th February 1943.

CHANEL – REINAD

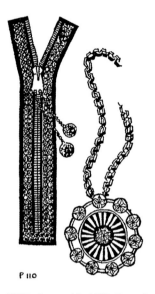

P 110

WWD, August 16, 1935: Reinad Novelty Co. A slide fastener and a gold finished necklace.

Collectors and dealers have always wondered whether the items marked Chanel – in script, with what looks like the signature of Gabrielle "Coco" Chanel – have anything to do with the French designer.

The problem was resolved by some information that appeared in *WWD* in the brief period between 10th January to 28th February 1941. *WWD*, 10th January 1941, starts with the title: "Sets of three In Enamel, Metal" and continues:

"A new costume jewelry source in the $1 to $3 retail price ranges, and one which is of special interest because the firm does its own designing as well as all manufacturing, is Chanel Novelty Co., which previously has worked exclusively in jewelry and ornaments for the garment trades. This firm is a metal house, and in its first retail collection concentrates on enamelled and jewelled pins either in flower designs or in novelty motifs, emphasizing the point that the designs shown are not popular price copies of higher priced jewelry successes but patterns made from original sketches, and interpreting what are considered important style trends for volume selling. One of the style ideas, which the firm likes, is the graduated 'series' pin in sets of three. There is a whole group of little animals to be worn together on dress or lapel. Those may be had either in polished metal or in colored enamels. There is a lively fawn, with jewelled eyes, a dachshund, a penguin, a cat, a blue bird and similar motifs, all in graduated sizings.

"The line, which is said to be registering best in initial orders, is of flower sprays in hand-painted enamels with either colored stones or satinore. There is another group of tropical birds in stones, and the hand-painted enamel, and one of big dragonflies with realistically colored wings and a single large stone for a body. Individual novelties include a jewelled 'fiddling grasshopper,' which is movable. Where the designs make it practical, earrings will be designed to match the pins.

"The firm is at present showing at 256 West 38th Street, although planning to open a Fifth Avenue show-room in the near future."

In the same edition of 10th January 1941 we learn that Al Marks joined the Chanel Novelty Co., as sales director for New York and New Jersey.

Shortly after, a month later, on 21st February 1941, *WWD* wrote: "Chanel Novelty Co announces change of name" and continues "Chanel Novelty Co. is changing its name to Reinad Novelty Co., Inc., in order to avoid confusion with firms of similar names. The organization will continue otherwise unchanged, operating out of the new 347 Fifth Avenue show-room." On the same page an advertisement appears with: "Reinad Novelty Co. Inc., (formerly Chanel Novelty Co.) 256 west 38th Street, New York. Show-room 347 Fifth Avenue, New York."

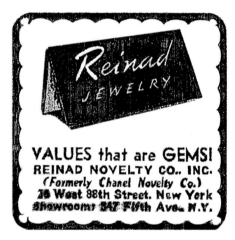

VALUES that are GEMS!
REINAD NOVELTY CO.. INC.
(Formerly Chanel Novelty Co.)
256 West 38th Street. New York
Showroom: 347 Fifth Ave., N.Y.

WWD, February 28, 1941: advertisement by Reinad, formerly Chanel Novelty Co.

Therefore Reinad, which already existed since 1922 for wholesale production and was perhaps already a shareholder in the "Chanel Novelty Co.," in 1941 wanted to start its own production for retail by using or founding the Chanel Novelty Co. It seems that there is no relation between Reinad or the Chanel Novelty Co. and the Maison Chanel of Paris which had its own representatives in the United States. Moreover, the maison Chanel had suspended production during the German occupation of France (1940). However, the fact that one month later Chanel Novelty Co. was forced to change its name to avoid confusion with other companies of the same name, leads to the conclusion that when some items under the name Chanel came out, there was a reaction either on the part of Chanel France, or their American representatives. Therefore items marked Chanel are American and were manufactured by Chanel Novelty Co. in only one collection: that of spring 1941. This explains the limited number of designs and the rarity of the items, all of which are of excellent quality. Reinad then continued to produce for wholesale and retail under the mark of Reinad making good quality collections.

Reinad, it seems, still worked for other companies such as Boucher, Hattie Carnegie, Eisenberg, using the same designs and stamps. In fact, the fish (Ch5.) apart from the Chanel make, exist in a very similar version, with the mark MB; the "African Mask" (Ch11.) exists both with the Chanel mark and the Eisenberg Original mark; the "Oriental Princess" (Re1. and HC1) has both Reinad and HC (Hattie Carnegie) marks.

A patent for a pair of earrings designed by William Wienner, New York, was issued to Reinad on 20th September 1949, n° 155,326.

There is no further information about Reinad after the mid-1950s.

Ch1. "Flamingo," Chanel 1941*****
Manufacturer Chanel Novelty Co.
Gold-plated metal brooch, azure and red stones, rhinestones, in the shape of a flamingo. 8x5cm.
Marked *Chanel*

Ch2. "Turkey," Chanel 1941*****
Manufacturer Chanel Novelty Co.
Gold-plated metal brooch with rhinestones in the shape of a turkey. 8x7.5cm.
Marked *Chanel*

Ch3. "Eagle," Chanel 1941***
Manufacturer Chanel Novelty Co.
Gold-plated metal brooch, rhinestones, red and green pendant stones, in the shape of an eagle. 5.5x8cm.
Marked *Chanel*
A patriotic version of this brooch also exists, with red, white and blue enamel on the wings.

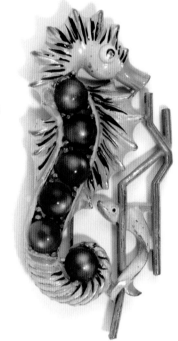

Ch4. "Sea Horse," Chanel 1941****
Manufacturer Chanel Novelty Co.
    Pot metal brooch, pink, black and white
enamel, pink satinore cabochons, depicting
a Sea Horse. 8.5x4cm.
    Marked *Chanel*

Ch5. "Fish," Chanel 1941****
Manufacturer Chanel Novelty Co.
    Pot metal brooch, yellow enamel and
rhinestones, in the shape of a fish.
7x6cm.
Marked *Chanel*.
    An almost identical brooch exists
with the mark MB by Boucher. This
confirms the hypothesis that Reinad/
Chanel also worked for Boucher.

Ch6. "Paradise Bird," Chanel
1941*****
Manufacturer Chanel Novelty Co.
    Pot metal brooch, pink and
sky-blue enamel, navette stones in
amethyst color, represents an exotic

Ch7. "Frog," Chanel 1941*****
Manufacturer Chanel Novelty Co.
   Pot metal brooch, green, red and black enamel,
rhinestones, in the shape of a frog. 7x7.2cm.
Marked *Chanel.*

Ch8. "Pierced Heart," Chanel 1941****
Manufacturer Chanel Novelty Co.
   Pot metal brooch with red enamel, depicting a heart pierced by an arrow, with two little hearts hanging from it. 7.5x9.5cm.
   Marked *Chanel.*
   There is also a necklace with the same motif which has eight little hearts hanging from it.

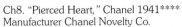

Ch9. "Pussy in Boots," Chanel 1941*****
Manufacturer Chanel Novelty Co.
   Rhodium-plated metal brooch, black and
red enamel, rhinestones, depicting a cat
in boots playing a violin. Legs and violin
quiver (*en tremblant*). 6.5x4.5cm.
Marked *Chanel.*

Ch10. "Mexican on a Palm," Chanel
1941*****
Manufacturer Chanel Novelty Co.
   Gold-plated metal brooch, sky-blue, yellow
and pink enamel, baguettes, depicting a Mexican on a palm. The figure moves. 8x6cm.
   Marked *Chanel.*

Ch11. "African Mask" Chanel 1941*****
Manufacturer Chanel Novelty Co.
   Gold-plated metal brooch, white crystals, rhinestones and pendant baroque pearl, depicting an African face. 9.5x5cm.
   Marked *Chanel*. An identical brooch exists with colored crystals marked Eisenberg Original, which is prove that Reinad/Chanel was one of the New York producers who worked for Eisenberg.

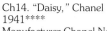

Ch14. "Daisy," Chanel 1941****
Manufacturer Chanel Novelty Co.
   Pot metal brooch, green, brown and yellow enamel, white satinore stones, rhinestones, in the shape of a daisy. 9.5x4.5cm.
   Marked *Chanel*.

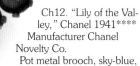

Ch12. "Lily of the Valley," Chanel 1941****
Manufacturer Chanel Novelty Co.
   Pot metal brooch, sky-blue, green and brown enamel, blue satinore stones, rhinestones, depicting a lily of the valley. 8x6.5cm.
   Marked *Chanel*.

Ch13. "Rose," Chanel 1941*****
Manufacturer Chanel Novelty Co.
   Gold-plated metal brooch, pink, red and green enamel, rhinestones, in the shape of a rose. 8x4.5cm.
   Marked *Chanel*. Pat. Pend.
   Probably inspired by a design by the Duke of Verdura. Despite the mark Pat. Pend. the design was never patented.

Ch15. "Agave," Chanel 1941****
Manufacturer Chanel Novelty Co.
   Pot metal brooch, green and pink enamel, pink satinore stones, rhinestones, depicting an agave flower. 10.5x8cm.
   Marked *Chanel*.

Ch18. "Flower Head with Ribbon," Chanel 1941****
Manufacturer Chanel Novelty Co.
　Pot metal brooch, sky-blue and green enamel, blue satinore stones and rhinestones, depicting a flower with a ribbon. 8.8x6.3cm.
　Marked *Chanel.*

Ch16. "Flower Bouquet," Chanel 1941****
Manufacturer Chanel Novelty Co.
　Gold-plated metal brooch, green enamel, green stones, depicting a bunch of flowers. 11x6.7cm.
　Marked *Chanel.*

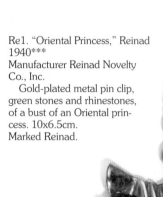

Re1. "Oriental Princess," Reinad 1940***
Manufacturer Reinad Novelty Co., Inc.
　Gold-plated metal pin clip, green stones and rhinestones, of a bust of an Oriental princess. 10x6.5cm.
Marked Reinad.

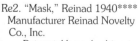

Re2. "Mask," Reinad 1940****
Manufacturer Reinad Novelty Co., Inc.
　Pot metal brooch, rhinestone pavé, red stones, green and blue baguettes, in the shape of a mask. 5.8x5.3cm.
　Marked Reinad.

Ch17. "Double Daisy," Chanel, 1941*****
Manufacturer Chanel Novelty Co.
　Gold-plated metal brooch, green and white enamel, white crystals, navette crystals in pink and sky-blue, depicting two daisies. 9x8.2cm.
Marked *Chanel.*

CORO

The history of the company, which is the largest in the world in this sector, is described in detail in documents of the time, and perfectly exemplifies the evolution of costume jewelry, jewelry making and fashion in the course of the decades.

The firm was founded in 1901 by Emanuel Cohn and Carl Rosenberger as Cohn & Rosenberger Co., and was based in New York. Coro Inc., the company's most well-known name, which was a fusion of both the founders' surnames, registered as a trademark in 1921, was used from the very beginning of production, and was adopted in 1943. The news of the change in company name was given by the company itself in a communiqué published in *Women's Wear Daily* on 4th June 1943.

WWD, October 29, 1931: Carl Rosenberger.

Carl Rosenberger was born in Germany in 1872 and emigrated to the United States in 1886 at the age of 14. For sixteen years he worked as a sales agent for various jewelry companies, then, in 1900, he joined E. Cohn & Co. as partner of the company, which became Cohn & Rosenberger Co. the following year.

In 1910 Coro became incorporated. The workshop and sales office were moved to 536 Broadway – a modest ground floor and basement – while the first factory was opened in Providence, R.I., at 46 Chestnut Street, in a one-story work space of about 5,000 square feet, which remained in use until 1929. From an initial twenty workers, the company grew to one hundred at the beginning of the 20s. In 1910, Emanuel Cohn died and Carl Rosenberger became chairman of the company, a position he held until he died on 7th October 1957 at 85 years of age.

In 1912, Royal Marcher, a twenty-two year old from New York, who had started working as an errand boy when he was thirteen, was hired as a sales agent. Marcher remained at Coro until 31st December 1959, building a brilliant career that saw his first great step forward in 1946, when he was appointed sales manager and culminating with his appointment as executive vice president in 1950. The company owed its great commercial development to his organization capacity, his marketing skills, and his capacity to understand and anticipate the public's tastes, as well as spot opportunities and find

original slogans and fashionable subjects. In 1926 Royal Marcher had the brilliant idea – or so he maintains – of giving a fantasy name to each line or piece of jewelry, often registering such names as trade names and using them in advertising. This proved a winning strategy in attracting new customers, who could identify and recognize the various items, the value of which increased with their growing popularity. This practice remained and was adopted by most costume jewelry makers.

At that time, costume jewelry was modest in price and mediocre in design, and appealed only to a small, low level market segment, because it was not considered elegant. Costume jewelry lines comprised only a few items, which were banal imitations of the "real" jewels that only the higher classes could afford, and were sold in textile stores and in a few department stores where they were relegated to the least visible areas, in baskets placed at the end of counters. Costume jewelry design was unheard of, and, moreover, would not have been commercially appreciated. Cohn & Rosenberger was no exception. The company manufactured trimmings for hats, brooches, buckles for shoes and belts, pendants, sliding brooches to secure chains, bead appliqués for blouses, glass bead necklaces and mourning jewelry. The use of mourning jewelry had originated in London, especially when Queen Victoria imposed a long period of mourning on her subjects after the death of Prince Albert. Thereafter, the designs of mourning jewelry, characterized by use of black and white and jet (made of granules of lignite in Britain and glass beads in France) multiplied.

In the 1920s, in the wake of Parisian fashion and of the style launched by Chanel, Cohn & Rosenberger began to abandon traditional designs, and became more and more successful, thanks to the contribution of Adolph Katz, a brilliant designer and intuitive product manager, who joined the firm in 1924 and stayed at Coro all his professional life, until the end of the 1960s. After working for thirteen years in various departments, in 1937 he became head designer and product manager, in 1948 vice president and in 1960 executive vice president, replacing Marcher.

In those years Cohn & Rosenberger strengthened their productive and commercial structure. In order to find skilled labor at low prices and have ready access to rhinestones and colored stones, it opened a factory in Czechoslovakia which closed down in the year of Nazi occupation (1938). A sales office was opened in Toronto, Canada, followed by a branch firm, Coro Canada Ltd., at 77 York Street and 110 Wellington Street, which remained operational and played an important role in the firm's economy. It is still in operation today with the lines Coro, Vendome, and Oscar de la Renta.

The headquarters remained in New York with offices and a showroom in the Marbridge Building, 1328

Broadway. A new, larger showroom, comprising several elegantly furnished rooms, was opened in June 1926. The showroom occupied the third store of the Marbridge Building with an entrance at 47 West 34th Street, which was the permanent address of Coro.

In 1929 the largest and most modern costume jewelry factory in the country, which would later be known as the Coro Building, was built in Providence, R.I., 177 Point Street. It was a three-storey building and basement for a total of 107,000 square feet. The building was H-shaped for greater luminosity, with ceiling-to-floor windows and featured a ventilation system. Large investments were made in modern machinery, new production lines were added and the total work force grew to over one thousand. The new structure became operational on 10th June 1929, beginning its activity with the delivery of the Fall collection.

In order to finance investment, Cohn & Rosenberger, for the first time in the history of the costume jewelry industry, turned to shareholding, a move which implied the publication of the company balance sheet. The operation, which, in the middle of the Depression, appeared to many as a huge risk, was actually justified – in the words of Carl Rosenberger in an interview given to *Women's Wear Daily* on the day of the inauguration – by the unprecedented growth of costume jewelry in the previous five years, boosted by the new fashion of "coordinates," i.e. the possibility of matching clothes to beautiful, albeit inexpensive jewels. A telltale sign of the growing popularity of costume jewelry was represented by the fact that these items were gaining larger and better floor space in department stores, where they were now displayed on the ground floor, after years of neglect lying among miscellaneous items on counters, or on the upper floors.

In any case, it was a winning strategy. Cohn & Rosenberger were ready for the boom in the sales of costume jewelry registered during the Depression, around the mid-1930s, and were ahead of the competition. The company had the space, machinery, technical know-how and the inventive capacity to meet demand and this abundance of resources enabled the company to grow and increase its production and sales volumes both in the USA and abroad.

In 1933 a branch office was opened in London, G.B., Cohn & Rosenberger Ltd., at 1 Argyll Street, as a first incursion in the European market and the Commonwealth. Production was suspended during the war, but was resumed soon afterwards under the leadership of Henry Rosenblatt, albeit with some difficulties due to the economic crisis the country was going through at the time.

In 1936 Cohn & Rosenberger had a turnover of $2,900,000 with a net profit before tax of $141,600, and,

together with its subsidiary CoroGram, Inc., established in 1926 for the production of initials and monograms for bags and other items, had further extended its range and increased its volumes.

The company advertised almost weekly in *Women's Wear Daily* with the slogan "Popular Jewelry at Popular Prices" initially with the trademark Cohn & Rosenberger, then with Coro Creations from 1927 and Coro from 1935, whereas advertising at national level was still modest.

In 1935, with advertisements in three consecutive issues of *Vogue* (1st and 15th October and 1st November) the company launched its most successful product, "The Coro Duette." The patent for the Duette mechanism – Pat. No. 1,798,867 of 31st March 1931, stamped on all Duette mechanisms manufactured by Coro at that time – was held by Gaston Candas of Paris and had originally been created for precious jewelry. Cohn & Rosenberger bought it in 1933 for its metal and silver production. The Duette mechanism became a characteristic feature of Coro and, made in the most diverse and imaginative designs, remained a constant success for many years. Its novelty lay in the shape of the frame which suited all clip models, even large and heavy ones. The clips were inserted into the frame slots and fixed at the back. The first Duettes produced were made of white or rhodium plated metal, studded with rhinestones in deco-style geometric volutes. The success of the Duette was so great, that other firms started patenting mechanisms for mounting individual clips on a single frame, allowing them to be worn together, e.g. Trifari's clip-mates, and the frames designed by Marcel Boucher for Mazer.

In 1937, again with an advertisement in *Vogue* (1st December), Coro launched "Triquette by Coro," which however was never as successful as the Duette. The Triquette, a trademark registered in the same year, was a single jewel composed of various parts that could be taken apart, becoming a bracelet, a brooch and a pair of clips. The design was patented as a mechanism with patent No. 2,085,723 on 6th July 1937, filed on 18th November 1936, and assigned to Ignaz Adelsberger and Abraham Kraus, New York, for E. M. Gattle & Co. of New York. Obviously a production partnership or patent transfer was signed with Coro.

Later on this model was no longer replicated and, in 1944, the trademark Triquette was used to define the evolution of the Duette, i.e. a brooch with a frame mechanism composed of three graduated clips instead of two.

Production in the period between the mid-1920s and the mid-1930s was strongly influenced by Parisian fashion, and the designs of the great French designers were even openly copied. It is interesting to note that in

1927, Coro, which within a few years would denounce the problem of copying in jewelry design, supporting an initiative to establish a category association for design protection, presented the Jura Tyrol line with "Chanel-style" crystals and white and colored baguettes, with the openly expressed intent to create Chanel jewelry imitations that would sell at much lower prices. In 1930 Coro presented the "Grace Brinkley Rubber Jewelry," a long "rubber tube" necklace launched by Jean Patou and modified by Coro for Grace Brinkley, the leading lady of the musical *Flying High* by George Withe. The quote of the source of inspiration for this piece of jewelry appeared in the advertisements and was therefore considered a plus and a service to the clientele, in keeping with the current mentality that considered French fashion a supreme and unattainable paragon of elegance that could only be imitated as best as possible.

In the second half of the 1920s, Cohn & Rosenberger was already presenting two collections a year, mainly consisting of necklaces, bracelets, and brooches with a flat line, that only seldom displayed figurative subjects. The jewelry lines were given fantasy names. Among the pieces dating from 1926 are: "White Stone Jewelry," a line of rhinestone studded jewels, "Grotto Blu" of gold-plated metal filigree with dark blue stones, "Celestial Jade" of pink gold-plated metal filigree with Chinese jade, "Cherry Red" of matt gold-plated metal with red stones, "Royal Orchid" of gold-plated metal and imitation amethysts and "Russian Antique" of antiqued gold-plated metal and rococo-style faux topaz and amber.

Royal Marcher – in an article by Irwin Ross, *Every Woman a Queen*, published in *American Magazine* of February 1948 – recounted that the idea for the Russian Antique collection came to him one night in his hotel room, when, tired after a long day's work with customers, he was lying on his bed observing the antique gold and topaz glare of the light reflected by the burnished metal of the chandelier. The name of the line had been suggested by a customer, who had observed that the gold plating looked antique and that the word "Russian" would give a touch of originality to the jewelry, although in reality, they had nothing to do with Russia. Thus, both a successful jewelry line and the idea of naming the various collections were born. It is also interesting to note that in 1948, some twenty years after these events, there was already a tendency to create a mythical aura for successful products, thus further enhancing the standing of the company and its management.

In 1927 Coro designers looked for inspiration to the Old World creating lines named "Venetian Art," with mosaic medallions, and "Golden Rod" with canary colored stones. Also a jewelry line for young girls was launched, under the name of "Debutante," which was a registered trademark. It consisted of necklaces of pearls and colored glass beads. In those years pearls were extremely fashionable: pearl ropes up to 60 inch (about 152 cm) long were worn full length, or wound around the neck like a choker with the remaining length left flowing. Another favorite was a novelty item presented in 1926, a triple strand necklace of graduated pearls like the one worn by Queen Mary during her visit to the States. The latter is one of the first examples of "topical jewelry," i.e. models inspired by current events of any kind: social, political, heroic etc. Topical jewelry remained a constant feature of Coro's production and of costume jewelry in general. Another important example of topical jewelry is the "Spirit of St. Louis," which was a rhinestone brooch shaped like an airplane, inspired by Captain Charles Lindberg's flight across the Atlantic in May 1927 that sold for 50 cents. Production of the brooches began as soon as news of the plane landing in Paris arrived and the items were ready for delivery at the time of Lindberg's triumphal return to the States. Trifari also produced two versions, single- or double-winged, of the "Spirit of St. Louis," with rhinestones and black enamel details and colored enamel flag, or with enamel wings and the word "Spirit."

Nor could the worlds of cinema and musicals be forgotten, "Rio Rita Chockers" was the name of a line of necklaces with the clasp worn in front, like a sort of portrait frame, similar to those worn by Florence Ziegfeld's *Senoritas of Rio Rita*. The "Betty Compton Collar," a "gold" and "silver" combination with a sand effect, was a homage to the main character of *Hold Everything* and the actress automatically became a testimonial. Coro's production for the cinema and theatre continued for a long time. In 1934, for example, the company produced a series of large, glittering brooches and pendants for Ziegfeld's *Follies*.

In 1930 Coro's production took an unexpected turn with the creation of jewelry – mainly bead necklaces and large bracelets – made of galalite, Bakelite, hematite and prystal, or Corolite. Prystal was one of the trade names

Spark plug: *Royal Marcher is credited with sparking the costume bauble business to dazzling brilliance. Behind him, model displays "tailored type" jewelry of polished metal*

American Magazine, February 1948: Royal Marcher.

of molded phenolic resin, a plastic material available in several glossy and matte colors, that could be used alone or in combination. Cohn & Rosenberger imitated this by producing a compound it called "Corolite," which became another patented trademark. The new collections featured black and white clips and jewels, metal barrettes with Corolite beads for the "Pompadour Line," engraved faux ivory roses for the line "Genuine Camellia," necklaces of barbarian inspiration for the line "The Barbarian Mode," chromium and Bakelite jewels for the "Neptune Blue Jewelry" line, for which a guaranteed rust-free chromium-like material, called "CoroChrome," was used. In 1931, engraved faux white coral and gold-plated metal; a revival of the antique look, with gold-plated filigree, marked the comeback of the "New Russian Antique" line of jade, marcasite, cameos: a triumph of the Victorian and second Empire style. The "New Serpentine Jewelry" line of 1930 is of particular interest, featuring sinuous "gas pipe" metal necklaces and bracelets. This line was again featured in 1948. The "Taylored Jewelry" line of 1931 featuring formal daytime jewels without stones is also worthy of mention. In 1934 the so-called "convertible" jewelry became all the rage. This jewelry could be used in several ways: e.g. pendants that could be transformed into brooches, or brooches whose central part could become a clip. Egyptian-inspired jewelry was also fashionable. The company was also producing children's jewelry. From the anonymous and banal "Peggy Jewelry" line of 1926, which included necklaces, small brooches, and bracelets sold in heart-shaped leather boxes, to the "Winnie the Pooh" line of 1931 inspired by the homonymous book by A. A. Milne which depicted a fantasy animal world, to the "Mickey Mouse Kiddie Jewelry" line of January 1932, produced under exclusive license of the Walt Disney company, to the series inspired by the "Three little pigs" and "Alice in Wonderland," which were the hits of Christmas 1934.

It was an exciting time, marked by a continuous search for the European styles and fashions described by the correspondents of major magazines – *Women's Wear Daily* had offices in Paris and Vienna – but Coro's production was then modest and of scarce personality if compared with that of the original European models. In those years Europe was the center of world culture and arts, the place where the philosophy of art applied to industry originated, a philosophy aiming at bringing art to the greatest possible number of people. With its schools of thought and applied arts, from Bauhaus to Darmstadt, Europe had spread and renewed the message of jewelry, whose artistic value was no longer determined by the preciousness of the materials, but by the artistic project, the harmonious relationship between material and formal perfection. "Modern style" in jewelry originated from this style and was interpreted in the best way by Theodor

Fahrner of Pforzheim, "the industrialist of art," as he was called, who cooperated with the Darmstadt artists in the production of pieces that were symbols of the perfect synthesis of quality, ideas, and form. Another important figure in this movement was Auguste Bonaz, a master in the production of chromium and red or black enamel jewels, which were famous for their pure and essential lines. Heinrich Grosse, of Henkel & Grosse, who in the 1950s worked for Christian Dior was another important figure. It was in Paris, in 1925, with the Exposition des arts décoratifs et industriels modernes, that art deco was officially born. It was an expression of geometric shapes, symmetry, strong chromatic contrasts and stylized decorative patterns. At the Exposition the Maison Tecla presented the first line of multiple jewelry which was then successively reproposed by Coro. European was the new fad *du jour*: Bakelite, or the combination of black and white, marcasite, ebony, and the fashion for clips, epitomized European jewelry tradition. At first, Paul Poiret and later Chanel, Schiaparelli, Patou, and Lelong dominated the scene. As American designers found inspiration in their work, likewise costume jewelry designers tapped into every successful line for inspiration. In this framework, the American copies appear as pale imitations of the European originals. Only a few attempts at originality were made, which drew inspiration from American culture and, for this reason, deserve to be mentioned. The "Spirit of St. Louis" and the "George Washington" line, created in 1932 for the bicentennial of Washington's birth, featuring miniature portraits of George and Martha Washington, are worthwhile mentioning on account of their historical significance. Also, the "Mickey Mouse Kiddie Jewelry" line, based on Walt Disney's design, can be considered an expression of American culture.

It was only during the second half of the 1930s that, with the boom of costume jewelry, a change in style – which was initially tentative and then more decisive – was apparent. In addition to its deco brooches and Duette jewels, Cohn & Rosenberger began producing jewelry with fantasy figurative designs and a hint of tridimensionality. From 1937 onwards the company began to systematically patent its designs. The newly acquired importance of design as a decisive factor coincided with the promotion of Adolph Katz, in 1937, to head designer, with the task of leading and coordinating not only company staff, but also the freelancers that collaborated with the firm. The quality of the materials and the workmanship was good and a careful observation of the pieces shows that it was constantly improving, although, in comparison with other manufacturers, such as Trifari, Cohn & Rosenberger appears lacking in both quality and design, probably because it was catering for a lower range market segment that was generally less demanding and reactive.

In 1937 it was still possible to find white metal clips and Duette with rhinestone pavé. In 1938 and 1939, in addition to small base metal alloy brooches with colored enamel and flowery and figurative rhinestone motifs, the first tridimensional Duettes with elaborate designs of enamel flowers and bows were available. The "Quivering Camellia" line dates from 1938 with the brooch selling for $15 and the necklace for $25. This line was one of the first great success stories and started the fad for "*en tremblant*" items and removable brooches. Another successful item was the "Camellia" bracelet.

Towards the end of 1939 Coro brooches became larger and tridimensional, were made of gold- or rhodium-plated metal, and had large colored stones and cabochons. In 1941 production included large Duettes with animal designs, and the last small enamel brooches, while glass stones were replaced by colored Lucite cabochons. Production of engraved wooden or plastic jewels – brooches in the shape of masks and South American idols – and of low-cost plastic jewels continued.

Rhodium- and gold-plated metals were used until 1942. Thereafter, due to quotas fixed for metals used in arms production, yellow or pink gold-plated (sterling) silver was used instead until about 1948. On 1st July 1942, the company presented with much fanfare – on a whole page of *WWD* – its first sterling silver collection, declaring itself to be the first company to accept the challenge of using non-priority materials in order to conform to Government rules. Therefore, the first line made entirely of sterling silver dates back to the fall of 1942, although a few cheap sterling lines with flower and animal subjects had already been produced back in spring, possibly to test the reactions of the public. Among these test items there are a few notable examples of brooches in which designs of birds and flowers are set in oval, round and square frames. This type of design was called Scandinavian style. This, together with the Scandinavian source of the silver, accounts for the "Sterling Genuine Norseland" trademark used for marking, which featured a typical Viking ship in the center.

During the war, 70% of the Coro plants was converted to military production. In spite of difficulties due to the war, the manufacture of costume jewelry continued, albeit on a smaller scale, until 1943 with good qualitative results and featured a series of very beautiful designs. Back in 1941 the Toronto factory, whose director, A. Manzer, was also a designer, had been enlarged. From 1943 part of the production had been transferred to Mexico, while the finishing process still took place in Providence, in order to assure the required quality standard. For the same reason the design and control stages were also carried out in Providence. The Mexican-made line, called Mexicraft, was manufactured in Taxco, in a Coro controlled factory with 200-300 workers. The earliest information about the "Andrée" line dates back

to 1944 (*WWD* 29th June). This line appears to have received a special mention for its Fall 1944 and Spring 1945 collections. From the description of the items reported in *Women's Wear Daily* it is evident that it was a secondary, low-priced line, produced using modern techniques, featuring wooden and metal necklaces with sequins and also historical designs. The lack of further information and the apparent absence of jewels with this trademark on the antique market, leave much uncertainty about the trademark used for marking ("Andrée" could be a trade name, while the items might be marked with the Coro trademark) and to the period in which the line had been produced.

In 1945, a year in which there were still tensions and economic difficulties, Coro sold shares for a second time in order to finance plans to add to its Providence factory another 60,000 square feet, with another 12,000 to follow in 1950, for a total of 172,000 square feet located in a four-story building, taking up most of the block.

In 1946 Coro was the largest manufacturer in the field, accounting for 16% costume jewelry production in the USA and it was the only company with the necessary means to cover an entire range of products, from the most expensive line; CoroCraft, to the low-priced items for the "five & dime," popular stores with outlets on all main roads in the United States. On the 4th December 1946, Coro was the first company to organize a jewelry fashion show broadcast on the TV-network WABD. This was tangible proof of its commercial and industrial leadership. It employed 2,100 people, mainly in Providence, had a consolidated turnover of $16,100,000 and a net profit before tax of $2,100,000 a year. Another sign of its affluence is the fact that 21 of its managers earned more than $20,000 a year. Coro had sales offices in New York, Toronto, and London, as well as in Chicago (from 1944), Los Angeles, San Francisco, Dallas, Montreal, and Miami. It was also represented in most Latin American countries. Production was carried out in the Providence and Toronto factories and consisted of two collections, a spring and a fall one, for which over one thousand designs were used, many of which were patented. Further evidence of the company's industrial power and development strategy is given by the news reported in *Women's Wear Daily* on 10th May 1946, of Coro's intention to build a factory in China, at Peiping, for the production of alabaster and glass beads, which were used as base for the manufacture of imitation pearls, that were greatly in demand. We do not know whether this project was finalized, since – according to Joseph M. Pearl, Coro's representative in China for many years – the company encountered many obstacles, whilst other locations, such as Shanghai and Soochow, had been turned down for the high cost of labor.

In 1944, Carl Rosenberger, aged 72, became chairman of the board of directors, leaving the position of president to his son, Gerald Rosenberger. The latter was born in 1904, and had joined the company in 1925, as Pacific Coast representative aged 21.

WWD, October 30, 1953: Gerald Rosenberger.

Royal Marcher was sales manager.

In 1948 two Coro veterans, Adolph Katz and Henry Rosenblatt (formerly import-export manager of the London branch office), became vice presidents and in 1951 the company leadership was the same with Royal Marcher as executive vice president, Jerome Oppenheimer the vice president and secretary and George Rosenberger the treasurer. In February 1948 Charles Rimsigeur, who had been with the company for twenty-seven years, was appointed president of Coro Canada Ltd.

WWD, November 26, 1948: Henry Rosenblatt.

WWD, November 26, 1948: Adolph Katz.

In 1948 Coro employed 2,500 people, and its workforce increased to over 3,000 by the end of the 1950s, compared with an average workforce of 100 people in the other companies in this sector. The company produced and sold about eight million items a year, to suit all tastes and pockets within a price range from $1 to $100, and was represented in almost all specialty shops and department stores. Coro jewelry was also selling very well in Europe, South America, Africa, and India. In Europe the London branch was still operative and, in spite of the inevitable decrease in sales due to the war, Coro still considered this market very important and in fact, as was hoped, it soon recovered. The company had a capillary sales network and a good commercial image, which it groomed with great national advertising campaigns.

The practice continued of giving a name to jewelry lines and using slogans that were often patented as trademarks. The patents were a protective measure to safeguard not only the products, but also the company image, and were often quoted in advertisements. One of these slogans was "Masterpieces of Fashion Jewelry" in use since 1944. While in 1947 the slogan used to advertise Coro's pearl creations was "For that priceless look." Finally, in 1946, the company began using the patented slogan "America's best dressed women wear Coro jewelry" in connection with celebrity spokeswomen wearing Coro jewels, such as Loretta Young, the star of the movie *The Stranger*, who appeared in an advertisement published in *Harper's Bazaar*, June 1946, Maggi McNellis, a radio character, in *Harper's Bazaar*, May 1947, Mrs. Bertrand L. Taylor III of New York in *Vogue*, April 1947, Cynthia McAdoo, daughter of Mr. T. McAdoo and niece of William Gibbs McAdoo, treasury secretary under President Wilson, in *Vogue*, 15th May 1947, Antonia Drexel Earle, leading member of high society in Philadelphia and Newport, in *Harper's Bazaar*, September 1947. Coro frequently cooperated with Revlon, the famous cosmetics company, with advertisements presenting jewelry and make-up in matching colors.

Ongoing research and experimentation in the course of the years meant the highest possible degree of optimization of the production process was achieved, resulting in highly competitive products. In particular, the best efforts of the company engineers were aimed at perfecting the process of plating, lacquering and varnishing, in order to obtain perfectly gold-plated jewels which would remain unaltered in time. The difficulties of the post-war period – the high cost of sterling silver and the consequent creation of new metal alloys, high production costs, strong competition from small companies that had cropped up in great numbers, a shift in demand from top-notch products to items in the medium and low price ranges – obliged Coro to undergo a rapid mechanization process, change its products and sustain large promotional expenses in order to maintain large sales volumes that, for example in 1947, still held in terms of quantity, but reaped smaller profit margins. In 1948 Coro left sterling silver, which had become too expensive, for a good quality metal alloy, which was heavier for some lines and lighter for others and, in the wake of the new fashion, simplified its design, with a preference being given to necklaces and bracelets rather than brooches, which became smaller and lighter. The company managed to save on production costs through process mechanization, by using cheaper materials and "real look," often banal designs. Through these measures it could even lower its prices compared with the pricelists of the previous years, while at the same time meeting a changed demand. However, precisely for these reasons, items of jewelry made in the following years are only seldom considered collector items. An exception to this was a special high quality collection created in 1951 to celebrate the company's "Golden Jubilee."

Carl Rosenberger died in 1957, aged 85, and his son Gerald took over the leadership of the company.

WWD, November 29, 1957: Gerald Rosenberger, left, Coro president, is shown receiving an oil painting of his father, Carl, from Max Sentlowitz of B. Altman & Co.

The decline of Coro started in 1960. Royal Marcher left the company and was replaced by Adolph Katz as executive vice president. The balance sheets were in the red. In 1963 Gerald Rosenberger resigned from his position as company president and was succeeded by Michael Tancer, who had been with the company since 1959 as head of the "trends section." Rosenberger kept for himself only the position of chairman of the board of directors. In 1967, at the age of 63, he died suddenly of a heart attack.

In 1964 Coro had a loss of $906,964 on a turnover of $22,600,448 and, in 1968, its losses amounted to $2,043,442.

In 1969 Richton International Corporation of New York, chaired by Frank M. Ricciardi, who founded the company in the spring of the same year, gained control of Coro and, in an attempt to revive its fortunes, sought the collaboration of fashion designer Oscar della Renta with license to use his name. Coro and Richton merged at the beginning of 1970 and in 1979, following the deep crisis that hit the American costume jewelry industry, Coro ceased operations, went bankrupt and closed the Providence factory. The reason for its decline and bankruptcy was the same that had determined its success: changing fashion and social appreciation of costume jewelry.

As already explained, the company manufactured jewelry to suit all pockets. "Coro" was the cheapest line, "CoroCraft," most probably launched in 1935, the most expensive. However, a massive presence of the CoroCraft line was first recorded at the same time as the fall 1942 collection which coincided with the beginning of the use of sterling. The few CoroCraft items made before that date are made of metal and date from the period between 1939 and 1941. Moreover, in the years from 1939 to 1942, the company manufactured some items of very high quality, which, in spite of being expensive at the time, were marketed with the Coro trademark. The "Dragonfly" of 1940 (C39.) or the "Blazing Lily" (C38.) of 1941 sold for 25 dollars. For collectors there are no differences in terms of price between items of the two lines and only in the later production years – 1948, 1950-51 – do CoroCraft items stand out for their better quality.

WWD, July 21, 1939: New Cohn & Rosenberger Showroom at 47 W 37th Street.

Coro availed itself of the collaboration of a great number of designers, some of whom were employees, whilst others were freelancers. These designers all worked under the guidance of Adolph Katz, who was also responsible for design. Many of these professionals remain unknown, others are known only by their names that were reported on the patents they were awarded on behalf of the company, and others are better known for being mentioned in magazines of the time. In any case, they were all good or even extraordinary jewelry design professionals who were endowed with artistic sensibility. They interpreted to perfection the tastes of the times, by combining art and technique. The best known designers were:

Adolph Katz, who has already been mentioned. Katz, of German origin, was one of the principal authors of Coro's success story. He worked for the company for almost forty years, with his last year in the role of supervisor of the "Vendome" line. He was a talented artist both in his work as a designer and in his ability to spot innovative motifs. He possessed both inventiveness and technical know-how, and produced many of the most beautiful Coro creations. Most of the numerous Coro design patents are his.

As already mentioned in the section on item dating and attribution, it is likely that Adolph Katz, in his role as head designer, also patented in his own name designs created by the company in-house staff. For this reason, it has been claimed that he was given more credit than he deserved. However, the responsibility of choosing the lines, subjects, and designs was entirely his and therefore the merit of the continuous innovation and variety so appreciated nowadays is all his.

Katz's skills as a designer were questioned after an interview with Gene Verrecchio, now Gene Verri, which appeared in the winter 2001 issue of *Vintage Fashion & Costume Jewelry*. In this interview Verrecchio claimed to be the only author of the majority of Coro's most famous designs, not only of those patented in his name, but also of those patented in Katz's name. According to Verri, Katz – in his position as company manager – only prepared and signed patent applications. As already stated, Katz, similarly to Philippe at Trifari, was probably not the material author of all the designs patented in his name, but to claim that he was no designer at all, is equally wrong. In addition to the observation already made, further strength is given to the argument in defense of Katz's designing skills in the following section quoted in full about Katz from an article entitled *Every Woman a Queen*, by Irwin Ross, published in "American Magazine" in February 1948:

> ...Adolph Katz the irrepressible, bouncy little man who is Coro's top designer and factory manager.
>
> A lover of pastoral delight Katz once drove into the countryside of Providence, parked his car near a pond on which a few ducks were idly paddling. "Within five minutes" – Katz reported – "I had dozen

of duck ideas, duck pins, duck earrings, duck necklaces. They were sensational. We dashed right back to the office."

Katz is quick to point out, however, that he is no mere photographic artist. "Let's say I'm having lunch," he says. "I find myself next to a coffeepot. I'm staring at it. I suddenly decide that what we need more than anything else in the line is a coffeepot. But do I just make a common, ordinary model of a coffeepot? Not on your life. I glamorize that old coffeepot, and it may make us $1,000,000."

Year after year, Katz and Marcher have glamorized an endless series of everyday objects. Two horse heads done up into a double clip, festooned with ruby ears, aquamarine eyes, and dubbed "Thorobreds," swamped the country a few years ago, and became another million-dollar seller. Almost equally popular was a pair of owls, "Hoots," which sparkled with rubies and huge sapphire eyes. The pin was a great success because of those startling eyes. "I got the idea for the owl from my fish," Katz says. "What made the fish was the big stone in its mouth. It was colossally attractive." ... This year, as soon as the first rumor was heard of the impending marriage of Princess Elizabeth, Katz started designing a series of crowns...

This text speaks for itself and practically demolishes the thesis, according to which Katz was not a skilful designer.

Gene Verrecchio (known later on as Gene Verri). His real surname was actually Verrecchia. His parents emigrated to the States from Italy in 1904. His father was a goldsmith who worked for the best companies in Providence. In 1911 twin brothers Alfeo and Eugenio (Gene) were born. The family returned to Italy in 1916 but, after a few misfortunes – the twins' mother died and their father was taken prisoner during the Great War – in 1924 the three surviving family members went back to Providence. In 1925 Gene enrolled at the Rhode Island School of Design where his talent soon emerged. In 1933, at the age of 19, he was hired by Coro where he worked until 1948 when, together with his brother Alfeo (who died in 1978), who also held a few design patents, he founded his own company, initially called Craftsman, then Sample Art and, then Gem-Craft Corporation, which is the name it still has today.

Verrecchio, who also collaborated in the creation of the "Vendome" line, created many designs for Coro. These designs were often patented, and consisted of different subjects and various styles. In addition to his famous "Quivering Camellia" and many other Duettes and brooches with animal or flower subjects, he became famous for his generous use of colored or milky cabochons set in enamel frames in delicately shaded colors.

Charles E. Pauzat, lived in New York until 1941, although he remained a French citizen. He collaborated with the company from 1939 to the mid- 40s. He did not produce many designs, but the jewelry that he did produce is considered very beautiful. In 1938 he collaborated with the Brody Novelty Jewelry Manufacturing Co., founded in the same year by A. Brody.

Oscar Placco, an American living in Providence, worked continuously for Coro at least from 1938 to the mid-1940s, designing good quality items. In 1945 he patented three designs for sterling jewelry made by Bates & Bacon of Attleboro, Massachusetts (BB1, BB2).

Robert Geissman, an American living in New York, where he worked as a freelance designer, only created three brooch designs for Coro in June 1938: "Screech Owl" (C9.), "Parrot" (C11.) "Mallard" (C10.).

Carol McDonald, an American living in New York, created only one design for Coro in 1940, which was a brooch of a balloon vendor (des. n° 119,830, April 2nd, 1940).

Sidney Pearl, an American living in New York, collaborated with Coro at the beginning of the 40s (patent No. 126,630 of 15th April 1941) and then established his own firm, the Sidney Pearl Co., with offices in New York, 366 Fifth Avenue, which became operative in 1945.

Lester Gaba, an American living in New York, was asked by the magazine *Ladies' Home Journal* to design the brooch "Emblem of the Americas" (PC2.) for Coro. The brooch design was patented on 31st December 1941. Gaba also collaborated with the Albert Manufacturing Co. in designing jewelry (*see* specific section). In 1948 Gaba prepared an advertising campaign for Coro to relaunch the Duette. More information can be found on Lester Gaba in the notes on "Emblem of the Americas."

"National Button Bulletin," 1948: Marion Weeber.

Marion Weeber, an American citizen, born in Albany N.Y and resident in New York, was a freelancer who gained her reputation while working for Twentieth Century Fox and by designing accessories on an exclusive basis for Macy's and Lord & Taylor.

In 1940 Weeber designed a collection of brooches, necklaces and bracelets in delicate red, white and blue enamel for Coro. She also designed a remarkable series of "ceramic charms," which were thin enamel dishes resembling old American, Dutch and French china, with tiny golden knives, spoons, forks and cups. Two other patented designs by Weeber are of a military cadet hat with a high plume (des. n° 120,925 of June 4th 1940) and a miniature airplane with a parachutist suspended from a golden

chain (des n° 124,125 of December 17th 1940).

In 1941 Weeber achieved additional fame with her jewelry inspired by the song "Wise Old Owl" written by Joe Ricardel of Broadcast Music, Inc. and made by Volupte Inc. of New York. Weeber worked not only for Volupte and Coro, but also for the National Silver Company and Eisenberg-Lozano.

Marion Weeber is also famous for her button designs, in particular for the large series of buttons made in 1948.

Victor Di Mezza, an American from Ozone Park, New York, designed a series of emblem pins in 1950, for Coro which were patented on 16th May 1950 (Pat. n° 158,559 through 158,562).

Several trademarks were deposited in the name of Cohn & Rosenberger and of Coro, however, as already mentioned, most of them are trademarks that were not used for jewelry marking. The markings visible on the items are reproduced hereunder. Some of them come from the merging of two trademarks or are variants of previous trademarks. Though trademarks do not indicate the dates of jewelry with absolute certainty, it is useful to know the different markings, since they followed one another with a certain regularity.

The Marks

Coro – mark No. 1 - in use since 1919, registered in 1921, still valid. It is the oldest mark and was used almost exclusively from the beginning of production until the fall 1942 collection, when use of sterling began and mark No. 7 replaced No. 1. During this period the marks were stamped so lightly that they were sometimes difficult to read and, for a brief period in 1942, they were very small too. This mark remained practically always in use and is found, though rarely, on Duette clips or earrings from the mid-40s. It reappeared in 1948, when sterling was no longer in use and therefore can be found on metal pieces, where it was initially engraved and later marked in relief on an oval plate. The hallmark punch is larger then the one initially used.

Coro – mark No. 2 –is a graphic variant of mark No. 1, from which it differs in its more slender line. The lettering is still thin and light and is indifferently used in 1941 and 1942 as an alternative to No. 1.

Coro DUETTE – mark No. 3 – a combination of the basic mark No. 1 and the Duette mark. The latter was in use from 1929, was registered in 1930, and is still valid and exclusively used for marking Duette brooches. It is stamped on the mechanism joining the clips together with the patent number of the mechanism. The mark has always been in use.

CoroCraft – mark No. 4 – in use  from 1935, registered in 1937, used for a relatively small number of pieces from 1939 to 1941.

Coro-Craft – mark No. 5 – a variant of mark No. 4 and equally little used for marking.

Both mark No. 4 and mark No. 5 were variously combined with the word **STERLING** or with the figure of Pegasus and were largely used in these combinations.

Sterling CRAFT Coro – mark No. 6 – inscribed in a square plate, a variant of mark No. 2; it was little used and mainly in the second half of 1942.

CoroCraft STERLING – mark No. 7 – mark No. 4 combined with the sterling hallmark and inscribed in an oval plate; it was used for items made of sterling, for which marking was required by the law. It was in use from the second half of 1942 to the spring of 1944.

Coro-Craft Sterling with Pegasus figure – mark No. 8 – mark No. 5 started to be combined with the sterling hallmark and the Pegasus mark, and the whole mark was inscribed in a rectangular plate applied to the item. It was used from the second half of 1942, initially with mark No. 7, until about 1945.

CoroCRAFT Sterling inscribed in a square plate held by Pegasus – mark No. 9 – registered in 1945, in use from the second half of 1944 to the end of

1947, when Coro suspended all sterling jewelry production.

Coro inscribed in a plate held by Pegasus – mark No. 10 – was occasionally used in 1948 on metal items.

CoroCraft inscribed in a square plate – mark No. 11 – the lettering is different from that of marks No. 4 and 5 with the words placed one on top of the other. It was used in 1940-41 and again from 1948.

CoroCRAFT inscribed in a square plate without the figure of Pegasus – mark No. 12 – is a variant of mark No. 2 and was in use from 1948.

The Pegasus figure was one of the company trademarks in use from 1938. It was registered in 1956 as only a figurative trademark of Pegasus holding a rectangular plate with no lettering on it, in order to protect the design and the name. It was often used in advertising and on the jewelry it was always combined with one of the trademarks with the company name. The subject was used for a jelly belly brooch designed by Adolph Katz and patented (JB74.).

Although Coro frequently patented its designs, it only rarely and randomly stamped the patent numbers on the jewels.

C1. "Charlie McCarthy," Coro
1937****
Manufacturer Cohn & Rosenberger, Inc.
Design not patented.
Mechanism patent n° 2,038,343 Gaston Candas, New York, 21st April 1936, filed on 25th July 1935.

Card for photo of Edgar Bergen and Charlie McCarty.

Charlie McCarthy was "born" during Bergen's high school years. Although someone else carved the dummy's head, Bergen crafted the body himself. His ventriloquism and feats of magic allowed him to pay his collegiate expenses at Northwestern University. Bergen broke into show business by way of vaudeville and eventually headlined in nightclubs across the United States and Europe. He was the father of the actress Candice Bergen.

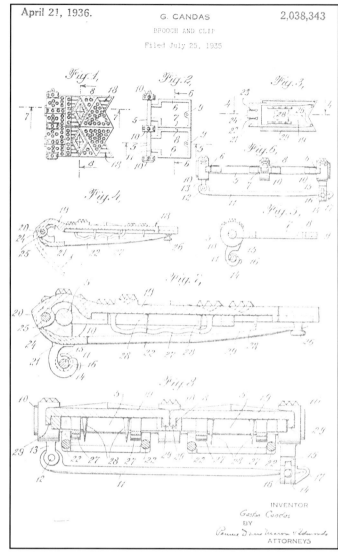

C1a. *WWD*, October 29, 1937: "Charlie McCarthy" by Coro.

The American ventriloquist Edgar Bergen (1903-1978) was born in Chicago as Edgar John Bergren and developed his unusual talent while still in grade school.

"My Diminutive Little Chum" Enters Jewelry

T 386

Charlie McCarthy, the dummy of the radio, enters the jewelry field in this amusing clip with a press clip which moves the lower lip and chin exactly in the fashion of the original. It is shown here in actual size.
Cohn & Rosenberger, Inc.

Gold-plated metal pin clip, white, black and pink enamel, of the upper body of Charlie McCarthy, the dummy in a tuxedo, wearing a monocle and a top hat. A little lever at the base of the figure meant that the dummy's bottom lip and chin could be moved in a similar fashion to the original dummy. 3.5x2cm.

Marked Mf'd under exclusive license from Edgar Bergen and Charlie Mc-Carthy Inc. Charlie McCarthy was the ventriloquist Edgar Bergen's dummy, which, after first participating on the "Rudy Vallee Radio Show" on 17th December 1936, became so popular that he immediately won a contract to have his own show: "The Edgar Bergen and Charlie McCarthy Show" also know as "The Chase and Sanborn Hour," which was the coffee producing company that sponsored the program on the NBC network from 9th May 1937 to 26th December 1948. Edgar Bergen then moved to CBS and the new sponsor of the show was Coca–Cola, from 2nd October 1949 to 1st June 1952.

From then on the program had various other sponsors until the last series aired from 2nd October 1955 to July 1956. In 1939 Edgar Bergen had created another dummy named Mortimer Snerd. Charlie McCarthy also appeared in numerous films and on television. Among his most famous jokes were: "Ambition is just an excuse for those without the good sense to be lazy" and "Hard work never killed anyone, but why take the chance?"

The brooch was featured in *WWD* 29th October 1937 where it was written that it was produced by Cohn & Rosenberger.

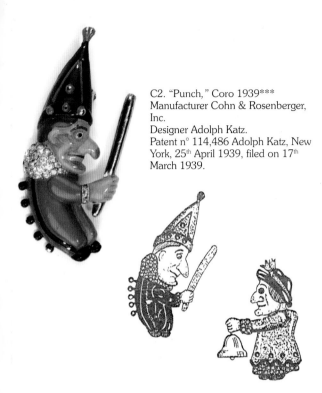

C2. "Punch," Coro 1939***
Manufacturer Cohn & Rosenberger, Inc.
Designer Adolph Katz.
Patent n° 114,486 Adolph Katz, New York, 25th April 1939, filed on 17th March 1939.

C3. "Juliette," Coro 1939**
Manufacturer Cohn & Rosenberger, Inc.
Designer Adolph Katz.
Patent n° 114,484 Adolph Katz, New York, 25th April 1939, filed on 17th March 1939, assignor to Cohn & Rosenberger, Inc., New York.

Rhodium and gold-plated metal pin clip with azure, burgundy, pink, brown and black enameling and rhinestones, of the "Punch" puppet. 7x3.9cm. Marked Coro (mark n° 1).

"Punch" and his wife "Judy" (des. n° 114,483 of 25th April 1939) are a married couple.

The Punch and Judy show is a popular British glove puppet show (although string puppets were used in the older shows) for children, starring Punch and his wife, Judy. The show consists of a series of brief scenes played by just two characters. The show is traditionally put on by a single puppeteer, called the "Professor," who, for obvious reasons, can only do two characters at a time (one puppet for each hand).

Punch wears a colorful jester outfit, has a hunchback and a beaky nose which almost touches his jutting chin. He holds a stick almost as tall as he is, which he liberally uses to strike other characters. He speaks in a bizarre rasping voice, produced with the aid of a device known as a swazzle or swatchel, which the Professor holds in his mouth while speaking, and through which he produces the merry chatter which gave birth to the well-known saying: "as pleased as Punch."

The roots of the Punch and Judy show go very deep indeed, since the show is based on the Italian *commedia dell'arte*. The Punch character comes from the stock character of Pulcinella. Judy was originally called "Joan".

The 9th May 1662 is considered to be Punch's date of birth, because on that date the diarist Samuel Pepys wrote that he had attended a Punch and Judy show near St. Paul's Church, in London's Covent Garden. The puppeteer was an Italian, Pietro Gimondi, who went by the pseudonym of "Signor Bologna".

Small base metal clip, with enameling and rhinestones, of Juliet at the balcony. 5.5 x 2.3cm.
Marked Coro (mark n° 1).

According to Katz the "Juliet" and "Romeo" clips (des. n° 114,485, 25th April 1939) were to be worn together so as to emulate the famous balcony scene from Shakespeare's tragedy. The quality of the clips, especially in their detail, is not very high, however the cultural nature of the subjects chosen and the realism conveyed by the combined image, as well as their rarity, make them very an interesting collector's items. Katz designed "Punch" (see C2.) & "Judy," two characters from popular American tradition, and two brooches to be worn together, representing the king and queen in a deck of cards for the same collection. These items were also decorated with enamel and rhinestones.

The "Romeo" clip was remade in 1948 in a gold-plated, smaller version.

C4. "Cowboy and Cowgirl," Coro 1939****
Manufacturer Cohn & Rosenberger, Inc., New York.
Designer Adolph Katz.
Patents: cowboy n° 114,219; cowgirl n° 114,220 Adolph Katz, New York, 11th April 1939, filed on 8th March 1939, assignor to Cohn & Rosenberger, Inc., New York.

Pair of rhodium-plated metal brooches with maroon and black enameling (boy), and pink, red and black enameling (girl); round moonstones were used for their faces, an oval green cabochon was used for the boy's torso, and a pink round one was used for the girl's torso, with rhinestones. The two figurines represent a cowboy and a cowgirl holding a lasso. 6x5.3cm (boy), 6x5.1cm (girl).

Mark Pat. No D 834 (boy), Pat. No D 83421 (girl). These are the file numbers of the respective patent applications.

The patented cowboy figurine is slightly different from the actual brooch. In the design above, the cowboy is holding the lasso (represented in full) with the end of the rope pointing downwards, while in the real brooch, the end of the rope points upwards. This is one of the rather frequent variants that were made in the production phase.

C5. "Dutch Peasants," Coro 1940****
Manufacturer Cohn & Rosenberger, Inc., New York.
Designs by Marion Weeber, not patented.

Right:
WWD, March 1, 1940.

Pair of base metal pin clips with blue, red, yellow and green
enameling, representing a couple of Dutch peasants carrying two
vases (boy) and a flower spray (girl), respectively. 4.5x3.9cm (boy),
4.5x3.7cm (girl).
   Marked Coro (mark n° 1).
   The pins were featured in *WWD*, 1st March 1940 issue, which stated that they belonged to a series of "doll figurines of natives of various countries. The figurines are to be worn as a set". Furthermore,
WWD, loc. cit. and in the issue of 23rd February 1940, explained that
the spring collection designed by Marion Weeber for Coro included,
in addition to these, other brooches, bracelets and necklaces representing miniature dishes, knives, forks, cups and spoons. This series
is called "ceramic charms" because the dishes were enameled in
such a way as to look like Dutch, French and English china. These
motifs were used individually on the brooches, while they were used
as charms on the bracelets, other charms being gold-plated knives,
forks, cups and spoons.

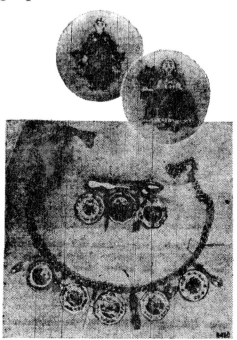

Doll-Like—Figurines or Tiny Equipment for Charm Bracelet

Two lapel ornaments, tiny
enamel doll figures of natives of
various countries, are to be worn
sets as Cohn & Rosenberger,
feature them. The charm
celet and its matching pin
on two fashion ideas of
r — the feeling for minia-
tures, and the feeling for porce-
lains. Here Marion Weeber,
whose collection for this manufacturer has been discussed previously in these pages, uses tiny
plates in enamel each complete
with its tiny gold spoon, knife or
fork or cup.

C6. "Dutch People," Coro 1940**
Manufacturer Cohn & Rosenberger, Inc.
Designer Adolph Katz.
Patents n° 119,306 and 119,307 Adolph Katz,
New York, 3rd March 1940, filed on 24th January
1940, assignor to Cohn & Rosenberger, In.,
New York.

A pair of small pin clips of rhodium-plated base metal,
with enameling and tiny rhinestones, in the shape of a
Dutch couple. Dutch girl 4.4x2.7cm; Dutch boy 4.6x2cm.
   Marked Coro (mark n° 1). Only the Dutch boy is
marked.
   The patented design is much larger than the manufactured clips.

C9. "Geissmann Screech Owl," Coro 1938***
Manufacturer Cohn & Rosenberger, Inc.
Designer Robert Geissmann.
Patent n° 110,141 Robert Geissmann, New York, 21st June 1938, filed on 20th May 1938, assignor to Cohn & Rosenberger, Inc., New York.

C7. "Mr. & Mrs. Pig," Coro 1934-40***
Manufacturer Cohn & Rosenberger, Inc.
Designer Adolph Katz (?)
Not patented.
    Rhodium-plated base metal brooches with chatelaine, representing a pair of little, pink enameled pigs; the male is in a brown enameled barrel, the female has a movable red enamel basket under her arm. 4.7x2cm.
    Marked Coro (mark n° 1).
    In 1934 Cohn & Rosenberger produced some items inspired by the tale of the *Three little pigs* for its children's jewelry line. However there is no proof – regarding either the subject or documentation referring to this piece – to indicate that this particular brooch belongs to that series, although, the materials used and its light weight indicate that it might date from 1934.

Rhodium-plated base metal alloy brooch, with blue and azure enameling and rhinestone pave, depicting a screech owl in the act of swooping down on its prey. 5.5x6cm.
    Marked Coro (mark n° 1).
    For a similar brooch – which was most probably a contemporary imitation, but which had a *tremblant* head - *see* U35. Robert Geissmann patented three brooch designs in 1938 and all on behalf of Cohn & Rosenberger. No other information is available about this designer, except that he was of German origin, and lived in New York. He was probably a freelancer who occasionally worked for Coro and the jewelry sector. He was an inventive designer, with an extremely realistic style which he combined with a touch of irony giving his chosen subject matter an almost fantasy-like appearance and a strongly defined expressivity. The barely hinted three-dimensionality of the subject is emphasized by its position and the materials and colors used.

C8. "Rooster and Hen Chatelaine," Coro 1940**
Manufacturer Cohn & Rosenberger, Inc.
Designer Adolph Katz (?)
Not patented.
    Rhodium-plated metal chatelaine brooches of a hen and a rooster, with red, yellow, sky blue and pink enamel and small rhinestones. 3x2.5cm.
    Marked Coro (Hen mark n° 1).

C10. "Geissmann Mallard," Coro 1938****
Manufacturer Cohn & Rosenberger, Inc.
Designer Robert Geissmann.
Patent n° 110,142 Robert Geissmann, New York, 21st June 1938, filed on 20th May 1938, assignor to Cohn & Rosenberger, Inc., New York.

Rhodium-plated base metal brooch, with blue, azure, green, yellow, pink and black enameling, green baguettes and rhinestones. The brooch represents a mallard in flight. 7.8x6.5cm.
Marked Coro (mark No. 1).

Rhodium-plated base metal alloy brooch, with blue, azure, white and brown enameling and rhinestones. The brooch represents a parrot perched on a branch. The rhinestone pavé is present only on its head, while the rest of its body is enameled. 7.5x4.5cm.
    Marked Coro (mark No. 1).

C11. *"Geissmann Parrot,"* Coro 1938**
Manufacturer Cohn & Rosenberger, Inc.
Designer Robert Geissmann.
Patent n° 110,143 Robert Geissmann, New York, 21st June 1938, filed on 20th May 1938, assignor to Cohn & Rosenberger, Inc., New York.

C12. *"Horned Owls Duette,"* Coro 1941***
Manufacturer Cohn & Rosenberger, Inc.
Designer Adolph Katz.
Patent n° 129,437 Adolph Katz, New York, 9th September 1941, filed on 31st July 1941, assignor to Cohn & Rosenberger, Inc., New York.

Rhodium-plated metal Duette with brown and yellow enameling and rhinestones, representing two horned owls. Their eyes are made of small Lucite half-spheres with two tiny black pellets set in the yellow to emphasize the jutting effect and an owl's fixed stare. 6x4.5cm.
Marked Coro Pat. No. 129437 (mark n° 2).
The mechanism is marked Coro Duette Pat. No. 1798867.
    From 1938 to 1950 Coro manufactured several owl-shaped single and Duette brooches. The most famous Duette using owls is "Hoots" made in 1944 (see C94.).

Rhodium-plated metal Duette, with azure enameling and rhinestone pavé; the Duette represents a calopsitta – a cockatoo- like parrot with a raised crest and a long tail – the body of the bird is studded with rhinestones. 9.2x6cm.
    The mechanism is marked Coro Duette Pat. No. 1798867 (mark n° 3).
    The clips are not marked. It is a quality piece that was probably produced in large quantities, since it is still easily found and available in several color variants.

C13. *"Calopsitta Duette,"* Coro 1941**
Manufacturer Cohn & Rosenberger, Inc.
Designer Gene Verrecchio.
Patent n° 126,490 Gene Verrecchio, Providence, R.I., 8th April 1941, filed on 3rd March 1941.

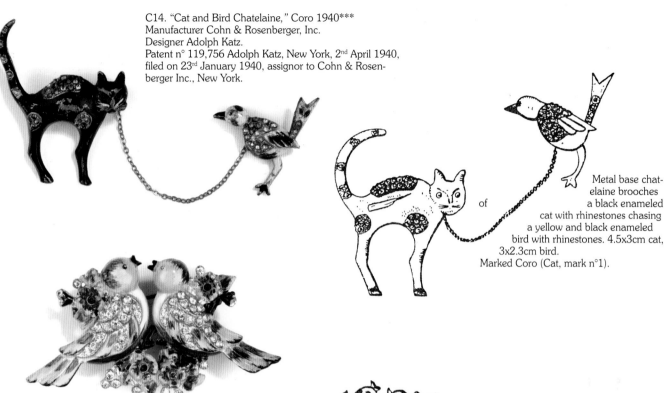

C14. "Cat and Bird Chatelaine," Coro 1940***
Manufacturer Cohn & Rosenberger, Inc.
Designer Adolph Katz.
Patent n° 119,756 Adolph Katz, New York, 2nd April 1940, filed on 23rd January 1940, assignor to Cohn & Rosenberger Inc., New York.

Metal base chatelaine brooches a black enameled cat with rhinestones chasing a yellow and black enameled bird with rhinestones. 4.5x3cm cat, 3x2.3cm bird.
Marked Coro (Cat, mark n°1).

Base metal Duette, with blue, azure, brown, pink, and red enameling and rhinestones, representing two birds. 6.6x3.5cm.
    The mechanism is marked Coro Duette (mark n° 3) Pat. No 1798867. Clips are marked Coro (mark n° 1) and Coro Pat. No 127909.

C15. "Lovebirds Duette," Coro 1941***
Manufacturer Cohn & Rosenberger, Inc., New York.
Designer Adolph Katz.
    Patent n° 127,909 Adolph Katz, New York, 24th June 1941, filed on 24th May 1941, assignor to Cohn & Rosenberger, New York.

C16. "Mr. & Mrs. Bird," Coro 1941**
Manufacturer Cohn & Rosenberger, Inc.
Designer Gene Verrecchio.
Patent n° 125,976 Gene Verrecchio, Providence, 18th March 1941, filed on 11th February 1941, assignor to Cohn & Rosenberger, Inc. New York.

Small rhodium-plated base metal brooches, with blue, azure, black, red and yellow enameling, cream-white milky cabochon and rhinestones. The brooches are of a pair of birds. The male is wearing a top hat and holding a cane with black and red enameling, the female is bareheaded. Their bodies are made of milky cabochons and are completely enameled. Male 5x3cm; female 5x2.5cm.
Marked Pat. No. 125976.
    The patent number and the existence and identity of the design of this piece of jewelry, indicate beyond doubt that these are Coro items. Only the male has the Coro stamp on its tail. In the patent design the birds are joined together by a thin chain.
    Between March and April 1941, Gene Verrecchio patented three brooch designs portraying "anthropomorphic" birds: "Hunting Bird," a small brooch of a bird dressed like a hunter (des. n° 126,922 of 29th April 1941) and "Ma Bird & Sons," a mother bird followed by two chicks joined together by a small chain (des. n° 126,923 of 29th April 1941). He also designed other items of this kind, which however were not patented. This line was especially delightful because of its combination of an inventive, almost childish design with a skilful use of enamel.
    Compared to previous enamel lines, these items stand out for their emphasized three-dimensionality, (underlined by the large central cabochon) and for the good enameling technique used, particularly evident in the accuracy of details.

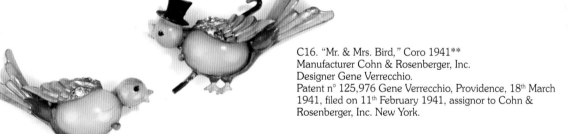

C17. *"Quivering Camellia Set,"* Coro
1938*****
Manufacturer Cohn & Rosenberger,
Inc.
Designer Gene Verrecchio.
Patent n° 110,296 Gene Verrecchio, Providence, R.I.,
26th June 1938, filed on
9th May 1938. The patent
covers the Duette brooch,
but the design was used
for the creation of the
complete set.

Mechanism patent n° 1,798,867 granted to Gaston Candas, Paris, 30th March 1931, filed on 31st May 1930.

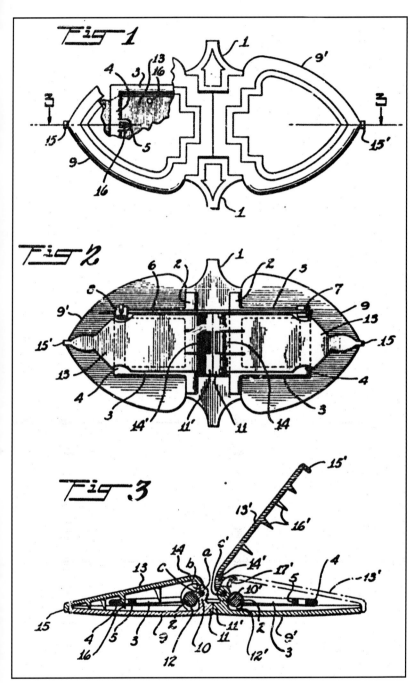

Set composed of Duette brooch, necklace, bracelet and earrings. The items are rhodium-plated on the inside and gold-plated on the outside, with blue and white baguettes, green enameling and rhinestones, in the shape of a camellia with a *tremblant* pistil.

The necklace is made of rhodium-plated metal with gold-plated metal camellias. The chain consists of jointed links with rhinestone-studded, green-enameled leaves, alternating with rhinestone-studded washers and joined by blue baguettes. The central motif is of two camellias with tremblant pistils, decorated with white baguettes and a blue central crystal. The flowers are joined to the chain by two large green enameled, rhinestone-studded leaves containing a leaf-shaped green enameled pendant with rhinestones and blue baguettes. The necklace has a hidden clasp decorated with a blue baguette. 46cm, central motif 6.5x6cm.

Gold-plated metal Duette brooch with rhodium-plated metal joining mechanism. Camellias with *tremblant* pistils decorated with white baguettes and blue central crystal, stem with green enameled leaves decorated with rhinestones and blue baguettes. 7.5x3.8cm.

Jointed bracelet with three camellias. Hidden clasp and safety chain. Size: 19cm. Gold-plated screw earrings. 2.5cm.

Necklace mark: D. Pat. 110296 Reg. U.S.A. Pat. Off. V. Brooch: Reg. U.S.A. Pat. Off. D. Pat. 110296. Mechanism: Coro Duette Pat. No. 1798867 (mark n° 3). Bracelet: D. Pat. Reg. U.S.A. Pat. Off. Earrings: D. Pat. 110296 Reg. U.S.A. Pat. Off.

The "Quivering Camellia" set was produced in the color variants red, blue and white, always with green enameled leaves, while the principal color is determined by the color of the baguettes. The most common variant is the one with red baguettes.

The rarest of the set pieces is the necklace (****), followed, in this order, by the earrings (**), the bracelet (***) and the Duette (*). Two versions of the bracelet were made: one with three camellias and another with only one camellia.

The advertisement for the "Quivering Camellia" set appeared in *Vogue* in 1938. The pieces were on sale at the following prices: $14.95 for the Duette and $25 for the necklace. A similar advertisement, however featuring only the Duette, appeared in *Harper's Bazaar*, in December 1938. The Duette was worn by Jeannette McDonald in a photograph of 1941.

This design began the tremblant effect line and was such a great commercial success, that it is said to have resulted in 500,000 dollars in sales even before production had started. Indeed, it proved to be one of Coro's best-sellers, and production continued for a long time and was resumed again and again in the following years.

The mark "Quivering Camellia," written in italics, was registered by Cohn & Rosenberger, Inc., and was used from 1939. It is the trademark of the line used for advertising campaigns and for sales, and the fact that it was deposited after production had started, is indicative of the line's success.

C18. *"Hidden Treasure,"* Coro 1938***
Manufacturer Cohn & Rosenberger, Inc.
Designer Adolph Katz.
Patent n° 112,148 Adolph Katz, New
York, 15th November 1938, filed on
5th October 1938, assignor to Cohn &
Rosenberger, Inc., New York.

Gold-plated metal deco brooch, consisting of an oval frame decorated with small palm trees and a barrette, also decorated with
palm trees, that, when rotated reveal two portrait frames.
4x5.5cm.
   Not marked.
   The brooch attribution to Coro is confirmed by the
patent on the design and by the existence of marked
exemplars. The brooch was featured in *Mademoiselle*, September 1938, with the name "Hidden Treasure" and was on sale at Saks 34th Street for $1.98.

C19 *"Placco Deco Duette,"* Coro 1938**
Manufacturer Cohn & Rosenberger, Inc.
Designer Oscar Placco.
Patent n° 111,087 Oscar Placco, Cranston,
R.I., 30th August 1938, filed on 21st July 1938,
assignor to Cohn & Rosenberger, New York.

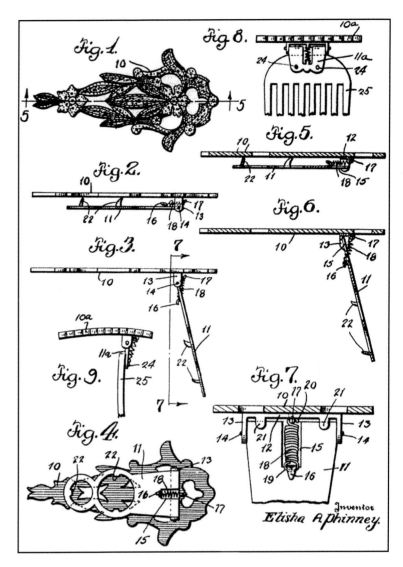

Mechanism patent n° 1,798,867 Gaston Candas, Paris, 30th March 1931, filed on 31st May 1930.

Clip mechanism patent n° 1,852,188 Elisha A. Phinney, South Attleboro, Massachusetts, 5th April 1931, filed on 17th February 1931, assignor to Geo H. Fuller & Son Company, Pawtucket, Rhode Island, a company founded in 1858 for the production of jewelry components. The company is still in business.

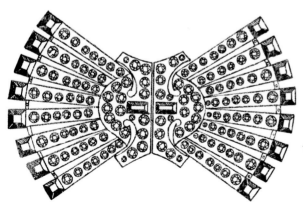

Rhodium-plated base metal Duette studded with rhinestones and baguettes, with deco design. 7.5x5cm.

Coro Duette mechanism mark Pat. No. 1798867 (mark n° 3).

Clip mark Pat. 1852188. This patent covers both the design of a flowery motif clip and the clip mechanism. In this Duette only the mechanism is used.

C20. "Deco Duette," Coro 1935***
Manufacturer Cohn & Rosenberger, Inc.
Designer Adolph Katz (?)
Design not patented. Mechanism patent n° 1,798,867 Gaston Candas, Paris, 30th March 1931, filed on 31st May 1930. Clip patent n° 1,852,188, Elisha A. Phinney, South Attleboro, Massachusetts, assignor to Geo. H Fuller & Son Company, of Pawtucket, Rhode Island, 5th April 1932, filed on 17th February 1931.
   Rhodium-plated metal Duette with rhinestones pavé, with two deco-line clips. 7.3x4cm.
   Marked mechanism Coro Duette Pat. No. 1798867 (mark n° 3), clips pat. 1852188.

C21. "Katz Quivering Camellia," Coro 1939**
Manufacturer Cohn & Rosenberger, Inc., New York.
Designer Adolph Katz.
Patent n° 116,478, Adolph Katz, New York, 5th September 1939, filed on 26th July 1939, assignor to Cohn & Rosenberger, Inc., New York.

Duette patent n° 1,798,867 Gaston Candas, Paris, 30th March 1931, filed on 31st May 1930.
   Clip mechanism patent n° 1,852,188, Elisha A. Phinney, South Attleboro, Mass., 5th April 1932, filed on 17th February 1931, assignor to Geo H. Fuller & Son Company, Pawtucket, Rhode Island.
   Gold-plated metal Duette with azure enameling and azure baguettes and rhinestones. The brooch is shaped like a camellia with a quivering pistil. 7.3x4.5cm.
   Mechanism mark: Coro Duette Pat. No. 1798867 (mark n° 3). Clip mechanism mark: Pat. No. 1852188.
   There were several color variants of this brooch: azure, white and pink with green enameling, pink stones and rhinestones. It is similar in design and materials used to the "Quivering Camellia," from which inspired Adolph Katz to create this smaller, refined brooch, in the wake of the former's success.

C22. *"Flower Pot,"* Coro 1938*
Manufacturer Cohn & Rosenberger, Inc.
Designer Gene Verrecchio.
Patent n° 110,469 Gene Verrecchio,
Providence, R.I., 12ᵗʰ July 1938, filed on
3ʳᵈ June 1938.

Rhodium-plated base metal brooch, with enameling and rhinestones, representing a vase of flowers inserted into a rectangular frame with rounded corners. 5x3.8cm.
  Marked Coro D. Pat. 110469 (mark n° 1).
  There is another version of this design with more rhinestones and with baguettes in the frame corners. In the 1938, 1939 and spring 1940 collections Coro presented, in addition to the Duettes and to large, three-dimensional brooches made of heavy rhodium or gold-plated metal, small rhodium-plated brooches with colorful enameling and figurative or flowery subjects, in keeping with the fashion of the time. Similar items were also manufactured by Trifari, Pennino, Du Jay, Albert Manufacturing and other companies whose names are unknown, because they were not in the habit of marking their jewelry pieces. All of them are interesting collector items because they are rare examples of an old, refined type of production that, once it had gone out of fashion, was no longer included in later collections. They are all small, light, flat, with glossy enameling and without any stones, or with a few very small rhinestones. The subjects, often fantasy figures and almost childish, were made with an abundance of enamel details. At Coro this kind of jewelry belonged to the low-price range, with designs that were not always refined, due to the imprecision of the enameling technique used.

C23 *"Tulips,"* Coro 1939***
Manufacturer Cohn & Rosenberger, Inc., New York.
Designer Adolph Katz.
Patent n° 115,043 Adolph Katz, New York, 30ᵗʰ May 1939, filed on 21ˢᵗ April 1939, assignor to Cohn & Rosenberger, Inc., New York.

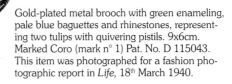

Gold-plated metal brooch with green enameling, pale blue baguettes and rhinestones, representing two tulips with quivering pistils. 9x6cm.
Marked Coro (mark n° 1) Pat. No. D 115043.
This item was photographed for a fashion photographic report in *Life,* 18ᵗʰ March 1940.

Rhodium-plated metal pin clip, green enamel with rhinestones, in the shape of a rose. 6.5x4.5cm.
    Marked Coro Pat. No 122437 (mark n° 1).
    The brooch was inspired by a Fulco Della Cerda Duke of Verdura design and was photographed for the Sears catalogue for the summer of 1944.

C24. "Rose," Coro 1940***
Manufacturer Cohn & Rosenberger, Inc.
Designer Adolph Katz.
Patent n° 122,437 Adolph Katz, New York, 10th September 1940, filed on 8th August 1940, assignor to Cohn & Rosenberger Inc., New York.

Rhodium-plated metal Duette, with pale green enameling and white and blue rhinestones, representing two roses. 7.7x5.5cm.
    The mechanism is marked Coro Duette Pat. No 1798867 (mark n° 3). The clips are not marked.

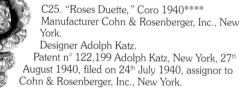

C25. "Roses Duette," Coro 1940****
Manufacturer Cohn & Rosenberger, Inc., New York.
    Designer Adolph Katz.
    Patent n° 122,199 Adolph Katz, New York, 27th August 1940, filed on 24th July 1940, assignor to Cohn & Rosenberger, Inc., New York.

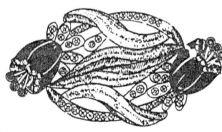

Base metal Duette (rhodium-plated mechanism), with green, azure and blue enameling and rhinestones, representing two tulips. 7.2x3cm.
    The mechanism is marked Coro Duette Pat. No 1798867 (mark n° 3). The clips are not marked.

C26. "Tulips Duette," Coro 1942***
Manufacturer Cohn & Rosenberger, Inc., New York.
Designer Gene Verrecchio.
Patent n° 131,976 Gene Verrecchio, Providence, R.I, 7th April 1942, filed on 19th February 1942, assignor to Cohn & Rosenberger, Inc., New York.

C27. "Camellia Set," Coro 1939*****
Manufacturer Cohn & Rosenberger, Inc.
Designer Adolph Katz.
Patent n° 116,288 Adolph Katz, New York,
22nd September 1939, filed on 21st July
1939, assignor to Cohn & Rosenberger,
Inc., New York.

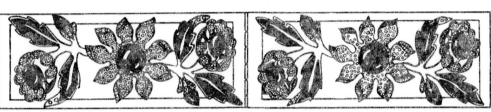

Set composed of a bangle and a barrette-shaped brooch with camellia motif. The bangle is a rigid band made of gold-plated sterling, with green enameling, red, green and blue cabochons and rhinestones, with a camellia motif applied in relief along the whole length of the bangle. The bangle is hinged and has a clasp with a safety chain. 4cm h.

The brooch is made of gold-plated metal in a rectangular frame. It features the same applied camellia motif as the bangle. 9.5x4cm.

Bracelet is marked CoroCraft Sterling Band (mark n° 5).

The brooch is marked CoroCraft (mark n° 4).

The patent refers to the bangle and the design was used also for the manufacturing of Duettes and clips. This model was made of different metals and the original pieces were probably made of metal, while the sterling items are 1942-43 versions. The bangle was remade in 1965 in the Vendôme line. This time, it was made of black plastic with white stones and rhinestones and featured significant changes from the original.

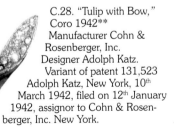

C.28. "Tulip with Bow,"
Coro 1942**
Manufacturer Cohn &
Rosenberger, Inc.
Designer Adolph Katz.
Variant of patent 131,523
Adolph Katz, New York, 10th
March 1942, filed on 12th January
1942, assignor to Cohn & Rosen-
berger, Inc. New York.

Large rhodium-plated metal brooch, with shaded red-purple, brown and green enameling, red stones and rhinestones, in the shape of a tulip with a large bow studded with rhinestones and a central red stone. The corolla has red-purple enameling with a rhinestone border; the leaves have shaded green enameling and rhinestones, the stem has brown enameling and yellow veins. The brooch consists of two separately cast components joined by two small screws: the corolla was made separately and then assembled. 11x5cm. Marked Coro (mark n° 1).

This is a variant of the patented design, from which it differs only in the stem. The two component assembly allowed for various combinations.

C29. "Trembling Flowers Duette," Coro 1939*****
Manufacturer Cohn & Rosenberger, Inc.
Designer Adolph Katz.
　　Patent n° 115,852 Adolph Katz, New York, 25th July 1939, filed on 9th June 1939, assignor to Cohn & Rosenberger Inc., New York.

Gold-plated metal Duette, green and brown enamel, rhinestones and small red cabochons, in the shape of flowers with trembling pistils. 6.5x9cm.
　　Marked Coro Duette Pat. No. 1798867 (mark n° 3).

Rhodium-plated metal brooch, sky blue and green enamel, rhinestones and blue drop shaped stones, representing a mobile corolla with five dangling pendants. 6.2x5.5cm.
　　Marked Coro (mark n°1).

C30. "Nodders Flower," Coro 1939***
Manufacturer Cohn & Rosenberger, Inc.
Designer Adolph Katz.
Patent n° 116,233 Adolph Katz, New York, 22nd August 1939, filed on 13th July 1939, assignor to Cohn & Rosenberger Inc., New York.

C31. "Quivering Bell Flowers," Coro 1939***
Manufacturer Cohn & Rosenberger, Inc., New York.
Designer Adolph Katz.
Patent n° 116,607 Adolph Katz, New York, 12th September 1939, filed on 4th August 1939, assignor to Cohn & Rosenberger, Inc., New York.

Mechanism patent n° 1,798,867 Gaston Candas, Paris, 30th March 1931, filed on 31st May 1930.
　　Clip mechanism patent 1,852,188 Elisha A. Phinney, South Attleboro, Mass., 5th April 1932, filed on 17th February 1931, assignor to Geo H. Fuller & Son Company, Pawtucket, Rhode Island.
　　Rhodium and gold-plated metal Duette with green enameling, green stones and rhinestones, representing two bell-flowers with a quivering central flower. 8x3.5cm.
　　Marked Coro Duette Pat. N° 1798867 (mark n° 3).

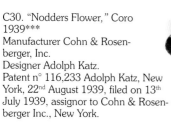

C32. *"Hyacinth Duette,"* Coro 1941****
Manufacturer Cohn & Rosenberger, Inc.
Designer Adolph Katz (?)
Not patented.
   Rhodium-plated metal Duette, green and lilac enamel, rhinestones, representing two hyacinths. 7.5x5.5cm.
   Marked Coro Duette Pat. No. 1798867 (mark n° 3).

C33. *"Bell Flower Necklace,"* Coro 1939****
Manufacturer Cohn & Rosenberger, Inc.
Designer Adolph Katz.
Patent n° 115,266 Adolph Katz, New York, 13th June 1939, filed on 4th April 1939, assignor to Cohn & Rosenberger, Inc, New York.
   Gold- and rhodium-plated metal necklace, green enamel, rhinestone pavé and red baguettes. The chain is rat-tail type. The middle pendant is composed of three little bells with trembling pistils. The motif in the centre is 5x11cm.
   Marked Pat. No. D. 115226.
   The patent refers to a Duette of the same theme (s. C36.)

🐦 CORO 🐦

Rhodium-plated metal brooch,
enamel in various colors and tones,
rhinestones, in the shape of a
thistle. 8x6.5cm.
  Marked Coro (mark n° 1).

C34. "Thistle," Coro 1942***
Manufacturer Cohn & Rosenberger, Inc.
Designer Adolph Katz.
Patent n° 131,559 Adolph Katz, New York,
10th March 1942, filed on 14th January 1942.

Base metal brooch, pink, sky blue
and green enamel, representing a
barrel used as a vase for flowers.
5.5x4.8cm.
  Marked Coro (mark n° 1).

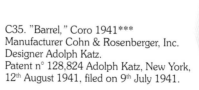

C35. "Barrel," Coro 1941***
Manufacturer Cohn & Rosenberger, Inc.
Designer Adolph Katz.
Patent n° 128,824 Adolph Katz, New York,
12th August 1941, filed on 9th July 1941.

Mechanism patent 1,798,867 Gaston Candas, Paris, 30th March 1931, filed on 31st May 1930.
Rhodium-plated metal Duette with green enameling, white pearls and rhinestones, shaped like bell flowers with tremblant pistils. Each pistil is composed of a drop-shaped pearl and rhinestone-studded flowers. 9x6cm.
Marked Coro Duette Pat. No. 1798867 (mark n° 3).
This is one of the first examples of large Duettes. The line is still flat, but the quality is good and the Duette flowery subject is new. For successive production Coro went on to develop this motif in all possible manners.

C36. "Bell Flower Duette," Coro 1939***
Manufacturer Cohn & Rosenberger, Inc.
Designer Adolph Katz.
Patent n° 115,266 Adolph Katz, New York, 13th June 1939, filed on 4th April 1939, assignor to Cohn & Rosenberger, Inc., New York.

C37. "Calla Lily," Coro 1941***
Manufacturer Cohn & Rosenberger, Inc., New York.
Designer Gene Verrecchio.
Patent n° 125,647 Gene Verrecchio, Providence, R.I., 4th March 1941, 30th January 1941, assignor to Cohn & Rosenberger, Inc., New York.

Rhodium-plated metal brooch with green, brown and yellow enameling and rhinestones representing a bunch of calla lilies. The corollas have a pearlescent finish. 10x5.7cm.
Marked Coro (mark n° 1) Pat. No. 125647.

Large, massive yellow- and pink-gold-plated metal brooch in the shape of a lily with pistils with red marquis-cut stones and a rhinestone-studded corolla. 9.5x6cm.
Marked Coro (mark n° 1).
The advertisement for "Blazing Lily," its original name, was published in *Harper's Bazaar,* October 1941, where it was stated that the gold-plating used was the two-tone "Coroplate" (a special gold-plating technique invented by Coro) and that the brooch was on sale for $25, a very high price for the time.
In its fall 1941 collection Coro presented large, massive, gold-plated or bicolor brooches of excellent quality and craftsmanship.

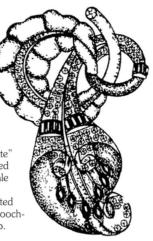

C38. "Blazing Lily," Coro 1941****
Manufacturer Cohn & Rosenberger, Inc.
Designer Adolph Katz.
Patent n° 129,435 Adolph Katz, New York, 9th September 1941, filed on 31st July 1941, assignor to Cohn & Rosenberger, Inc., New York.

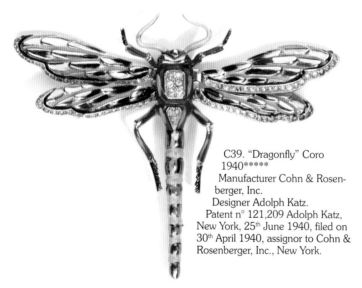

C39. "Dragonfly" Coro 1940*****
Manufacturer Cohn & Rosenberger, Inc.
Designer Adolph Katz.
Patent n° 121,209 Adolph Katz, New York, 25th June 1940, filed on 30th April 1940, assignor to Cohn & Rosenberger, Inc., New York.

Rhodium-plated brooch with rhinestones, yellow, green and dark brown enameling, in the shape of a dragonfly with mobile wings. The double wings of the dragonfly are mounted on a delicate mechanism controlled by a small screw that sets the wings in motion at the slightest touch. 9.5x7.5cm.
Marked Coro Pat. No. D. 116711 (mark n° 1).
The stamped patent number is wrong and refers to a Katz design of 19th September 1939 for a brooch representing a camellia with a stem and bow. The mistake was made by a worker during the punching phase; i.e., the worker mixed up the two punches used for the marking of two different pieces which were manufactured at the same time. Similar mistakes were made by other manufacturers, although this took place rarely, and usually involved only one or a few items in a series, with the rest of the items in the same series bearing the correct number. A similar mistake was made with Trifari's jelly belly "Orchid" that was stamped with the number of a daisy-shaped jelly belly, also by Trifari.
The piece appeared in *Glamour,* August 1940, and was on sale at Lord and Taylor, New York, for $5.

C40. "Brooch and Locket," Coro 1941**
Manufacturer Cohn & Rosenberger, Inc.
Designer Gene Verrecchio.
Patent n° 126,490 Gene Verrecchio, Providence, R.I., 3rd June 1941, filed on 16th April 1941.

Rhodium-plated metal brooch, with enameling and rhinestone pave, representing a flying bird holding a pendant in the shape of a cuckoo clock in its beak, which hides a picture frame that can be opened. 10x4cm.
Marked Coro (mark n° 1).

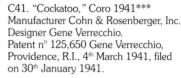

C41. "Cockatoo," Coro 1941***
Manufacturer Cohn & Rosenberger, Inc.
Designer Gene Verrecchio.
Patent n° 125,650 Gene Verrecchio, Providence, R.I., 4th March 1941, filed on 30th January 1941.

Rhodium-plated metal brooch with large blue cabochons and rhinestone pavé, representing a cockatoo, a parrot species with an upright crest, strong beak, and short, rounded tail. 5x4cm.
Marked Coro Pat. No. 125650 (mark n° 1).
Gene Verrecchio, on 4th March 1941, patented a series of three brooch designs – "Cockatoo," "Mallard" and "Paradise Fish" – which shared the same concept and materials: they all represented animals, were large, enameled and their bodies were made of several pearlized cabochons. Of the three items "Cockatoo" is the one most frequently found on the antique market, whereas "Paradise Fish" is the rarest. There are several color variants of all three.
In the same period Gene Verrecchio designed other brooches, including some Duettes, using flowery or abstract subjects, also made of large milky cabochons, which were however less interesting than the three items with animal subjects.

C42. *"Mr. & Mrs. Squirrel,"* Coro 1941**
Manufacturer Cohn & Rosenberger, Inc.
Designer Gene Verrecchio.
Not patented.
  Rhodium-plated base metal brooches with enameling, representing a pair of squirrels, the male is wearing a top hat, while the female is holding a flower spray in her paw and is wearing a hat with flower trimmings. 5x3.5cm.
  Marked Coro (mark n° 1). Both pieces are marked.
  They belong to the same series as the anthropomorphic birds and were made of the same materials. Therefore, it is possible to date them with certainty to the spring of 1941.

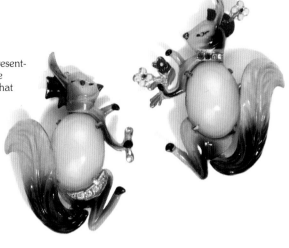

C43. "Lovebirds Duette", Coro 1941*****
Manufacturer Cohn & Rosenberger, Inc.
Designer Gene Verrecchio.
Patent n° 130,144 Gene Verrecchio, Providence, R.I., 28th October 1941, filed on 8th August 1941.

Rhodium-plated metal Duette, rhinestones, pink enamel and pink oval stones, representing two birds perched on a heart. 5.5x9.5cm.
  Marked Coro Duette Pat. No. 1798867 (mark n° 3).

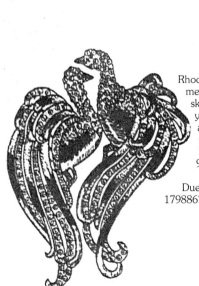

Rhodium-plated metal Duette, blue, sky-blue and yellow enamel, and rhinestones, representing two large pheasants. 9x7.5cm.
  Marked Coro Duette Pat. No 1798867 (mark n° 3).

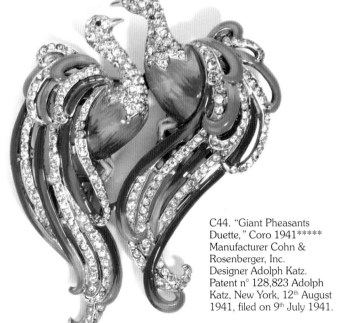

C44. "Giant Pheasants Duette," Coro 1941*****
Manufacturer Cohn & Rosenberger, Inc.
Designer Adolph Katz.
Patent n° 128,823 Adolph Katz, New York, 12th August 1941, filed on 9th July 1941.

C45. "Big Birds Duette," Coro 1941*****
Manufacturer Cohn & Rosenberger, Inc.
Designer Adolph Katz (?)
Not patented.
    Rhodium-plated metal Duette, green, burgundy and brown enamel, rhinestones and red and blue carved stones in the shape of a leaf, representing two birds perched on branches. 8.5x5cm.
    Marked Coro Duette Pat. No. 1798867 (mark n° 3).

C46. "Mallard," Coro 1941***
Manufacturer Cohn & Rosenberger, Inc.
Designer Gene Verrecchio.
Patent n° 125,652 Gene Verrecchio, Providence, R.I., 4th March 1941, filed on 30th January 1941.

Gold-plated metal brooch with pink, lilac and white enameling and large milky cabochons, representing a mallard in flight. 11x9.5cm.
    Marked Coro Pat. No 125652 (mark n° 1).

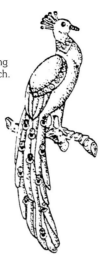

Gold-plated metal brooch, enamel in various colors and tones, rhinestones, representing a peacock perched on a branch. 10.5x4.5cm.
   Marked Coro (mark n° 1).

C47. "Peacock," Coro 1942****
Manufacturer Cohn & Rosenberger, Inc.
Designer Adolph Katz.
Patent n° 131,972 Adolph Katz, New York, 7th April 1942, filed on 19th February 1942.

C48. "Paradise Fish," Coro 1941****
Manufacturer Cohn & Rosenberger, Inc.
Designer Gene Verrecchio.
Patent n° 125,651 Gene Verrecchio, Providence, R.I., 4th March 1941, filed on 30th January 1941.

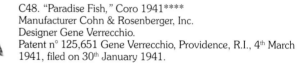

Rhodium-plated metal brooch in the shape of a fish with a body made of large milky white cabochons, pink, azure and shaded blue enameled fins, and rhinestone pavé snout. 7x 9cm.
Marked Design Pat.

C49. "Big Parrot," Coro 1941***
Manufacturer Cohn & Rosenberger, Inc.
Designer Adolph Katz.
Patent n° 128,822 Adolph Katz, New York, 12th August 1941, filed on 9th July 1941.

Gold-plated metal pin clip, blue, sky blue, yellow and green enamel, white and pink rhinestones, representing a parrot perched on a branch. 13x4.5cm.
    Marked Coro (mark n° 1).

C50. "Strass Pheasant," Coro 1942***
Manufacturer Cohn & Rosenberger, Inc.
Designer Adolph Katz (?)
Not patented.
    Rhodium-plated metal brooch with rhinestones, square red stones and black enameling, representing a pheasant completely studded with rhinestones and wings marked with a thin line of red stones, black enameled crest, collar and feet. The wing is a separate component joined to the body by means of a small screw. This assembly method emphasizes the brooch's tridimensionality which is further accentuated by the convex line of the pheasant's body. 10.5x6cm.
    Marked Coro (mark n° 1).

 C51. "Flamingo," Coro 1941****
Manufacturer Cohn & Rosenberger, Inc. New York.
Designer Adolph Katz (?)
Not patented.
    Rhodium-plated metal brooch, with pale blue, yellow and reddish enameling, representing a flamingo in flight. 11.5x7.3cm.
    Marked Coro (mark n° 1).

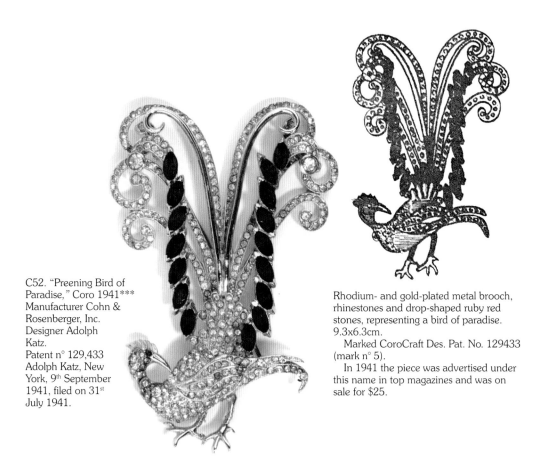

C52. "Preening Bird of Paradise," Coro 1941***
Manufacturer Cohn & Rosenberger, Inc.
Designer Adolph Katz.
Patent n° 129,433 Adolph Katz, New York, 9th September 1941, filed on 31st July 1941.

Rhodium- and gold-plated metal brooch, rhinestones and drop-shaped ruby red stones, representing a bird of paradise. 9.3x6.3cm.
    Marked CoroCraft Des. Pat. No. 129433 (mark n° 5).
    In 1941 the piece was advertised under this name in top magazines and was on sale for $25.

C53. "Fantastic Bird," Coro 1942****
Manufacturer Cohn & Rosenberger, Inc., New York.
Designer Adolph Katz.
Patent n° 131,772 Adolph Katz, New York, 24th March 1942, filed on 28th January 1942.

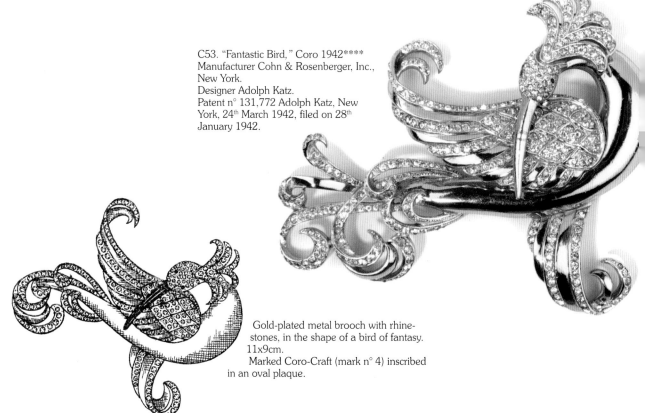

Gold-plated metal brooch with rhinestones, in the shape of a bird of fantasy. 11x9cm.
    Marked Coro-Craft (mark n° 4) inscribed in an oval plaque.

Rhodium-plated metal brooch with azure enameling, in the shape of a pheasant seen from the front, with large rhinestone pavé neck and tail. 8x4.5cm.
Marked Coro (mark n° 1).
This model is similar to a golden brooch with square stones on the tail, by Mellerio, or Meller, a famous Parisian jeweler, who made his brooch in the '40s (s. Melissa Gabardi, *Gioielli anni '40*, page 42).

C54. "Pheasant," Coro 1942 ****
Manufacturer Cohn & Rosenberger, Inc.
Designer Adolph Katz.
Patent n° 131,765 Adolph Katz, New York, 24th March 1942, filed on 22nd January 1942, assignor to Cohn & Rosenberger, Inc., New York.

C55. "Strass Turtle," Coro 1942****
Manufacturer Cohn & Rosenberger, Inc.
Designer Adolph Katz.
Patent n° 131,105 Adolph Katz, New York, 13th January 1942, filed on 15th December 1941, assignor to Cohn & Rosenberger, Inc., New York.

Rhodium-plated metal brooch, gold-plated in the front. The brooch represents a turtle studded with rhinestones and oval red stones, with gold-plated metal paws dotted with enamel. 9x7cm.
Marked Coro (mark n° 1).
The spring 1942 collection, still made of metal, includes several figurative items, with human, animal and flower shapes, manufactured with great care as individual brooches or Duettes. Human subjects were often of man-woman couples. The enameling is glossy or matte and the enamel was sometimes applied by hand for greater precision in rendering the details. Due to the sophistication and fantasy of the design, the high degree of workmanship and the delicacy of the materials used, these items are considered important collector pieces. In fact, it is reputed to be one of Coro's most beautiful series.

Rhodium-plated metal brooch with shaded brown enameling, representing a cock with rhinestone-studded crest and wattles 7.5x7cm.
Marked Coro (mark n° 2).

C56. "Rooster," Coro 1942****
Manufacturer Cohn & Rosenberger, Inc.
Designer Adolph Katz.
Patent n° 131,758 Adolph Katz, New York, 24th March 1942, filed on 19th January 1942, assignor to Cohn & Rosenberger, Inc., New York.

C57. "Mask," Coro 1941****
Manufacturer Cohn & Rosenberger, Inc.
Designer Adolph Katz (?)
Not patented.
Gold-plated metal pin clip, rhinestones, marquises and red baguettes, representing a mask with an elaborate hairstyle. 8.5x5.5cm.
Marked Coro-Craft (mark n° 5).

Large gold-plated metal and rhinestone brooch, in the shape of a mask with large door knocker pendant. 9.5x8cm. Marked Coro Pat. No. 129438 (mark n° 1).

C58. "Door Knocker," Coro 1941****
Manufacturer Cohn & Rosenberger, Inc.
Designer Adolph Katz.
Patent n° 129,438 Adolph Katz, New York, 9th September 1941, filed on 31st July 1941, assignor to Cohn & Rosenberger, Inc., New York.

C59. "Orchid," Coro 1941***
Manufacturer Cohn & Rosenberger, Inc.
Designer Adolph Katz (?)
Not patented.
  Bi-color yellow and pink-plated metal brooch, representing an orchid with petals, bordered by rhinestones and pistils covered with baguettes. 10x7.5cm.
  Marked Coro (mark n° 1).
  Large, heavy brooch, whose tridimensionality is emphasized by the superimposing of two components joined by a small screw; the overall effect, however, is not very harmonious.
  This subject became popular in the '40s; a popularity which started with an item of precious jewelry created by the Duke of Verdura (*Vogue* 1st October 1940), which was then copied not only by Coro but also by Alfred Philippe for Trifari (see T118.).

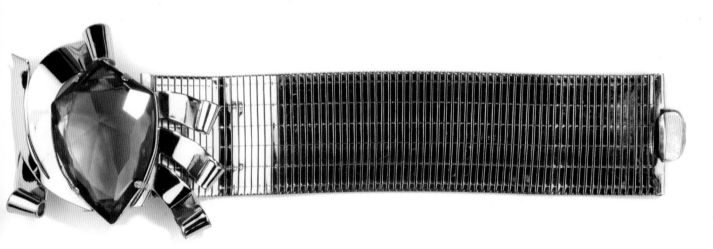

C60. "Topaz Bracelet," Coro 1941****
Manufacturer Cohn & Rosenberger, Inc.
Designer Adolph Katz (?)
Not patented.
  Gold-plated metal bracelet with large multifaceted topaz colored stone. 5.2x6cm motif in the center.

C61. "Grasshopper," Coro 1942****
Manufacturer Cohn & Rosenberger, Inc.
Designer Adolph Katz.
Patent n° 131,732 Adolph Katz, New York, 24th March 1942, filed on 17th January 1942, assignor to Cohn & Rosenberger, Inc., New York.

Rhodium-plated metal brooch, with shaded green and brown enameling, shaped like a grasshopper, with double rhinestone collar. 8x4.5cm.
  Marked Coro (mark n° 1).

C62. "Tarantula," Coro 1942****
Manufacturer Cohn & Rosenberger, Inc.
Designer Adolph Katz.
Patent n° 131,757 Adolph Katz, New York, 24th March 1942, filed on 17th January 1942, assignor to Cohn & Rosenberger, Inc, New York.

Rhodium-plated metal brooch with brown enameling, in the shape of a tarantula, with a rhinestone-studded body. 8x5cm.
  Marked Coro (mark n° 2).

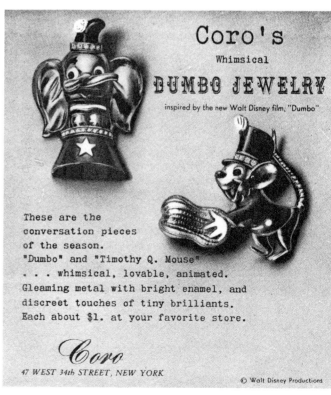

C63. "Dumbo Jewelry," Coro 1941****
Manufacturer Cohn & Rosenberger, Inc.
Not patented.

Mademoiselle, October 1941.

Gold-plated metal brooch, white, black, blue and red enamel, representing a ringmaster with a clown peeping out of a barrel and a giraffe. 4.2x7.2cm.
  Marked Coro (mark n° 1) ©W.D.P (Walt Disney Productions).
  As seen in an advertisement in *Mademoiselle*, October 1941, Coro produced the "Dumbo Jewelry" line which was inspired by Walt Disney's new movie; "Dumbo". Walt Disney productions had the copyright.

C64. *"Dumbo Jewelry,"* Coro 1941****
Manufacturer Cohn & Rosenberger, Inc.
   Not patented.
   Gold-plated metal brooch, white, red, green
and black enamel, representing the ringmaster
with Dumbo on a pedestal. 4x6cm.
   Marked Coro (mark n° 1) ©W.D.P.

C65. *"Dumbo Jewelry,"* Coro 1941****
Manufacturer Cohn & Rosenberger, Inc.
Not patented.
   Gold-plated metal pin clip, white, red and
blue enamel, representing a clown with a
tambourine. 6x4.5cm.
   Marked ©W.D.P.

C66. *"Dumbo Jewelry,"* Coro 1941****
Manufacturer Cohn & Rosenberger, Inc.
Not patented.
   Rhodium-plated metal brooch, with white enamel, representing a
small bear and two clowns, one of which is sucking his finger after
having bashed it with a hammer. 2.8x7.6cm.
   Marked ©W.D.P.

C67. *"Ubangi,"* Coro 1942****
Manufacturer Cohn & Rosenberger, Inc.
Designer Adolph Katz.
Patent n° 131,768 Adolph Katz, New York,
24th March 1942, filed on 22nd January
1942.

Gold-plated metal brooch, enamel in various
colors and tones, representing the female head
of a "Ubangi". 5.8x4.5cm.
   Marked Coro (mark n° 1).
   The Ubangi are the inhabitants of Ubangi
Shari, a French colony in Equatorial Africa which
chose the name of the Central African Republic
when it became independent. A distinguishing
feature of the Ubangi women is that they wear
numerous rings around their necks.

Rhodium- and gold-plated metal alloy brooch with pink, yellow, red, and black enameling and rhinestones. The brooch represents the head of a Chinese man with a large pagoda hat. 6.5x5cm.
Marked Coro (mark n° 2).

C68. "Chinaman," Coro 1942****
Manufacturer Cohn & Rosenberger, Inc.
Designer Adolph Katz.
Patent n° 131,959 Adolph Katz, New York, 7th April 1942, filed on 14th February 1942, assignor to Cohn & Rosenberger, Inc., New York.

C69. "Fujiman," Coro 1942****
Manufacturer Cohn & Rosenberger, Inc.
Patent n° 131,736 Adolph Katz, New York, 24th March 1942, filed on 19th January 1942, assignor to Cohn & Rosenberger Inc., New York.

Rhodium-plated metal pin clip, in the shape of a Fujiman's head with a long black enameled beard, yellow enameled face and blue enameled hat with red, yellow and blue ribbons and a motif made of rhinestone pavé triangles. 7.5x4cm.
Marked Coro (mark n° 1).

C70. "Mr. and Mrs. Dog," Coro 1942**
Manufacturer Cohn & Rosenberger, Inc.
Designer Adolph Katz.
Patent Mr. Dog n° 131,525, Mrs. Dog n° 131,526 Adolph Katz, New York, 10th March 1942, filed on 14th January 1942, assignor to Cohn & Rosenberger Inc., New York.

Gold-plated metal brooches, red, white and black enamel, rhinestones, representing two small puppies. Mr. Dog 4x2.8cm, Mrs. Dog 3.8x3.5cm.
Marked Coro (mark n° 1).

C71. "Apache & Putain," Coro 1942*****
Manufacturer Cohn & Rosenberger, Inc.
Designer Adolph Katz.
Patents Apache n° 131,735, Putain n° 131,755 Adolph Katz, New York, 24th March 1942,
filed on 17th January 1942, assignor to Cohn & Rosenberger, Inc., New York.

Gold-plated metal Duette with black, yellow and red enameling, and rhinestones, representing a typical couple of the old Parisian underworld, an "Apache" and his "Putain". 6x7.5cm.
   Marked CoroDuette Pat. n° 1798867 (mark n° 3).
   Rhodium-plated base metal alloy pin clip with pink, red, yellow and black enameling and rhinestones, representing an "Apache" with a cigarette in his mouth and a neckerchief. 6x4cm.
   Coro mark (mark n° 2).

C72. "American Indian Couple," Coro 1942*****
Manufacturer Cohn & Rosenberger, Inc.
Designer Adolph Katz.
Patent Squaw n° 131,759, Brave n° 131,760
Adolph Katz, New York, 24th March 1942, filed on
19th January 1942, assignor to Cohn & Rosenberger,
Inc., New York.

Gold-plated metal Duette with yellow, black and red enameling, red stones and rhinestones, representing a couple of American Indians, probably of the Navajo tribe: 8.5x6cm.
   Marked CoroDuette Pat. n° 1798867 (mark n° 3).
   Rhodium-plated base metal alloy pin clip with pink, red, black and white enameling and rhinestones, in the shape of the head of a Navajo Indian squaw. Size: 8.5x3cm.
   Marked Coro (mark n° 1).

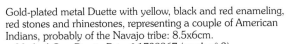

C73. "Ethnic Face," Coro 1942***
Manufacturer Cohn & Rosenberger, Inc.
Designer Adolph Katz.
Patent n° 133,741 Adolph Katz, Providence,
R.I., 8th September 1942, filed on 12th
August 1942, assignor to Cohn & Rosen-
berger, Inc., New York.

Gold-plated sterling brooch with black
and red enameling, blue cabochon and
rhinestones. The brooch represents a
woman's face in profile. 7.4x4cm.
Marked CoroCraft Sterling (mark
n° 7).

C74. "Zulu," Coro 1942*****
Manufacturer Cohn & Rosenberger, Inc., New York.
Designer Adolph Katz (?)
Not patented.
Gold-plated sterling brooch with brown and
yellow enameling, amethysts and rhinestones,
representing a standing Zulu warrior holding a
shield and spear. 8.5x4cm.
Marked CoroCraft Sterling (mark n° 7).

C75. "Black Head," Coro 1943*****
Manufacturer Coro, Inc.
Designer Adolph Katz.
Patent n° 136,311 Adolph Katz, Providence,
R.I., 7th September 1943, filed on 7th August
1943.

Gold-plated sterling brooch and earrings, rhinestones,
brown, red, green, white and black enamel, representing
the head of a black woman with an elaborate hairstyle
made of feathers. 10x6cm brooch, 3.5x2.5cm earrings.
Marked brooch CoroCraft Sterling (mark n° 7), earrings
Sterling.
　　Like other brooches that figure the head of black women
with various hairstyles (s. C67. and C73.) this item is often
erroneously named "Josephine Baker". In reality, these
brooches have nothing at all to do with Josephine Baker
who, at the time, was not very popular in America.

C76. *"Southern Belle,"* Coro 1942****
Manufacturer Cohn & Rosenberger, Inc.
Designer Adolph Katz (?)
Not patented.
    Gold-plated sterling brooch, pink, red, yellow, green and brown enamel, representing the head of a woman with long locks of hair, wearing a large straw hat tied under her throat with a bow ribbon. 6x5cm.
    Marked CoroCraft Sterling (mark n° 7).

C77. *"Mexican Woman,"* Coro 1942****
Manufacturer Cohn & Rosenberger, Inc.
Designer Adolph Katz.
Patent n° 133,473 Adolph Katz, Providence, R.I., 18th August 1942, filed on 15th July 1942.

Gold-plated sterling brooch, enamel in various colors, rhinestones, representing a Mexican woman holding an infant and carrying a jar. 7x4.3cm.
    Marked CoroCraft Sterling (mark n° 7).

C78. *"Harpist,"* Coro 1942****
Manufacturer Cohn & Rosenberger, Inc.
Designer Adolph Katz.
Patent n° 133,740, Adolph Katz, Providence, R.I., 8th September 1942, filed on 12th August 1942, assignor Cohn & Rosenberger, Inc., New York.

Gold-plated sterling brooch with brown and blue enamel and rhinestones, representing a harpist in Egyptian dress, with her hair tied up in a pony-tail with a rhinestone band, and fanning out at the ends. The girl's complexion is rendered with brown enamel, her large eyes with white and black enamel, and her lips and nails with red enamel. She is wearing "golden" bangles. The brooch is composed of two parts: the woman's figurine and the harp, assembled by means of two small screws. 7x6.5cm.
    Marked CoroCraft Sterling (mark n° 7).

C79. *"Mexican Flowergirl,"* Coro 1942****
Manufacturer Cohn & Rosenberger, Inc.
Designer Adolph Katz.
Patent n° 133,737 Adolph Katz, Providence, R.I., 8th September 1942, filed on 12th August 1942, assignor to Cohn & Rosenberger, Inc., New York.

Gold-plated sterling brooch with red, green, yellow, pink, azure, violet enameling, little colored rhinestones, representing a Mexican girl carrying a flower basket on her head. 5x8cm.
    Marked CoroCraft Sterling (mark n° 7).

C80. "Sparrow Duette," Coro 1942***
Manufacturer Cohn & Rosenberger, Inc.
Designer Adolph Katz.
Patent n° 133,472 Adolph Katz, New York, 18th
August 1942, filed on 13th July 1942, assignor to
Cohn & Rosenberger, Inc., New York.

Gold-plated sterling and enamel Duette, representing two sparrows with rhinestone pavé bodies, perched on a twig with green leaves. 8x4cm.
    The mechanism is marked Coro Duette Pat. No. 1798867 Sterling (mark n° 3). The clip is marked Sterling Craft Coro (mark n° 6).
    The fall 1942 collection featured the use of rather light sterling silver, which was smooth and compact, plated with vivid yellow gold and varnished to preserve the items' color and gloss, giving a still-new look. The weight of the Duette is heavier. The Duette also features glossy enameling applied with sophisticated craftsmanship. For successive collections Coro used heavier sterling silver with bright yellow or, at times, pink gold-plating.

Gold-plated sterling Duette with enameling, in the shape of flying sparrows. 7.5x4.5cm.
    Clip marked CoroCraft Sterling (mark n° 7). The mechanism is marked Coro Duette Sterling Pat. No. 1798867 (mark n° 3).

C81. "Flying Sparrow Duette," Coro 1943**
Manufacturer Cohn & Rosenberger, Inc.
Designer Adolph Katz.
Patent n° 134,981 Adolph Katz, Providence, R.I., 9th
February 1943, filed on 15th January 1943, assignor to Cohn & Rosenberger, Inc., New York.

C82. "Queen Bees," Coro 1942**
Manufacturer Cohn & Rosenberger, Inc.
Designer Adolph Katz.
Patent n° 133,477 Adolph Katz, Providence, R.I., 18th
August 1942, filed on 15th July 1942, assignor to Cohn & Rosenberger, Inc., New York.

Set composed of bee-shaped Duette and earrings with yellow enameling with brown and black shading and rhinestones. The Duette is made of gold-plated sterling. 7x2.8cm. The screw earrings are made of gold-plated metal 2.8cm.
    Clips are marked CoroCraft Sterling (mark n° 8).
    The mechanism is marked Coro Duette Sterling Pat. No. 1798867 (mark n° 3).
    Earrings are marked Coro (mark n° 3).
    "Queen Bees" is the original name and was registered by Coro as a trademark. The set appeared in the Jewelers' Circular Keystone, September 1943, with an indication of retail prices: $16.95 for the brooch and $7.50 for the earrings. The Duette also appeared in an advertisement in the Sears spring-summer 1944 catalog together with other Coro brooches under the slogan "Heirloom Quality". The earrings appeared together with other Coro earrings in the same catalog. The brooch was also featured in a drawing published in Women's Wear Daily, 17th July 1942, as an anticipation of the fall-winter collection. The Duette was featured in Vogue, 1st December 1943, as part of the magazine's Christmas gift suggestions, on sale at Stern's for $16.50. The use of different metals for the brooch (sterling) and the earrings (metal) can probably be explained by the fact that the period when they were manufactured – June 1942 – was a time of transition from metal to sterling.

Gold-plated sterling Duette, with white and shaded blue enameling and rhinestones, in the shape of blue jays. 7x5.5cm.
   The mechanism is marked Coro Duette Sterling Pat. No. 1798867 (mark n° 3).
   The clip is marked Sterling.

C83. "Blue Jay Duette," Coro 1942***
Manufacturer Cohn & Rosenberger, Inc.
Designer Adolph Katz.
Patent n° 133,479 Adolph Katz, Providence, R.I., 18th August 1942, filed on 16th July 1942, assignor to Cohn & Rosenberger, Inc., New York.

C84. "Birds Triquette," Coro 1942****
Manufacturer Cohn & Rosenberger, Inc.
Designer Adolph Katz.
Patent n° 133,478 Adolph Katz, Providence, R.I., 18th August 1942, filed on 15th July 1942.

Gold-plated sterling Triquette, rhinestones and dashes of enamel, representing three birds perched on branches. 4x8cm.
   Marked clips Sterling, mechanism Coro Duette Sterling Pat. No. 1798867 (mark n° 3).
   The patent refers to a single brooch.

C85. "Heavenly Swallows," Triquette, Duette & Earrings, Coro 1944****
Manufacturer Coro, Inc.
Designer Adolph Katz.
Patent n° 138,961 Adolph Katz, Providence, R.I., 3rd October 1944, filed on 20th July 1944.

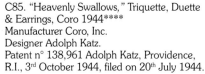

Gold-plated sterling Triquette, Duette and earrings studded with rhinestones, in the shape of flying swallows. Triquette 4.5x10cm, Duette 5x6cm, earrings 2cm.
   Marked Triquette and Duette clips Sterling CoroCraft (mark n° 8), mechanism Coro Duette Sterling Pat. No. 1798867 (mark n° 7), earrings Sterling.
   The model was elaborated in Triquette, Duette and a single brooch in three different sizes, earrings and small brooch. The entire series was published in *Harper's Bazaar*, March 1945, under the name of "Heavenly Swallows."

Gold-plated sterling brooch with azure, yellow, green red and brown enameling and rhinestones. The brooch is of a crane perched on a branch with flowers. 7x6.5cm.
    Marked CoroCraft Sterling (mark n° 7).

C86. "Perching Crane," Coro 1942****
Manufacturer Cohn & Rosenberger, Inc.
Designer Adolph Katz.
Patent n° 133,742 Adolph Katz, Providence, R.I., 8th
September 1942, filed on 8th August 1942.

C87. "Butterfly," Coro 1942*
Manufacturer Cohn & Rosenberger, Inc.
Designer Adolph Katz.
Patent n° 133,474 Adolph Katz, New York, 18th
August 1942, filed on 13th July 1942, assignor to
Cohn & Rosenberger, Inc., New York.

Gold-plated sterling brooch with enameling, in the shape of a butterfly, with wings decorated with red and blue marquis-cut stones. 3.5x8.5cm.
    Marked CoroCraft Sterling (mark n° 7).

Swan-shaped gold-plated sterling brooch with white, various shades of blue and brown enameling, and a large oval blue crystal at the center of the swan's body. 6x3cm.
    Marked CoroCraft Sterling (mark n° 7).

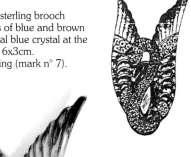

C88. "Swan," Coro 1942**
Manufacturer Cohn & Rosenberger, Inc.
Designer Adolph Katz.
Patent n° 133,744 Adolph Katz, Providence, R.I., 8th September 1942, filed on 12th August 1942 assignor to Cohn & Rosenberger, Inc., New York.

C89. "Lovebirds," Coro 1942**
Manufacturer Cohn & Rosenberger, Inc.
Designer Adolph Katz.
Not patented.

Sterling brooch representing two birds perched on a branch inside a circle. 5.5x5.5cm.
Marked Coro (mark n° 1) Sterling Genuine Norseland with a sketch of a Viking ship, Reg. U.S. Pat. Off.
The brooch belongs to the first sterling series of items produced by Coro in the spring of 1942. The mark "Genuine Norseland" with a sketch of a Viking ship is registered and indicates that the item is made of Norwegian silver. An almost identical brooch was patented under the name of Adolph Katz with the number 132,335 on 5th May 1942.

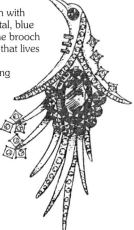

Gold-plated sterling brooch with a prong-set large blue crystal, blue stones and rhinestones. The brooch represents a dunlin, a bird that lives in swamps. 11x5.5cm.
Marked CoroCraft Sterling (mark n° 7).
The design is stylized and emphasizes the head with its large eye and the body by means of the large crystal, while the other body parts appear roughly sketched.

C90. "Dunlin," Coro 1944***
Manufacturer Coro, Inc.
Designer Adolph Katz.
Patent n° 137,353 Adolph Katz, Providence, R.I., 22nd February 1944, filed on 26th January 1944 assignor to Coro, Inc., New York.

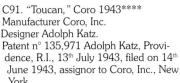

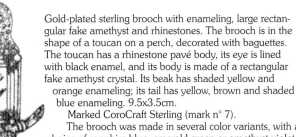

C91. "Toucan," Coro 1943****
Manufacturer Coro, Inc.
Designer Adolph Katz.
Patent n° 135,971 Adolph Katz, Providence, R.I., 13th July 1943, filed on 14th June 1943, assignor to Coro, Inc., New York.

Gold-plated sterling brooch with enameling, large rectangular fake amethyst and rhinestones. The brooch is in the shape of a toucan on a perch, decorated with baguettes. The toucan has a rhinestone pavé body, its eye is lined with black enamel, and its body is made of a rectangular fake amethyst crystal. Its beak has shaded yellow and orange enameling; its tail has yellow, brown and shaded blue enameling. 9.5x3.5cm.
Marked CoroCraft Sterling (mark n° 7).
The brooch was made in several color variants, with a choice of sapphire blue, emerald green or amethyst violet for the central crystal.
The brooch appeared in a Coro advertisement in *Vogue*, 15th December 1943, with the name "Toucan," with information concerning the retail price – about $30 - and the fact that it was made of sterling.

C92. "Crane," Coro 1944*****
Manufacturer Coro, Inc.
Designer Adolph Katz.
Patent n° 137,780 Adolph Katz, Providence, R.I., 23rd April 1944, filed on 26th January 1944, assignor to Coro, Inc., New York.

Gold-plated sterling brooch with red-orange enameling and rhinestones, representing a stylized crane with rhinestone-studded *tremblant* head; its neck and wings are emphasized with pink-orange enamel lines and rhinestones. 8.5x5.5cm.
    Marked CoroCraft Sterling (mark n° 7).
    The "Crane" appeared with this name in Sears' spring-summer 1944 catalog under the letter "H" at a retail price of $35.50.

C93. "Crane Head," Coro 1944*****
Manufacturer Coro Inc.
Designer Adolph Katz.
Patent n° 137,349 Adolph Katz, Providence, R.I., 22nd February 1944, filed on 26th January 1944, assignor to Coro, Inc., New York.

Gold-plated sterling brooch with red burnished and yellow enameling, green stones for its eyes and rhinestones. The brooch represents a crane's head with rich plumage. 10.6x6.1cm.
Marked CoroCraft Sterling (mark n° 7).
This piece seems to be a variant of the "Crane" (C92.)

Set composed of gold-plated metal alloy Duette and clip earrings with brown, blue and yellow enameling, large faceted blue stones for the eyes and rhinestones. The set represents two owls perched on a tree branch (Duette) and two owl heads (earrings). 4.5x4.8cm (Duette); 1.7cm (earrings).
    Mechanism mark: Coro Duette Pat. No 1798867 (mark n° 3); clip (only one is marked) with the Coro mark on a plaque with Pegasus (mark n° 10). Earring clip mark Pat. No 1967965.

C94. "Hoots," Coro 1944 (1947)*
Manufacturer Coro, Inc.
Designer Adolph Katz.
Patent n° 138,960 Adolph Katz, Providence, R.I., 3rd October 1944, filed on 20th July 1944, assignor to Coro, Inc., New York.

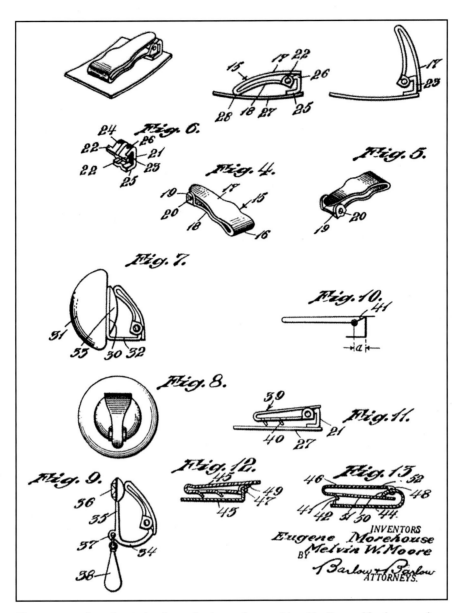

The patent number refers to the clip mechanism and was registered by Eugene Morehouse and Melvin W. Moore, Providence, R.I., 24th July 1934, filed on 30th March 1934, for B. A. Ballou & Co., Inc., Rhode Island. Ballou was an important Providence based company set up in 1876 by Barton A. Ballou. The company produced golden and gold-plated jewelry and jewelry components. This is further evidence of the fact that the mechanisms, on account of their very function, remained in use for a long time. The same mechanism was used by Réja for the "Nubian Head" which was part of the "Africana" (R34.) series and for the "Cuban Dancer" earrings by Grayce Norato (U25.).

"Hoots" is one of Coro's most famous pieces, and was made as a set complete with gold-plated sterling earrings (1944 – 1946) or, as in this case, it was made of gold-plated metal alloy (1947 – 1948) and in different enamel and stone color variants: azure, blue, green, yellow and, more rarely, red. The sterling version is marked CoroCraft, like all other pieces dating from 1943 – 1944. There are small but significant differences between the two versions: for example in their respective dimensions (the sterling version is slightly smaller and more compact). The name "Hoots" – an onomatopoeic word – is the original name and appears in a whole-page color advertisement of the CoroCraft line published in *Vogue*, 1st August 1944, and in an advertisement which appeared in *Mademoiselle*, February 1944, where it stated that the Duette was on sale for about $30 and the earrings for $15. They were also advertised in a 1943 sales catalog. Katz himself identified these pieces with the name "Hoots" in the article "*Every Woman a Queen*" by Irwing Ross, published in *American Magazine*, February 1948, in which he talked about some of his most famous pieces of jewelry, mentioning "Rockfish" (C116.) as being the source of inspiration for "Hoots." Since "Hoots" was one of Coro's best-sellers, it was produced in large quantities, and is nowadays among one of the best known and most easily found items.

C95. "Owl," Coro 1944*****
Manufacturer Coro, Inc.
Designer Adolph Katz.
Patent n° 137,002 Adolph Katz, Providence,
R.I., 11th January 1944, filed on 25th November
1943, assignor to Coro, Inc., New York.

Gold-plated sterling pin clip with brown
and yellow enameling, white stones for
its eyes, rhinestones and a large faceted
pink stone for its body. The pin is of an
owl. 7x4cm.
    Marked CoroCraft Sterling (mark n°
7).

C96. "Night Owls Triquette," Coro 1944***
Manufacturer Coro, Inc.
Designer Adolph Katz.
Patent n° 138,612 Adolph Katz, Providence, R.I., 22nd August
1944, filed on 9th June 1944, assignor to Coro, Inc., New York.

Gold-plated sterling Triquette and earrings with blue marquis-cut
stones and white baguettes, representing a night owl which is a
common species of owl. Triquette 3.8x5cm; screw earrings: 3cm.
    Triquette mark: CoroCraft Sterling (mark n° 8).
    The mechanism is marked Coro Duette Sterling Pat. No.
1798867 (mark n° 3). Earring sterling mark.
    The design was made in several stone color variants: blue, red
and green.
    The name is the original name with which it was registered by Coro Inc. in May
1944. The Triquette mark was registered by Cohn & Rosenberger in 1937 and was initially
used for the design of bracelets that could be disassembled in three pieces (bangle, brooch
and two clips) and later on for the brooches that could be taken apart, in three clips of decreasing size, which were made in a limited number.
    The "Night Owls" Triquette with matching earrings was mentioned in a magazine article
(WWD, 29th June 1944) as a beautiful example of "Triquette […], a development of the Duette presented by Coro several seasons before. The Triquette is a patented design consisting
of three clips of decreasing size that can either be worn individually or attached to a frame for
use as a single brooch." The Triquette was mentioned again in WWD, 4th January 1946.

C97. "Pansy Duette," Coro 1942****
Manufacturer Cohn & Rosenberger, Inc.
Designer Adolph Katz.
Not patented.
    Rhodium-plated metal Duette, rhinestones, red stones and green enamel, representing two pansies. 6.5x6.5cm.
    Marked clips Coro (mark n° 1), mechanism Coro Duette Pat. No. 1798867(mark n° 3).
    This Duette is not patented but a bracelet (Des. 131,778), necklace (Des 131,779), and brooch (Des. 131,877) using an identical design are patented.

C98. "Flowers Deco Duette," Coro 1942***
    Manufacturer Cohn & Rosenberger, Inc., New York.
    Designer Adolph Katz.
    Patent n° 133,468 Adolph Katz, Providence, R.I., 18th August 1942, filed on 15th July 1942.

Deco style gold-plated sterling Duette with fake amethysts and rhinestones, representing two flowers. 7x4cm.
    The mechanism is marked Coro Duette Pat. No 1798867 Sterling (mark n° 3). The clips are marked CoroCraft Sterling (mark n° 7).

C99. "Roses Bracelet," Coro 1942 ****
Manufacturer Cohn & Rosenberger, Inc., New York.
Designer Massa Raimond (?)
   Massa Raimond, Malden, Mass., patented a similar design in 1942 (des. n° 133,966, 29th September 1942, filed on 1st September 1942).
   Sterling silver bracelet composed of five large roses in relief. The roses are joined by thin hooks. Insert clasp. Length: 19cm; each rose measures 3cm.
   Marked Coro (mark n° 2).
   Due to the elaborate design and sophisticated craftsmanship, combined with the rarity of Coro bracelets dating from this period, this is considered to be an important collector's item.

C100. "Horse Head," Coro 1942***
   Manufacturer Cohn & Rosenberger, Inc.
   Designer Adolph Katz.
Patent n° 133,729 Adolph Katz, Providence, R.I., 8th September 1942, filed on 12th August 1942, assignor to Cohn & Rosenberger, Inc., New York.

Gold-plated sterling pin clip with pink enameling, red baguettes and rhinestones, in the shape of a horse's head with three flowers around its neck. 6.8x4.5cm.
   Marked CoroCraft Sterling (mark n° 7).

C101. "Thorobreds," Coro 1943**
Manufacturer Coro, Inc.
Designer Adolph Katz.
Patent n° 135,970 Adolph Katz, Providence,
R.I., 13th July 1943, filed on 14th June 1943,
assignor to Coro, Inc., New York.

Set composed of gold-plated sterling Duette and screw earrings with black and red enameling, red and green stones and rhinestones, representing two horses' heads. 5.8x5.6cm (brooch); 3.5cm (earrings).
   The mechanism is marked Coro Duette Pat. No 1798867(mark n° 3). The clip is marked (only one clip is marked) Sterling CoroCraft (mark n° 8). Earrings are not marked.
   The Duette appeared in an advertisement in *Harper's Bazaar*, December 1943, with the original name "Thorobreds," which is also its registered trademark. Together with the earrings it appeared in an advertisement in "Vogue, 1st August 1944 and in the spring 1944 edition of the "Sears" catalog, at the price of $32. It was also photographed for *Fortune*, December 1946, as a visual accompaniment for an article entitled "Costume Jewelry".
   It was a very successful item and, unlike most articles, was produced for some years and, for this reason, is still one of the most widespread Coro pieces of jewelry.

Gold-plated sterling Duette, green enamel, rhinestones and two large multifaceted stones in the color of topaz, representing two sunflowers. 5x8cm. Marked clips CoroCraft Sterling (mark n° 7), mechanism Coro Duette Sterling Pat. No. 1798867 (mark n° 3)

C102. "Sunflowers Duette," Coro 1944****
Manufacturer Coro, Inc.
Designer Adolph Katz.
Patent n° 138,694 Adolph Katz, Providence, R.I., 5th
September 1944, filed on 22nd June 1944.

Gold-plated sterling brooch, with red marquis-cut stones, ruby and rhinestones. The brooch is of a spray of flowers. 8.6x4.2cm.
Marked CoroCraft Sterling (mark n° 8).
The brooch was advertised with the name "Bouquet" in the spring 1944 edition of the "Sears" catalog, priced at $27.

C103. "Bouquet," Coro 1944***
Manufacturer Coro Inc.
Designer Adolph Katz.
Patent n° 137,781 Adolph Katz, Providence, R.I., 25th April 1944, filed on 26th January 1944.

C104. "Pike," Coro 1943**
Manufacturer Coro, Inc.
Designer Adolph Katz.
Patent n° 136,312 Adolph Katz, Providence, R.I., 7th September 1943, filed on 7th August 1943, assignor to Coro, Inc., New York.

Gold-plated sterling brooch representing a pike, with rhinestone pavé snout, red enameled open mouth, small blue rhinestone for an eye, gold-plated sterling scales on its tail, and tridimensional fretwork fins. There is an empty space for the contoured body which has no central stone. 6.5x7.5cm.
Marked CoroCraft Sterling (mark n° 7).
Almost stylized design with very light contours and the same skilful use of "full and empty" as in the fins of the "Rockfish" (C116.). It is unusual that the center of the body was left empty, but this was done so that the fabric of the dress underneath was visible. The same technique was used for two other brooches; a cock (des. n° 136,313 of 7th September 1943) and a flying duck, (not patented).

Gold-plated sterling and rhinestone brooch in the shape of a French poodle, with rhinestones on the front part of its body, around its paws and on its tail, to simulate the poodle's characteristic curly hair. 6x5.8cm.
Marked CoroCraft Sterling (mark n° 7).

C105. "Poodle," Coro 1943***
Manufacturer Cohn & Rosenberger, Inc.
Designer Adolph Katz.
Patent n° 134,983 Adolph Katz, Providence, R.I., 9th February 1943, filed on 15th January 1943, assignor to Cohn & Rosenberger, Inc., New York.

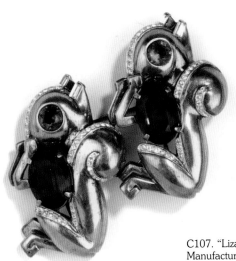

C106. "Squirrels," Coro 1944****
Manufacturer Coro, Inc.
Designer Adolph Katz (?)
Not patented.
   Gold-plated sterling Duette, with red and green faceted stones and rhinestones, of two squirrels in profile, rubbing their snouts with their front paws.
   7.6x6.6cm.
   Marked CoroCraft Sterling (mark n° 7).

C107. "Lizard," Coro 1942*****
Manufacturer Cohn & Rosenberger, Inc.
Designer Adolph Katz.
Patent n° 133,469 Adolph Katz, Providence, R.I., 18th August 1942, filed on 15th July 1942.

Sterling brooch, green enamel, rhinestones, representing a lizard holding a large white pearl in its mouth. 5x7.5cm.
   Marked CoroCraft Sterling (mark n° 7).

C108. "Mouse," Coro 1945*
Manufacturer Coro, Inc.
Designer Adolph Katz.
Patent n° 141,457 Adolph Katz, Providence, R.I., 5th June 1945, filed on 13th March 1945, assignor to Coro Inc., New York.

Gold-plated sterling brooch with green stone and rhinestones, representing a crouching mouse. 3x2cm.
   Marked Sterling CoroCraft inscribed in a rectangular plaque with Pegasus (mark n° 8).
   This is a typical scatter pin; a pin intended to be worn as part of a group with other scatter pins, as in an advertisement published in *Vogue,* June 1945, where three pins are worn together.

C109. "Monkeys Duette," Coro 1945*****
Manufacturer Coro, Inc.
Designer Adolph Katz.
Patent n° 141,687 Adolph Katz, New York, 26th June 1945, filed on 13th March 1945, assignor to Coro, Inc., New York. Patent covers the individual clip.

Gold-plated sterling Duette with green crystals and rhinestones, of two monkeys sitting on a branch. The body and ears are made of large faceted green crystals. The eyes are made of Lucite half-spheres with small black pellets set in yellow irises. 5.5x4cm.
   The mechanism is marked Coro Duette Sterling Pat. No. 1798867 (mark n° 3). The clips bear only the Sterling mark.
   There are at least two known versions of this piece of jewelry, i.e. with green and red stones.
   This item appeared in a Coro advertisement – a full color page – in *Vogue,* June 1943, with the CoroCraft mark, together with the "Marlin" and "Fox" jelly bellies (s. JB92. and JB79.), a flamingo-shaped brooch and a small mouse-shaped brooch (C108). On 12th January 1945, *Women's Wear Daily* announced that the novelty items of the season were the small, refined brooches with animal or flower subjects in the CoroCraft line. Brooch dimensions began to change from 1945: they became smaller and more harmonious, thereby the excesses of the previous years were abandoned; this change was apparent not only in Coro's production, but was a general trend.

C110. "Squirrel," Coro 1943*****
Manufacturer Coro, Inc.
Designer Adolph Katz.
Patent n° 136,833 Adolph Katz,
Providence, R.I., 14th December
1943, filed on 6th November 1943.

Gold-plated sterling
pin clip, grey and
brown enamel, red
rhinestones and
marquises, repre-
senting a squirrel on
a branch. 8x4cm.
    Marked CoroCraft
Sterling (mark n° 7).

C111. "Gazelle," Coro 1944*****
Manufacturer Coro, Inc.
Designer Adolph Katz.
Patent n° 137,003 Adolph Katz, Providence, R.I.,
11th January 1944, filed on 25th November 1943,
assignor to Coro, Inc., New York.

Gold-plated sterling brooch in the shape of a gazelle with grey-
blue enameled body, white enameled horns and rhinestone
pavé neck. The gazelle is depicted standing on top of a rock
made of a large square red crystal. 10x6cm.
    Marked CoroCraft Sterling (mark n° 7).
    This item was featured in *WWD*, 16th July 1943, in the
presentation of Coro's fall collection.
    It is an extraordinary item in many respects: for its beauty,
elegance and dimension. The same features are apparent in
the "Elephant" (C112.) and "Squirrel" (C110.).

C112. "Elephant," Coro 1944*****
Manufacturer Coro, Inc.
Designer Adolph Katz.
Not patented.
    Gold-plated sterling brooch representing an elephant
with a gray-blue enameled body, a rhinestone pavé
head and large green rectangular crystal in its trunk.
5.5x5cm.
    Marked CoroCraft Sterling (mark n° 7).

C113. "Bill and Coo," Coro 1945****
Manufacturer Coro, Inc.
Designer Adolph Katz.
Patent n° 140,014 Adolph Katz, New York, 16th January 1945, filed on 18th November 1944, assignor to Coro, Inc., New York.

Set composed of gold-plated sterling Duette and screw ear-rings, in the shape of love birds with bodies made of blue crystal, enamel and rhinestones on their wings and on the branch. Duette 6.5x3cm; earrings 3cm.

The clips are marked CoroCraft Sterling (mark n° 8). The mechanism is marked Coro Duette Sterling Pat. No. 1798867 (mark n° 3). The earrings are marked Sterling.

The Duette featured in *Mademoiselle* with this name in May 1944, at a sales price of $25. "Bill and Coo" is a familiar expression to describe two people in love.

C114. "Fighting Cocks," Coro 1945***
Manufacturer Coro, Inc.
Designer Adolph Katz.
Patent n° 140,326 Adolph Katz, New York, 13th February 1945, filed on 16th December 1944, assignor to Coro, Inc., New York.

Pair of gold-plated sterling brooches with drop-shaped red stones on the wings and wattles and rhine-stones. The brooches represent two cocks with spurs in a fighting position. Each brooch 4.5x4cm.

Mark (both are marked) CoroCraft Sterling (mark n° 8).

Set composed of gold-plated sterling Duette and earrings with azure and pink enameling, in the shape of two open-mouthed fish, each holding a blue crystal in its open mouth. Duette 7x5cm. Screw earring 2.5cm.

The clips are marked CoroCraft Sterling (mark n° 8), The mechanism is marked Coro Duette Sterling Pat. No. 1798867 (mark n° 3). Earrings are marked Sterling.

The design was made in at least two versions: with the fish mouth made of blue crystals or white pearls.

The Duette, with the name "Jeweled Dolphins," appeared in *Mademoiselle*, July 1944, and was on sale for $30.

C115. "Jeweled Dolphins," Coro 1944*****
Manufacturer Coro, Inc.
Designer Adolph Katz.
Patent n° 139,101 Adolph Katz, New York, 10th October 1944, filed on 29th July 1944, assignor to Coro, Inc., New York.

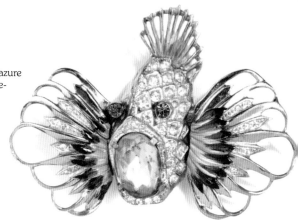

C116. "Rock Fish," Coro 1944****
Manufacturer Coro, Inc.
Designer Adolph Katz.
Not patented.
   Gold-plated sterling brooch of an open-mouthed fish with azure
and pink enameling, large azure crystal in its mouth and rhinestones. 8x6cm.
   Marked CoroCraft Sterling (mark n° 8). In an interview
with Irwin Ross (*American Magazine*, February 1948, *Every
Woman a Queen*) Adolph Katz talked about the "Rock Fish,"
of the success it gave him and of how it inspired him to
design "Hoots". Therefore, its attribution to Adolph Katz is a
certainty and it is entirely probable that the design was made
for the spring-summer 1944 collection. It exists in at least two
color variants: blue and red.

C117. "Frog Duette," Coro 1944*****
   Manufacturer Coro, Inc.
   Designer Adolph Katz.
   Patent n° 138,958 Adolph Katz, Providence, R.I., 3rd October
   1944, filed on 19th July 1944, assignor to Coro, Inc., New York.
   The patent refers to the "Frog Duette Jelly Belly" (s. JB85.), of
   which the exemplar with crystals is a contemporary variant.

Frog shaped gold-plated sterling Duette, with large, oval, azure, faceted crystal,
yellow, green, and red enameling, and rhinestones. The protruding eyes are
made of Lucite half-spheres with a small black pellet in the middle. 5x5cm.
   Clip mark Coro Sterling (mark n° 1). The mechanism is marked Coro Duette
Sterling Pat. No. 1798867 (mark n° 3).
   There are matching earrings that go with this model, whose design was
made in at least two color variants; azure and green. The version with crystals
appeared in an advertisement for the CoroCraft line in *Vogue*, 1st December
1944; the jelly belly version appeared in *Harper's Bazaar*, February 1945. The
subject was mentioned by *WWD*, 29th June 1944, to introduce the Coro fall
collection. It is an exceptionally rare item.

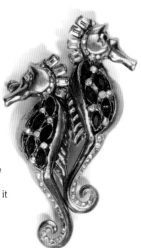

C118. "Sea Horses Duette," Coro 1944-45***
Manufacturer Coro, Inc.
Designer Adolph Katz (?)
Not patented.
   Sea-horse shaped gold-plated sterling Duette with small red
oval stones and rhinestones. 6x4cm.
   Clip is marked CoroCraft Sterling (mark n° 8). The mechanism
is marked Coro Duette Sterling Pat. No. 1798867 (mark n° 3).
   In 1941 Charles E. Pauzat patented (n° 127,445) a gold-plated
Duette in the shape of sea-horses which were larger than the sea-
horses in this one, and without the stones. This model was probably
revised to suit the fashion of the day that required smaller brooches
with more elaborate designs. It was not patented, probably because it
was just a new version of an existing model.

C119. "Bunnies," Coro 1945****
Manufacturer Coro, Inc.
Designer Adolph Katz (?)
Not patented.
   Gold-plated sterling Duette with blue stones, red baguettes and rhinestones representing two bunnies' heads with upright ears. 4.5x5.5cm.
   The mechanism is marked Coro Duette (mark n° 3) Sterling Pat. No 1798867. The clips are marked CoroCraft Sterling; the mark is inscribed in a rectangular plaque with Pegasus (mark n° 9).
The heads of the bunnies resemble the head of "Bugs Bunny," a

C120 "Rabbits Duette," Coro 1945****
Manufacturer Coro, Inc.
Designer Adolph Katz.
Patent n° 142,483 Adolph Katz, Providence, R.I., 2nd October 1945, filed on 22nd May 1945.

Gold-plated sterling Duette and earrings, green cabochons, red stones and baguettes, representing two rabbits. 5.5x5cm Duette, 2.5x1.2cm earrings.
   Marked clips CoroCraft Sterling (mark n° 7), mechanism Coro Duette Sterling Pat. No. 1798867 (mark n° 3), earrings Sterling.

Gold-plated sterling brooch with chatelaine, with red enameling, rhinestones and red, green and blue stones, representing a knight in the act of piercing a heart with his sword. Knight size 6.2x5cm, sword 8.5x2.5cm. Mark CoroCraft Sterling (mark n° 9).

The sword follows a design patented by Katz, on 20th March 1945, filed on 9th January 1945, n° 140,604. This same sword, with earrings also shaped like swords, appeared in an advertisement in 1945 with the name "jeweled rapiers".

The chatelaine appeared in an advertisement in *Harper's Bazaar,* November 1945.

C121. "Knight Chatelaine," Coro 1945****
Manufacturer Coro, Inc.
Designer Adolph Katz.
Knight Patent n° 143,219 Adolph Katz, Providence, R.I., 18th December 1945, filed on 21st July 1945.

Gold-plated sterling chatelaine brooch, red enamel, rhinestones, representing a bullfighter holding up a cape in front of a bull. Torero 4.2x2.5cm, bull 3x4.5cm Marked CoroCraft Sterling (mark n° 7).

C122. "Torero Chatelaine," Coro 1946****
Manufacturer Coro, Inc.
Designer Adolph Katz.
Patent n° 144,194 Adolph Katz, Providence, R.I., 19th March 1946, filed on 12th October 1945.

C123. "Tragedy and Comedy Chatelaine & Duette," Coro 1946****
Manufacturer Coro, Inc.
Designer Adolph Katz
Patent n° 144,198 Adolph Katz, Providence, R.I., 19th March 1946, filed on 12th October 1945, assignor to Coro, Inc., New York. Patent covers the chatelaine.

Gold-plated sterling brooches with chatelaine, black enameling, rhinestones and red and green stones, representing comedy and tragedy masks. 3.5x3cm.
    Marked CoroCraft Sterling (mark n° 9).
    Gold-plated sterling Duette with black enameling and rhinestones in the shape of comedy and tragedy masks. 3.5x5.5cm. The clip is marked (Tragedy) CoroCraft Sterling (mark n° 9). The mechanism is marked Coro Duette Sterling Pat. No. 1798867 (mark n° 3).
    The Duette appeared in an advertisement published in *Mademoiselle,* February 1946, and in *Town & Country,* April 1946. The Chatelaine version is mentioned in *WWD,* 10th August 1945.

C124. "Chinese Warrior," Coro 1945***
Manufacturer Coro Inc.
Designer Adolph Katz.
Patent n° 143,218 Adolph Katz, Providence, R.I.,
18th December 1945, filed on 21st July 1945, assignor to Coro, Inc., New York.

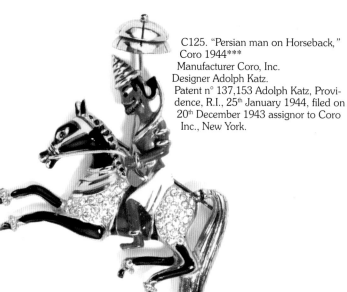

Gold-plated sterling brooch, black enamel
details, red, green and black stones, portraying a Chinese warrior in dueling stance.
6.5x5.5cm.
Marked Sterling CoroCraft inscribed in a
rectangular plaque with Pegasus (mark n° 8).

C125. "Persian man on Horseback,"
Coro 1944***
Manufacturer Coro, Inc.
Designer Adolph Katz.
Patent n° 137,153 Adolph Katz, Providence, R.I., 25th January 1944, filed on
20th December 1943 assignor to Coro
Inc., New York.

Gold-plated sterling brooch with black, white, and green
enameling and rhinestones, in the shape of a Persian knight
with a parasol . 6.7x7cm.
Marked CoroCraft Sterling (mark n° 7).
With this brooch, the only one made in 1943-44, Adolph
Katz returned to a theme he had already developed in his
1942 fall collection which had similar characteristics. The
collection included ethnic figurines decorated with enamel
and rhinestones, made in a miniaturist's style and with a
clear intent to analyze the culture the figurines represented.
(s. "Harpist" C78.).

C126. *"Pixie,"* Coro 1947***
Manufacturer Coro, Inc.
Designer Adolph Katz.
Not patented.
 Gold-plated sterling brooch with red, green and azure citrine crystals, and rhinestones, portraying an imp. 5.5x4cm.
Marked CoroCraft Sterling (mark n° 9).
 There is also a brooch of only the imp's head.

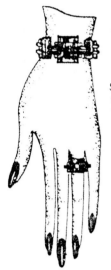

Set composed of gold-plated sterling pin clip, brooch, screw earrings with colored stones and rhinestones, portraying a hand with varnished nails, wearing a ring and bangle with red and blue stones. Pin clip 9.5x3.5cm; brooch 6.5x2.2cm; earrings: 3cm.
 Marked CoroCraft Sterling (mark n° 9). Earrings with Sterling mark.
 The pin clip appeared in a Coro advertisement in *Mademoiselle*, October 1945, with the CoroCraft mark and the caption "Friendship […] beautifully symbolized in this romantic creation by Coro. Glowing jewel color […] sterling, gold finish."

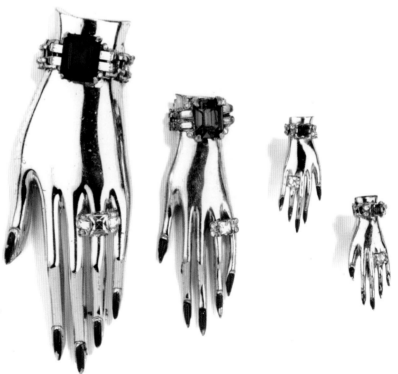

C127. *"Friendship,"* Coro 1944****
Manufacturer Coro, Inc.
Designer Adolph Katz.
Patent n° 139,075 Adolph Katz, Providence, R.I., 10th October 1944, filed on 2nd August 1944, assignor to Coro, Inc., New York.

Crown-shaped brooch and screw earrings set made of sterling silver (the brooch) and gold-plated metal (the earrings) with red and green cabochons, azure baguettes, and azure and green stones and rhinestones. 4.3x4.3cm (brooch); 3cm (earrings).
The brooch is marked CoroCraft Sterling; the mark is inscribed in a rectangular plaque with Pegasus (mark n° 9); the earrings are marked Coro (mark n° 1).
From 1943 onwards, the crown became one of the most popular subjects in costume jewelry: the most famous model is the one designed by Alfred Philippe for Trifari (T182.), but all manufacturers made crowns: see, for example, Castlecliff (Ca4.).

C128. "Crown Set," Coro 1944***
Manufacturer Coro, Inc.
Designer Adolph Katz.
Patent n° 139,100 Adolph Katz, Providence, R.I. 10th October 1944, filed on 20th July 1944, assignor to Coro, Inc., New York.

C129. "Siren," Coro 1945****
Manufacturer Coro, Inc.
Designer Adolph Katz.
Patent n° 142,644 Adolph Katz, Providence, R.I., 23rd October 1945, filed on 4th July 1945, assignor to Coro, Inc., New York.
Patent covers the individual pin and, based on the same design, the pin, Duette and earrings were made.

Gold-plated sterling set consisting of two pin clips, Duette, and screw earrings with sunburst arranged baguettes for the hair, red enameling and rhinestones for the siren's head. The pin clips are decorated with red baguettes; Pin clips 4.5x4cm. The Duette and earrings feature blue baguettes and white marquise-cut stones, measuring 6x4cm and 2.5cm, respectively.
The pin clips are marked CoroCraft Sterling (mark n° 8). The mechanism is marked Coro Duette Sterling Pat. No. 1798867 (mark n° 3). The earrings are marked Coro Sterling (mark n° 1). The Duette clips bear only the Sterling mark.
Pin clip and earrings appeared in a small black and white advertisement published in *Vogue*, 1st December 1945, with the name "Siren by Coro". The advertisement was for Rapphel Jewelers, 47 W 57th St., New York, a shop where this jewelry was on sale for $25 for the pin clip and $20 for the earrings. A company advertisement appeared in *Mademoiselle*, September 1945.

Gold-plated sterling brooch shaped like a half-moon bordered by rhinestones, on which an imp is sitting. The imp's face is made of a red cabochon, the pointed hat is a yellow stone, the shoes two small white marquise-cut stones, while the dress features black enamel buttons and a red enamel heart on the imp's chest. The imp and half-moon are two separate pieces joined by means of a small screw. 5.5cm.

Marked CoroCraft Sterling mark (mark n° 9).

There are also earrings with the same design. This design drew inspiration from the precious brooches – gold, moon-stones as decorations for the moon, and rubies for the imp's head – made by Georg Jensen, Inc., Fifth Avenue, advertised in *Vogue*, 15th February 1945.

C130. "Man in the Moon," Coro 1945***
Manufacturer Coro, Inc.
Designer Adolph Katz.
Patent n° 142,184 Adolph Katz, Providence, R.I., 14th August 1945, filed on 10th May 1945, assignor to Coro, Inc., New York.

C131. "Dutch People Duette," Coro 1947****
Manufacturer Coro, Inc.
Designer Adolph Katz.
Patent n° 147,189 Dutch girl, n° 147,243 Dutch boy, Adolph Katz, Providence, R.I., respectively on 22nd July and 5th August 1947, both filed on 8th July 1946, assignor to Coro, Inc., New York.

Gold-plated sterling Duette, with azure and red faceted stones, red and white rhinestones, representing a Dutch couple holding hands and dressed in traditional Dutch costume. The joining mechanism is exactly the same shape as the figurines. 4.5x6cm.

Clips marked CoroCraft Sterling (Boy, mark n° 9), and Sterling (Girl), respectively. The mechanism is marked Coro Duette Sterling Pat. No. 1798867 (mark n° 3).

The item was featured in *WWD* of 5th July 1946, for the presentation of Coro's fall collection.

Sterling Duette, red enamel, rhinestones and green stones, portraying two female faces. 5x5.5cm.

Marked clips CoroCraft Sterling (mark n° 7), mechanism Coro Duette Sterling Pat. No. 1798867(mark n° 3).

The Duette was featured in an advertisement in *Mademoiselle*, February 1946, and in *Town & Country*, April 1946.

C132. "Women's Faces Duette," Coro 1946****
Manufacturer Coro, Inc.
Designer Adolph Katz.
Patent n° 146,032 Adolph Katz, Providence, R.I., 10th December 1946, filed on 9th March 1946.

C133. "King and Queen Duette," Coro 1946****
Manufacturer Coro, Inc.
Designer Adolph Katz.
Patent n° 144,195 Adolph Katz, Providence, R.I.,
19th March 1946, filed on 12th October 1945, as-
signor to Coro, Inc., New York.

Gold-plated sterling Duette with synthetic red stones, turquoise and rhinestones, portraying the busts of a king and queen wearing crowns. 4.5x5cm.
    Clip (King) is marked CoroCraft Sterling (mark n° 8). The mechanism is
marked Coro Duette Sterling Pat. No. 1798867 (mark n° 3).
    The Duette appears with other Duettes of the CoroCraft line, in an adver-
tisement in *Vogue,* 1st December 1945.

C134. "Dancing Donkey," Coro 1945***
Manufacturer Coro, Inc.
Designer Adolph Katz.
Patent n° 142,183 Adolph Katz, Providence, R.I., 14th August
1945, filed on 10th May 1945, assignor to Coro, Inc., New York.

Gold-plated sterling set composed of a brooch
and screw earrings, in the shape of a donkey,
with ears made of marquise-cut red stones, a
mane made of baguettes, a rhinestone-studded
tail and black enamel hooves. The earrings have
the same design, only smaller. Brooch 5x4cm;
earrings 2.5cm.
    Brooch marked CoroCraft Sterling (mark n° 8).
Earrings marked Sterling.
    There is also another, possibly contemporary, gold-
plated sterling version with the CoroCraft Sterling mark, which is larger, less
harmonious and less accurately manufactured, with a flatter outline, either with
the same identical design, or featuring a colored enamel flower garland around
the donkey's neck.
    The set appeared in an advertisement published in *Glamour,* July 1945, with
the name "Dancing Donkey" and an indication of the prices: $22 for the brooch,
$13 for the earrings.

Gold-plated sterling Duette with red marquise-cut stones, tiny green stones and
rhinestones, representing two parrots on a perch. The tails are decorated with red
marquise-cut stones, the wings and beaks are rhinestone studded, while the eyes
are made of green stones. 5.3x4cm.
    The clip is marked CoroCraft Sterling (mark n° 9). The mechanism is marked
Coro Duette Sterling (mark n° 3).
    There is also a precious, probably antique, version of this brooch, which was
made of gold, with sapphires on the bird's tail and small diamonds. The design
is identical, with the only difference being that the precious version features parrots with longer tails studded with precious stones. It was made as a Duette, that
could be disassembled into two individual pins. The joining mechanism is identical
to Coro's.
    It is the only known example of a precious brooch made as a Duette with a join-
ing mechanism with the same contour as the clips.
    The Duette appeared in an advertisement published in *Mademoiselle,* February
1946, and in *Town & Country,* April 1946.

C135. "Parrots Duette," Coro 1946***
Manufacturer Coro, Inc.
Designer Adolph Katz.
Patent n° 146,141 Adolph Katz, Providence,
R.I., 31st December 1946, filed on 21st March
1946, assignor to Coro, Inc., New York.

C136. "China Peacocks Duette," Coro 1946***
Manufacturer Coro, Inc.
Designer Adolph Katz.
Patent n° 146,036 Adolph Katz, Providence, R.I., 10th December 1946, filed on 9th March 1946, assignor to Coro, Inc., New York.

Gold-plated sterling Duette with faceted red and blue stones, in the shape of peacocks, with tails decorated with red and blue stones and sterling bodies engraved with heavy lines to create a plumage effect. 3x6cm.
    The clips are marked Sterling; the mechanism is marked Coro Duette Sterling Pat. No. 1798867 (mark n° 3).
    This Duette belongs to a series of brooches in the Coro line, inspired by ancient China and made of gold-plated sterling with aquamarine colored stones, that appeared in *Vogue*, 1st June 1946 and in *Town & Country*, July 1946. The series includes four other brooches of a salamander, a lobster, a Chinese water carrier (whole figure) and two hands holding a heart. The subjects were described as being exotic.

C137. "Lovebirds," Coro 1948**
Manufacturer Coro, Inc.
Designer Adolph Katz.
Patent n° 151,151 Adolph Katz, Providence, R.I. 28th September 1948, filed on 13th March 1948, assignor to Coro, Inc., New York.

Gold-plated metal set composed of a Duette and screw earrings, with green and pink enameling, central, marquise-cut red stone, representing two parakeets on a branch. 6.3x3.9cm (Duette); 3cm (earrings).
    The mechanism is marked Coro Duette (mark n° 3) Pat. No 1798867; the clips are marked Coro Pat. Pend. (mark n° 1). The earrings are marked Coro (mark n° 1).
    In 1948 Coro launched its Duette spring collection with great fanfare. On 2nd April 1948 *WWD* wrote: "Coro Inc., has announced a shop-window competition for the presentation of its "Duettes". The competition is to be featured in a whole page advertisement in *Life* magazine on 26th April.
    Prizes total $2,500. Competition judges are Lester Gaba, show-window decoration consultant, Cecilia Staples, shop-window manufacturer and Henry Callahan, head shop-window decorator at Lord & Taylor".
    The advertisement in *Life* also featured this set with the name of "Lovebirds," with retail prices of $4 for the Duette and $2 for the earrings.

Gold-plated sterling brooch with large central faceted aquamarine, red baguettes and rhinestones, of a lighted lamp. 4.7x5cm.
    Marked CoroCraft Sterling inscribed in a rectangular plaque with Pegasus (mark n° 9).
    The brooch appeared, with the name "Aladdin's Lamp" by Coro, in an advertisement in *Mademoiselle*, June 1945, where it stated that the central stone was available not only in aquamarine, but also in ruby red, emerald green and amethyst violet colors. The sales price was about $30 plus taxes. There are also matching earrings patented with n° 142,193.

C138. "Aladdin's Lamp," Coro 1945***
Manufacturer Coro, Inc.
Designer Adolph Katz.
Patent n° 142,189 Adolph Katz, Providence, R.I. 14th August 1945, filed on 18th May 1945, assignor to Coro, Inc., New York.

C139. "Shining Stars Duette," Coro 1947***
Manufacturer Coro, Inc.
Designer Adolph Katz.
Patent n° 147,410 Adolph Katz, Providence, R.I., 2nd September 1947, filed on 24th August 1946, assignor to Coro, Inc., New York.

Gold-plated sterling Duette of two stars studded with colored stones and rhinestones. 5x8cm.

Clips are marked CoroCraft Sterling (mark n° 9). The mechanism is marked Coro Duette Sterling Pat. No. 1798867 (mark n° 3).

A whole set – necklace, bracelet and Duette – was made using this design and the necklace was patented with n° 147,444 on 9th September 1947, filed on 24th August 1946.

The Duette appeared in an advertisement published in Vogue, 1st August 1946, with the CoroCraft mark and the name "Shining Stars," which means that it was the original name. The advertisement was made to launch the new line, which also included a necklace and earrings.

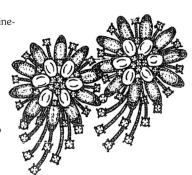

C140. "Mirror," Coro 1947**
Manufacturer Coro, Inc.
Designer Adolph Katz.
Patent n° 147,656 Adolph Katz, Providence, R.I., 14th October 1947, filed on 15th August 1946, assignor to Coro, Inc., New York.

Gold-plated sterling brooch of a mirror in an oval frame, decorated with rhinestones, red and blue stones, with a twisted hand-grip. 10x4cm.

Marked CoroCraft Sterling (mark n° 9). The brooch appeared in an advertisement in Mademoiselle, January 1947.

Gold-plated sterling brooch and clip earrings set with small colored stones and rhinestones, representing a lyre. Brooch 6.5x5cm; earrings 2.5cm.

The brooch is marked CoroCraft Sterling (mark n° 9). The earrings are marked Coro Sterling P.P. (mark n° 2).

The set appeared in an advertisement for the CoroCraft line published in Vogue, 1st November 1946, and in Fortune, December 1946, as an illustration for an article on costume jewelry and again in the Saturday Evening Post, 31st May 1947, as an illustration for an article by Elsie McCormick, Merchant of Glitter. The set also appeared in two advertisements in Mademoiselle, November 1946 and March 1947. In the 1947 advertisement only the brooch appeared as part of a series called "Carnegie Hall Jewelry," inspired by the movie Carnegie Hall.

C141. "Lyre Set," Coro 1947****
Manufacturer Coro, Inc.
Designer Adolph Katz.
Patent n° 147,183 Adolph Katz, Providence, R.I., 22nd July 1947, filed on 8th July 1946, assignor to Coro, Inc., New York.
Earring patent n° 148,304 Adolph Katz, Providence, R.I., 6th January 1948, filed on 29th October 1946.

C142. "Spoon," Coro
1948***
Manufacturer Coro, Inc.
Designer Adolph Katz.
Patent n° 148,792 Adolph Katz,
Providence, R.I., 24th February 1948, filed on 24th January
1947, assignor to Coro, Inc.,
New York.

Gold-plated sterling spoon-shaped
brooch, with a handle decorated
with rhinestones and red stones.
9.2x2cm.
    Marked CoroCraft Sterling
(mark n° 9).

C143. "Moyen Age Pipe," Coro 1948***
Manufacturer Coro, Inc.
Designer Adolph Katz.
Patent n° 150,624 Adolph Katz, Providence, R.I.,
17th August 1948, filed on 1st November 1947, assignor to Coro, Inc., New York.

Gold-plated metal brooch with red, green and
blue cabochons, with chatelaine and fringe,
representing a pipe. 7.6x9cm.
    Marked Coro inscribed in a rectangular
plaque with Pegasus (mark n° 10).

C144. "Moyen Age Lamp," Coro
1948***
    Manufacturer Coro, Inc.
    Designer Adolph Katz.
    Patent n° 150,611 Adolph Katz, Providence, R.I. 17th August 1948, filed on
1st October 1947, assignor to Coro,
Inc., New York.

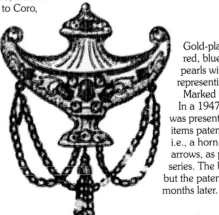

Gold-plated metal brooch with
red, blue and green cabochons,
pearls with chatelaine and fringe,
representing a lamp. 5.5x8.8cm.
Marked Coro (mark n° 1).
In a 1947 advertisement the piece
was presented together with other
items patented in the same period:
i.e., a horn, an axe and two crossed
arrows, as part of the "Moyen Age"
series. The brooch dates from 1947,
but the patent was granted several
months later.

C145. *"Chinese Duette,"* Coro 1947*****
Manufacturer Coro, Inc.
Designer Adolph Katz (?)
Not patented.

    Gold-plated metal Duette, with imitation-ivory white plastic, black and red enameling, small turquoise stones and imitation coral, drop-shaped white peals. The Duette represents royal Chinese masks with richly ornamented dress collars and hair. 5.5x6cm.

    The clips are marked Coro (mark n° 1 inscribed in relief in an oval plaque). The mechanism is marked Coro Duette Pat. No. 1798867 (mark n° 3).

    This is a high quality item and it is surprising that such an original, refined design was not patented, especially in a period when Coro was constantly patenting its products, even the most banal pieces. Its only fault lies in its size, which was slightly too large for the fashion of the time.

    All these facts suggest that the brooch had probably been made especially for the exhibition at Coro's showroom. In fact, in 1947 (*WWD*, 24th January and 27th June 1947), in line with a marketing policy which held that a showroom had the same power to attract customers as a shop-window, Coro installed 24 display cases along its showroom corridors and walls where display themes with figures, fabrics, colorful objects and, naturally, matching jewels, were on display. The display cases had been designed by Henry Altheimer, who was also responsible for the exhibition.

    In the spring, to emphasize the fact that Coro was commercially represented worldwide, the exhibition was dedicated to several countries, whose cultural identities were highlighted in combination with ethnically inspired Coro jewelry. China was one of the countries that featured in this exhibition. Its display case was decorated with embroidered silk from the Mandarin age, and jewelry with aquamarines, rubies and rhinestones. It is possible that the "Chinese Duette" had been specially designed for this event and had been manufactured in a limited number of pieces, as a promotional item. Among the many display cases, *Women's Wear Daily* drew its readers' attention to the following displays: "Coro in Paris" display case bearing the heading *Haute Couture*. This display was symbolized by a picture of Elsa Schiaparelli at work, papier maché model figurines, needles, yarn and shoes; "Coro at Montecarlo" or *The Winning Hand* with a roulette, tokens, dice and cards, and diamond jewels; "Little Old New York" with policemen's hats, Sweet Caporal cigarettes and souvenirs from the Knickerbocker Hotel with its trademark red and black percale table cloth used as background; "Coro in Morocco," featured a splendid Moor surrounded by golden satin, gold and ruby jewelry; "Coro in Rio de Janeiro," with colored seeds mixed with natives' shoes and hats with fruit decorations; "Coro in Salzburg," with musical instruments; "Coro in the Riviera," with General Foch's parade hat with its shiny silver braids: "Highland," with tartan wool gaiters and informal jewelry. Coro's fall exhibition features different themes: A display case was dedicated to the "Club 47W" with jewelry in the shape of keys, slippers and chandeliers; another one was entitled "Coro and Lace" and featured figurines with mink coats; another was inspired by cotton plantations and featured the figure of Mamie, from Gone with the Wind, and percale cloth; the "Boudoir" display case played with the theme of the eternal femme fatale with black satin and pink lace; while "Street Scene of Fashion Place" displayed lamé fabrics and diamond jewelry and "Reptile" showed snake skin items and jewels.

    Obviously, this was a lavish promotional campaign that required the creation of flashy jewelry which would attract the buyer's attention, even though customers would generally opt for more subdued pieces of jewelry; nevertheless customers chose Coro because they were attracted by the glamour of the exhibition.

C146. *"Maria Camargo,"* Coro 1951****
Manufacturer Coro, Inc.
Designer Adolph Katz.
Patent n° 162,419 Adolph Katz, Providence, R.I., 13th March 1951, filed on 12th January 1951, assignor to Coro, Inc., New York.

Gold-plated metal brooch with small red, blue and azure stones and rhinestones. The brooch portrays a ballet dancer with a wide "openwork" skirt, studded with stones and holding a flower spray in one hand. 6.7x5.5cm. Marked CoroCraft (mark n° 11).

    "Maria Camargo" is a made up name derived from the subject. The design was probably inspired by two portraits of Maria Camargo by Nicolas Lancret, one of which was exhibited at the National Gallery in Washington whilst the other was at the Hermitage in St. Petersburg. In both pictures, Maria Camargo was portrayed in the same dancing position as in this brooch. However the brooch subject bears more similarity to the Hermitage portrait, where she is dancing alone.

    Maria Camargo was the stage-name of Marie-Anne de Cupis de Camargo (Brussels 1710 – Paris 1770), a ballet dancer of Belgian origin, naturalized French, whose notoriety came from her capacity to alter the traditional role for women in ballet, by interpreting steps that were usually reserved for men. The same subject was developed by Van Cleef & Arpels in a series of platinum, diamond, ruby and emerald brooches designed by Maurice Duvalet and crafted by John Ruben in 1944.

C147. *"Black Women Duette,"* Coro 1948****
Manufacturer Coro, Inc.
Designer Adolph Katz.
Not patented.
   Gold-plated metal Duette, black and red enamel, pink stones and rhinestones, depicting the face of two black women with feathered turbans. 5x3cm.
   Marked clips CoroCraft (in a rectangular plate, mark n° 12), mechanism Coro Duette (mark n° 3)

C148. *"Golden Jubilee,"* Coro 1951****
Manufacturer Coro, Inc.
Designer Adolph Katz.
Patent n° 161,936 Adolph Katz, Providence, R.I., 13th February 1951, filed on 22nd November 1950.

Gold-plated metal brooch and Duette, rhinestones, red stones and white baguettes, in the shape of a royal crown. Brooch 3.8x4cm, Duette 3x5.5cm
   Marked brooch CoroCraft (mark 11), Duette clips CoroCraft (mark n° 11), mechanism Coro Duette Pat. No. 1798867 (mark n° 3).
   The patent is for the brooch. The name "Golden Jubilee" came from an advertisement published in *Vogue* in 1951 and referred to Coro's golden anniversary (1901-1951). The brooch was on sale for around $12.

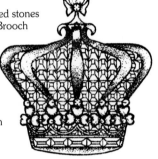

Gold-plated metal brooch, Duette and earrings, rhinestones, red stones and white baguettes, in the shape of acorns. Brooch 5.2x5.5cm, Duette 5.5x5cm, earrings 2.5cm
   Marked clips CoroCraft (mark 11), mechanism CoroDuette Pat. No. 1798867 (mark n° 3).
   The patent is for the brooch. The name "Royal Oaks" came from an advertisement published in *Vogue* in 1951 which presented the earrings and necklace.

C149. *"Royal Oaks,"* Coro 1951***
Manufacturer Coro, Inc.
Designer Adolph Katz.
Patent n° 165,166 Adolph Katz, Providence, R.I., 13th November 1951, filed on 30th July 1951

RALPH DeROSA

Ralph DeRosa was an Italian who gained American citizenship and lived in the Bronx, New York. In 1934 he set up the Ralph DeRosa Company, with an office in New York, in 404 Fourth Avenue.

Ralph (Raffaele) DeRosa was born in Naples in 1884 into a renowned family of jewelers. After studying at a school of design and the arts in Naples, in 1905 he emigrated to the United States.

In May 1935 his company presented a summer collection called "Point Venice" which was inspired by Venetian lace. The lace theme frequently cropped up in De Rosa's production and on 31st March 1947 Elsie McCormick, in an article entitled "Merchant of Glitter" in the *Saturday Evening Post*, wrote that Elvira De Rosa attributed the choice of this theme to a piece of ancient lace she had received as a wedding present from her Italian relatives. The "Point Venice" jewelry collection includes bracelets, clips, earrings, metal bands for watches, and brooches. The clips are shaped as shields or triangles with colored stones and clear rhinestones forming flowery motifs; in other items the rhinestones, baguettes, and colored stones are mixed with pearls. The collection also featured a "novelty brooch" of a golf bag with rhinestones and ice-colored stones.

Also in 1935, on August 15th, Ralph De Rosa registered a patent application for a support mechanism of a butterfly-shaped brooch. The patent was granted on 7th January 1936 and registered with n. 2,026,934. This was the first of the only two patents registered by the company. The second one, also in Ralph De Rosa's name, dated from 23rd September 1941 (des. n. 129,635) for a bracelet with hinged metal links.

Ralph De Rosa was one of the manufacturers who in 1939, spurred on by Trifari, tried to create an association to fight the widespread phenomenon of copying. He personally managed his firm until his death, caused by a heart attack, on 8th August 1942, at 58 years of age. He left a conspicuous inheritance that included the firm. Having left no will, his fortune was shared out equally between his wife Virginia and two daughters Elvira (Vera) and Teresa. After his death Elvira, who was also a designer, took over the running of the firm, with Virginia and Teresa De Rosa. The firm was operated with the assistance of Paul A. Green, De Rosa's right hand from 1934, who, in 1949, formed a partnership with Joseph Mazer to establish Jomaz.

On 17th September 1937 *Women's Wear Daily* printed a spiral-shaped clip with rhinestone pavé and sapphire accents. This clip is the first example of De Rosa's signature style: costume jewelry with the large size, accurate shape, and manufacture typical of precious jewelry.

News about the company's production was reported fairly regularly in the specialized press and in 1940 the company started advertising in national magazines such as *Vogue* and *Harper's Bazaar*. For these advertisements the firm used the trademark "Jewelry by De Rosa," replaced in 1946 by "De Rosa Designed Jewels" which was only registered in 1950. The jewelry was expensive: for example a 1940 brooch advertised in *Vogue* (15th October) cost 20 dollars.

In 1940 the company was manufacturing mainly flowery jewelry, including brooches shaped like bunches or baskets of flowers. In 1941 they made the first "retro" brooches set with large irregularly cut stones like topazes and amethysts (DR1.). All items in this period were made of metal, usually brightly gold-plated, sometimes with enamel accents, while the stones used were rhinestones and colored stones of all possible cuts and sizes.

In the summer of 1941 De Rosa presented a collection partly inspired by a Chinese art exhibition at the Metropolitan Museum (*WWD*, 22nd August). Among the most original subjects in this collection, were "Chinese King fisher group" and a series of birds with blue-green enamel bodies and gold-plated metal heads, variously used to ornate necklaces, earrings and bracelets. Several birds had wings studded with rhinestones and others held pearls in their beaks.

From the end of 1942 De Rosa began using sterling which became its most used metal even after the end of the war, until the end of 1949. The war-time sterling production included sets of brooches and earrings shaped like leaves, different sized bees that could be worn in twos or threes (1943), heart-shaped brooches with a space in the middle for initials, and disc-shaped brooches with flowers (1944).

A 1946 sterling collection was openly described as "Victorian" in advertisements while, in general, De Rosa continued to manufacture its typical "formal" jewelry which imitated precious jewelry and the styles of the past in typical "retro" style.

Figurative subjects were seldom featured: apart from those of the above mentioned 1941 collection, from the "Mayan Head" and the "Galleon" (DR4. and DR6.), there were some teenager brooches of a hatching chick (1947) and a hobby horse (1948). In keeping with the fashion of the time, which favored small jewelry, more figurative novelty brooches made of sterling and enamel were presented in 1949 with the name of "Tick, Tack, Toe." These were "scatter pins," i.e. pins that could be worn in bunches on lapels or on the front of dresses. These pins were of "Doves" (DR2.), various types of insects, bees, and frogs. Another 1949 collection was called "Botticelli" because of the seashell portrayed, which was one of main motifs and was similar to the one portrayed in

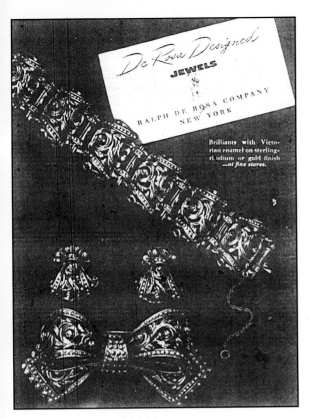

Harper's Bazaar, March 1947: De Rosa sterling Jewelry.

Vogue, December 1, 1941.

Gold-plated metal pin clip, large, multi-faceted and amethyst color middle stone, rhinestones. 8x5cm. Marked R. De Rosa.
　　This brooch appeared in an advertisement in *Vogue*, 1st December 1941, and was on sale for $16.

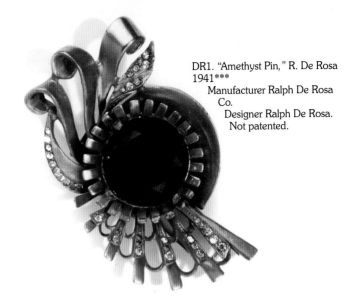

DR1. "Amethyst Pin," R. De Rosa 1941***
　　Manufacturer Ralph De Rosa Co.
　　　　Designer Ralph De Rosa.
　　　　Not patented.

Botticelli's painting *The Birth of Venus*, presently at the Uffizi in Florence. The latter items were made of gold- or rhodium-plated metal, because, although sterling was still being used for a large part of his production, De Rosa had reverted to the use of metal alloys as far back as 1947.

　　In 1949 De Rosa manufactured the gold-plated sterling brooches of the "Dearest" series, named after the initials of the stones hanging from a rhinestone studded frame surmounted by a motif of flowers and leaves (*see I gioielli della fantasia*, p. 158, n. 27): D(iamond), E(merald), A(methyst), R(uby), E(merald), S(apphire), T(opaz).

　　Every item of jewelry was marked: R. DE ROSA, in block letters with the addition, whenever was the case, of STERLING. This trademark was never registered, however it is identical to the block letter signature signed by Ralph De Rosa at the bottom of the company's two above mentioned patents.

　　After 1955 no further information about the firm is available.

DR2. "Doves," R. De Rosa 1949***
　　Manufacturer R. De Rosa Co.
　　　Designer Elvira De Rosa.
　　　Not patented.
　　　　Pair of rhodium-plated sterling brooches with pale green enamel. The brooches are of two doves with rhinestone-bordered wings and red stones for their eyes. 3x3.5cm. Marked R. De Rosa Sterling.
　　This item belongs to a series of sterling and enamel scatter pins which were featured in *WWD*, 11th March 1949, with the name of "Tick, Tack, Toe". The series included also scarabs, bees, frogs and flowers. The doves were designed to be worn with their beaks touching. A single dove appeared in *WWD*, 11th March 1949.
　　　　"Tick, Tack, Toe" is the American name for the British "noughts and crosses" game. Two players play this game, and they must decide which of them is the noughts and which is the crosses. Each player takes it in turns to write an x or a nought in one of nine spaces in a grid; the winner being the first player to complete a row of three noughts or of three crosses. This name may have been chosen for the scatter pins line because the way of wearing several of these scattered pins was visually similar to the game.

DR3. "Corolla," R. De Rosa 1941-42**
Manufacturer Ralph De Rosa Co.
Designer Ralph De Rosa.
Not patented.
    Gold-plated metal pin clip of a
flower with a pearl at the center,
surrounded by blue stones and
metal stamens with rhinestones
and red stones set at the extremities.
Diameter 5.8cm.
    Marked R. De Rosa.

DR4. "Galleon," R. De Rosa 1946-47****
Manufacturer R. De Rosa Co.
Designer Elvira De Rosa.
Not patented.
    Gold-plated sterling brooch of a Spanish galleon in full
sail. The ship has a red stone line on its side corresponding to the cannon ports. This was a rather unusual subject
for De Rosa, and it was designed with a painstaking care
for detail. 5.5x5.8cm.
    Marked R. De Rosa Sterling.

DR5. "Flower Basket," R. De Rosa 1944****
Manufacturer Ralph De Rosa Co.
Designer Elvira De Rosa.
Not patented.
    Gold-plated sterling pin clip of a flower pot,
represented by a triangular blue crystal, while
the flowers are made of rhinestones, red stones
and tiny white pearls. 5.8x5.5cm.
    Marked R. De Rosa Sterling.

DR6. "Mayan Head," R. De Rosa 1947*
Manufacturer R. De Rosa Co.
Designer Elvira De Rosa.
Not patented.
    Small gold-plated sterling brooch
of a Mayan prince's head, with a
row of pearls outlining his shoulders. 3.8x3cm.
    Marked R. De Rosa Sterling.

DR7. "Grapes Set," R. De Rosa 1949****
Manufacturer R. De Rosa Co.
Designer Elvira De Rosa.
Not patented.
　Set composed of necklace, brooch and
pendant earrings with clips, of gold-plated metal
alloy, black enamel and rhinestones with a motif
of vine leaves and grapes. Necklace 10.7x5.5cm
(central motif); 7.5x5cm brooch; 6x1.8cm earrings.
　Marked R. De Rosa.

DR8. *"Butterfly,"* R. De Rosa
1936***
Manufacturer Ralph De Rosa Co.
Designer Ralph De Rosa.
Patent n° 2,028,593 Ralph De Rosa,
New York, 21st January 1936, filed 15th
August 1935.

Rhodium-plated metal brooch with rhinestones, of a butterfly. 3.4x4cm.
Marked Pat. No. 2028593.

Ralph De Rosa obtained two patents for this mechanism, the first on 7th January 1936 with n° 2,026,934 and the second on 21st January 1936 with n° 2,028,593. The application was submitted on 15th August 1935 for both designs, and it is actually difficult to understand the reason for this double patent, since the designs and the specifications were identical. The mechanism designed allows for the brooch to be fastened to a dress or to hair, by folding the wings that are mounted on springs. When the wings are released, the two small pins at the back pierce the fabric with no need to apply any pressure. The design showed only the butterfly shape, since, as was stated in the specifications, the brooch could be decorated at will, with stones, spangles and the like.

Furthermore, in the specifications it was stated that the design could be changed during production without substantially altering the mechanism in any way.

Similar items do exist which present slight changes to the patent design (the antennae and the lack of baguettes on the body), whilst other items exist which are completely identical, but all of them bear the same patent number.

De Rosa also assigned this patent to others, including Ora, who used it in production without any changes, using patent No. 2,026,934. However the patent number was erroneously marked on items that bear the No. 2,026,924 instead of 934.

It is therefore reasonable to presume that items marked with the number of the second patent, had actually been manufactured by De Rosa.

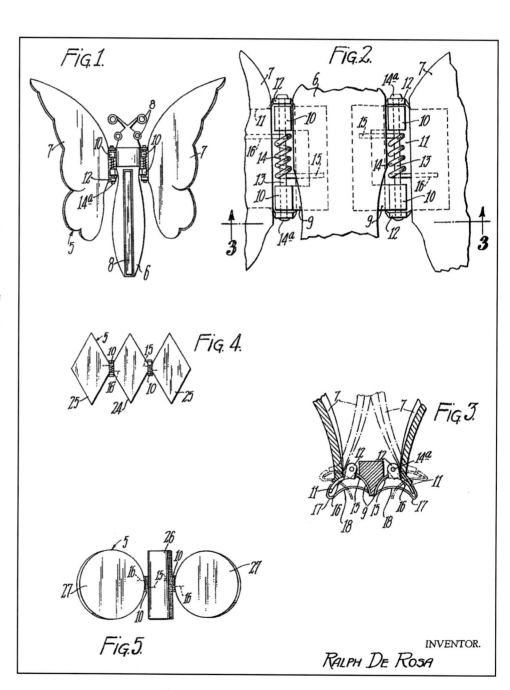

DU JAY

Du Jay Inc, was probably established in 1934 by Jules Hirsch and Jacques H. Leff as a division of Hirsch & Leff, a manufacturer of precious jewelry, and was operative from 1934 to 1972 with offices in New York, 37 West 47th Street.

The first information about the firm dates from 1935, when *Women's Wear Daily* presented its spring collection featuring brooches, huge single or double clips, large bangles, mesh bracelets (soft chains), bands and fobs (ribbons for pocket watches). The line was characterized by melon-cut imitation aquamarines and emeralds and semi-precious ox-blood stones and rhinestone pavés, as well as by tiny, closely set stones. The melon cut was considered extremely elegant, but the collection also included baguettes, cabochons and rhomboid stones, which was a novelty cut. The motifs featured a large central colored stone with a very minute rhinestone pavé frame. Some of the known pieces (see Deanna Farneti Cera, *Bijoux* page 121, bangle with red cabochon marked Du Jay) may belong to this collection. Another collection described in *WWD*, 23rd July 1937, was the fall 1937 collection, characterized by contrasting styles, for example large and small items, some of them elaborate, some simple.

This small company with a limited, top-notch production, was highly regarded by the industrial sector of costume jewelry – as shown by the fact that Jacques H. Leff and Jules Hirsch attended the 31st March 1939 committee meeting chaired by Nat Levy, of Nat Levy & Urie Mandel, for the establishment of a new Costume Jewelry Association. Du Jay came under the spotlight of the specialized press again in December 1940 when it won a legal case against Déja Inc. – who thereafter had to change its name to Réja – for the protection of the Du Jay company name.

Fortune, in an article in December 1946, described Du Jay as being one of the leaders in the field of costume jewelry. Information about the company is scarce and the most important source of such information is represented by the design patents which reveal the styles and names of the designers. In 1939 and 1940 Du Jay patented a series of designs in the name of J. Hirsch and J. H. Leff. In 1939 it presented a collection of small figurative brooches with minute rhinestone pavés or decorated with colored enamel and rhinestones. One of the most beautiful specimens of this collection is the "Band" series designed by Jacques H. Leff and composed of a "Majorette," a "Tuba Player," a "Drummer" (DJ4.) and of two other band players (trombone and bass drum).

Du Jay's jewelry displayed different styles and materials according to the period in which they were manufactured and the fashion of the time, but it was always characterized by an accurate, high-quality manufacture on the basis of artistic designs. The items are marked *Du Jay* and are very rare. Collectors should be cautious in dealing with several attributions of unmarked jewelry with characteristics similar to those described.

DJ1. "Butterfly," Du Jay 1939*****
Manufacturer Du Jay, Inc.
Designer Jacques H. Leff.
Not patented.
   Rhodium-plated metal brooch with yellow, red, blue and black enamel, red and blue cabochons and rhinestones, of a butterfly. 5x3.5cm.
   Marked Du Jay Pat. Pend. In spite of the Pat. Pend. mark, the design is unpatented.

DJ2. "Penguin," Du Jay 1939*****
   Manufacturer Du Jay, Inc.
   Designer Jules Hirsch.
   Patent n° 115,402 Jules Hirsch 21st June 1939, filed on 18th March 1939.

Rhodium-plated metal pin clip with black and yellow enamel, drop-shaped pearl and rhinestones, of a penguin. 3.5x2cm.
   Marked Du Jay Des. Pat'D.

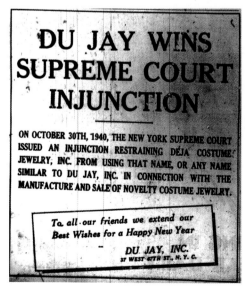

WWD, December 27, 1940: advertisement by Du Jay, Inc.

DJ3. "Strawberries", Du Jay 1939*****
Manufacturer Du Jay, Inc.
Designer Jacques H. Leff.
Not patented.
    Rhodium-plated metal brooch, red, green
and brown enamel, rhinestones, in the shape
of a bunch of strawberries. 6.5x6cm.
    Marked Du Jay Pat. Pend.

DJ4. "Band," Du Jay 1939*****
Manufacturer Du Jay, Inc.
Designer Jacques H. Leff
Patents: Drummer n° 117,925, Tuba Player n° 117,927,
Majorette n° 117,928 Jacques H. Leff, New York, 5ᵗʰ
December 1939, filed on 30ᵗʰ October 1939.

    Rhodium- and gold-plated metal pin clips, with red, black, blue, yel-
low, green and gold enamel, pearls for faces and heads, and rhinestones,
depicting a drummer, a tuba player and a majorette, respectively. Drummer
5.5x2.5cm, Tuba player 5.5x3cm, Majorette 5.5x2.2cm.
    Marked Drummer Du Jay Des. Pat'D 117925, Tuba player Du Jay Des.
Pat'D 117927, Majorette Du Jay Des. Pat'D 117928.
    These three items belong to the "Band" series designed by Jacques H.
Leff in 1939. The other designs are of a trombone player (des. n° 117,926)
and a bass drum player (des. n° 117,929).

    Rhodium-plated
metal brooch, enamel in
various colors, rhine-
stones, of a Chinese man
pulling a rickshaw, carrying a lady with a parasol.
The wheel can turn.
3.9x5cm.
Unmarked.

DJ5. "Rickshaw," Du Jay
    1939*****
    Manufacturer Du Jay, Inc.
    Designer Jacques H. Leff.
    Patent n° 113,634 Jacques H.
Leff, New York, 7ᵗʰ March 1939,
filed on 24ᵗʰ January 1939.

EISENBERG

Eisenberg Jewelry, Inc., was established in 1940 as a division of Eisenberg & Sons, Inc., with offices in Chicago, 847 Jackson Blvd. (from 1945, 222 North Bank Drive) and a showroom in Merchandise Mart.

Eisenberg & Sons was established in 1914 by Jonas Eisenberg and manufactured women's wear and perfumes. Around 1937, the company, at the time under the leadership of Jonas's sons, Harold and Samuel, started marketing brooches and, encouraged by an initial success, further developed its costume jewelry business, until a proper costume jewelry division was created.

WWD, February 7, 1936: Eisenberg & Sons advertisement showing that, at the time, they were not selling jewelry, nor had a jewelry division.

In 1958 the firm completely abandoned its clothing activity and concentrated on jewelry and, in 1977, became a division of Berns-Friedman. The company is still in business today under the leadership of Karl Eisenberg, Jonas's grandchild, and manufactures costume jewelry under the trademark Eisenberg Ice.

According to a rather fanciful story, which is probably only a company legend, the initial success of Eisenberg's jewelry was determined by the fact that women, enraptured by the beautiful items of jewelry, stole them from the dresses for which they had been created, thereby convincing the company that it would be a good idea to sell the jewelry separately. The real version of events was far removed from this tale; as clearly shown in a whole page communiqué published by the company in *Women's Wear Daily*, of 6th June 1941, which probably appeared in other papers too. The communiqué addresses American jewellery buyers and, in four lapidary statements, tells "the facts about Eisenberg's jewelry":

1) Each Eisenberg jewelry item is designed by Eisenberg, manufactured for Eisenberg, and sold exclusively to Eisenberg by a high quality jewelry manufacturer whose activity is closely related to Eisenberg's.

2) No Eisenberg jewelry item is manufactured in Chicago. This fact is emphatically stated as a reply to statements by Chicago manufacturers who claimed that they made "Eisenberg jewelry for Eisenberg."

3) Eisenberg jewelry is sold in franchising, only in shops where Eisenberg clothes are sold. No other shop is authorized to exhibit Eisenberg jewels, as clearly stated in a nationwide company advertisement.

4) Each "Eisenberg Original" item bears exactly these words on the back. The two words "Eisenberg Original," cast in each item, represent a permanent means of identification and is a guaranty of product originality. In the communiqué the trademark is reproduced in a size which is double its real format and customers are advised to: "Look for this trademark on all Eisenberg jewels."

The same concepts were reaffirmed in another advertisement of the same year.

WWD, June, 6, 1941: Eisenberg Jewelry, Inc.: the facts about Eisenberg Jewelry.

Moreover, in 1942 (*Women's Wear Daily*, 30th January), in another whole page communiqué, Eisenberg clearly stated that it intended to patent all designs and again stressed that each item bore the Eisenberg trademark, emphasizing that these precautions were necessary because non-authorized shops had been selling jewelry which was being passed off as Eisenberg items. In reality, the company, possibly discouraged by the scarce protection actually provided by patents, patented only one series of designs, but strictly adhered to its trademarking policy. Eisenberg's precautions and the warning of the existence of false Eisenberg jewelry in circulation, confirm the existence of contemporary non-marked copies that may still be found on the antique market today, which, if assessed on the basis of a stylistic criterion, might wrongly be attributed to Eisenberg.

The commercial policy of licensing the sale of jewelry on an exclusive basis only to one shop per town, was slightly altered in 1947 (*WWD*, 11th April), when Eisenberg

announced that Eisenberg jewelry and cosmetics would be available at another shop in each town, provided there were no conflicts with the existing franchisees.

Eisenberg & Sons was a prestigious name thanks to its strict commercial policy and advertising in the major magazines. Sometimes its clothes and jewelry were presented together, with the trademarks Eisenberg & Sons Original. Sometimes only the jewelry was presented with the trademark Eisenberg Ice, written in ornate italics. The trademark Eisenberg Ice, registered in February 1942, but definitely in use from November 1941, in the period being reviewed, was used for advertising purposes, but not for the stamping of the jewelry.

In the field of jewelry Eisenberg was a medium-sized company that manufactured high-quality, expensive jewelry. In 1941 a brooch cost $13 and a necklace $22,50 and, in February 1942, a brooch designed by Florence Nathan cost about $20.

Eisenberg jewelry consisted for the most part of brooches, whilst necklaces, bracelets, and rings were less represented. The jewelry was characterized by the high quality of the materials, in particular the white and colored crystals imported from Austria and Czechoslovakia, particularly Swarovski crystals, which were hand set. The items were generally large-sized, heavy and bulky, with abstract, flowery, geometric and spiral designs. These features give Eisenberg jewelry a distinct identity, but also make it somewhat repetitive. It is for this reason that the rarest and most precious jewelry items of this company are those with figurative subjects.

As already explained, Eisenberg neither designed nor manufactured their jewelry, but relied on external manufacturers who had their own designers or used freelancers for the designs.

From the start Eisenberg's main supplier was Fallon & Kappel Inc., a firm with headquarters in New York, 151 West 46th Street, which designed and created metal jewelry and accessories. The names of the other suppliers are not known, however one of them could have been Reinad, as shown by the absolute identical nature of an "African Mask" marked Chanel (see Ch11.) and one marked Eisenberg Original.

WWD, January 25, 1935: advertisement by Fallon and Kappel, Inc.

Fallon & Kappel was established in 1928 by Fallon, an Irish jeweler who died in the second half of the 1930s, and by August ("Gus") Kappel who ran the firm until the end of the 1940s, when it was purchased by two of its managers: Murray Silverman who joined the firm in 1945 and Florence Nathan who married Silverman in 1943. In 1943 Fallon & Kappel signed an exclusivity agreement with Eisenberg and from that time on worked only for the Chicago company which, in turn, only ordered its jewelry from F&K. The firm abruptly ceased operating in 1972 and apparently Florence Nathan Silverman ordered the destruction of all records, archives, designs, models, and molds.

The only designs patented for Eisenberg in March and May 1942 were signed by Florence Nathan (1908-1997) who worked for F&K from the start. The patented material included 27 designs – 26 brooches and 1 bracelet – with abstract, geometric, spiral and flowery subjects, and two bows, all studded with large crystals. The only exception was a brooch of a swan with open wings covered with marquise cut crystals, which had a large crystal in the middle of the body, and a metal head and neck. As reported in an advertisement published in *Vogue*, 1st February 1942, the items in this collection were made of metal and marked Eisenberg Original. According to available documentation they were the first of a long series of jewelry set with large crystals, which are often erroneously dated from the 1930s. In fact, in the late 1930s (the last 3 years) Eisenberg had a relatively small production and the few models it launched were made of a rather light metal alloy and were characterized by the use of cabochons, pearls, and imitation turquoise stones.

In an interview given in 1999 to Nicholas Tollemache and published in *VF&CJ*, winter 2000, Ruth Kamke stated that Florence Nathan was not a designer and that the designs she had patented, could have been made by Kamke herself or by one of the freelancers, on whom F&K was still relying at the time. Later on, Ruth Kamke told *VF&CJ* that she was the author of the designs. Herein lies a similar problem to that which arose with Coro designs patented by Katz. Although Mrs. Nathan was no designer (and in this respect she differs from Katz who definitely was a designer), she was nevertheless responsible for style in general, and, in Mrs. Kamke's words, it was Nathan, together with Gus Kappel, who chose the designs and suggested any necessary changes, and she was in contact with Eisenberg to decide which models should be designed for the company. For this reason Mrs. Nathan, if not the material author, can certainly be considered the person responsible for designs patented in her name.

Ruth Kamke (born 1925) was hired as an enameler by Fallon & Kappel in 1940 when she was 15, but soon became a designer, the only one belonging to the firm. In those years F&K made jewels for Eisenberg, but also for Hattie Carnegie, Chanel, Traina-Norell, and Schiaparelli and Mrs. Kamke designed jewels for all of them. For the whole period being reviewed, Ruth Kamke was Fallon & Kappel's only designer who, after the exclusivity agreement with Eisenberg, no longer used any freelance designers. Kamke remained with F&K until the business folded in 1972. From 1974 onwards, she worked at Panetta until she retired in 1987. Most of Kamke's designs were destroyed when Fallon & Kappel closed down, and, since none of them had been patented, there is no objective documentation, but only the author's memories to rely on. Generally speaking, only the Eisenberg designs from 1943 onwards could be attributed to Kamke, although some uncertainty remains, since, for example, she does not recall having designed the "Mermaid" (E26.). Among the pieces mentioned by Ruth Kamke in her interview are the "Pitcher," the "Cleaning Woman," the "Ballerina," and the "Fighting Cocks" (E33., E21., E22., E29.).

The jewels are marked:
• *"Eisenberg* Original" at least from 1938 (the first reporting of a bow-shaped brooch made of white metal and crystals appeared in *Vogue* in August of that year) to the first half of 1942. This trademark exhibits the same graphics and hatch letters simulating the stitching of the label-trademark *Eisenberg & Sons* Original, used in advertisements and probably on clothes. On items dating from 1940-41 the trademark is sometimes cast in relief on the metal base.
• *Eisenberg* Original Sterling in 1943 and 1944.
• *Eisenberg* Sterling from 1944-45 throughout 1948, when use of sterling ceased.
• *E*, in ornate capital italics identical to the initial of the trademark Eisenberg Ice. This trademark is little used and appears to be limited to a few sterling and metal items from the second half of the 1940s. The *E* appears also as capital block letter, sometimes together with the trademark *Eisenberg* Original or *Eisenberg* Sterling, on small items such as earrings and bracelet links which could not contain the trademark written in full.
• EISENBERG or EISENBERG ICE, in capital block letters from 1949 to about 1958.

E1. "Daisy," Eisenberg 1939****
Manufacturer unknown for
Eisenberg Jewelry, Inc.

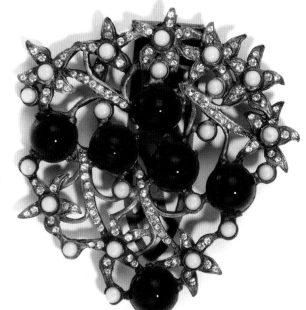

**Massive Jewelry in Smoky Stone Colors
Keys to a Costume Fashion for Pastels**

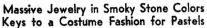

WWD, November 17, 1939: "Daisy" by Eisenberg.

 Gold-plated metal pin clip with moonstones
in the shape of a daisy. 11x8cm.
 Marked Eisenberg Original "B".
 The design was printed in *WWD*, 17th November 1939.

E2. "Berries," Eisenberg 1937-1939***
Manufacturer unknown for Eisenberg Jewelry, Inc.
 Large white raw metal clip with red cabochons, imitation turquoises and rhinestones, of a branch in bloom with berries. 8.5x7.3cm.
 Marked Eisenberg Original.
 The name Eisenberg was written in small segments to simulate how the trademark name 'Eisenberg & Sons Original' appears on the fabric labels used to advertise the clothing line.
 The items with cabochons, turquoises or similar stones and pearls date from the end of the 1930s.

E3. "King's Ransom," Eisenberg 1941****
Manufacturer unknown for Eisenberg Jewelry, Inc.

Vogue, November 1,1941: "King's Ransom pin for furs" by Eisenberg.

Large and heavy fur pin clip made of gold-plated metal, sapphire blue crystals and white crystals, of a flower. 11.5x7cm.
Marked Eisenberg Original "N".
The letter "N" refers to the stone setter.
Eisenberg was not in the habit of naming its lines or items. This is one of the few instances in which a name can be given to an Eisenberg item, based on an advertisement published in *Vogue,* 1st November 1941. The trademark Eisenberg & Sons Original was used to advertise clothes and jewelry, including this pin clip called "King's Ransom pin for furs". The pin clip was part of a set which also included a bracelet, earrings and a ring. The set shown in the *Vogue* advertisement was made of white crystals. The pin was on sale for $13.50.

E4. "Comet," Eisenberg 1939-1940***
Manufacturer unknown for Eisenberg Jewelry, Inc.
White metal brooch of a comet, with a large blue crystal at the center of the head and rhinestone pavé tail with a yellow crystal halo. 10x5cm.
Marked Eisenberg Original.
There was also a white crystal version of this design.

E5. "Four-Leaved Clover," Eisenberg 1937-39****
Manufacturer unknown for Eisenberg Jewelry, Inc.
Pot metal pin clip, green drop shaped crystals, coral cabochons, rhinestones, in the shape of a four-leaved clover. 7x5.5cm.
Marked Eisenberg Original "N".

E6. "Rétro Pin Clip," Eisenberg 1942****
Manufacturer Fallon & Kappel for Eisenberg Jewelry, Inc.
Designer Florence Nathan.
Patent n° 132,445 Florence Nathan, New York, 19th May 1942, filed on 14th February 1942, assignor to Eisenberg Jewelry, Inc., Chicago.

White metal pin clip with white crystals and rhinestones, with retro design. 5x5.5cm.
Marked Eisenberg Original.

E7. "Agave," Eisenberg 1940****
Manufacturer unknown for Eisenberg Jewelry, Inc.
Gold-plated metal brooch, black and white enamel, various colored crystals, of an agave plant in a pot. 9x6cm.
Marked Eisenberg Original.

White metal brooch with rectangular and square white crystals and rhinestones. The brooch is of a bowknot. 8.5x7.5cm.
Marked Eisenberg Original "CI".

E8. "Bow," Eisenberg 1942****
Manufacturer Fallon & Kappel for Eisenberg Jewelry, Inc.
Designer Florence Nathan.
Patent n° 132,435 Florence Nathan, New York, 19th May 1942, filed on 14th February 1942, assignor to Eisenberg Jewelry, Inc., Chicago.

E9. "Bowknot," Eisenberg 1942****
Manufacturer Fallon & Kappel for Eisenberg Jewelry, Inc.
Designer Florence Nathan.
Patent n° 131,688 Florence Nathan, New York, 24th March 1942, filed on 12th January 1942, assignor to Eisenberg Jewelry, Inc., Chicago.

White metal brooch with white crystals and rhinestones, of a bowknot. 7x6.5cm.
Marked Eisenberg Original.
The name "Bowknot" was taken from an advertisement published in *Vogue*, 1st February 1942, which stated that the jewelry designs were all originals as were Eisenberg clothes and that each item was marked Eisenberg Original and sold in only one major store in each city. The "Bowknot" was on sale for $15 and was photographed together with other patented jewelry made of white or colored crystals, designed by Florence Nathan. The picture also showed a bracelet, a ring and a pair of screwback earrings.

E10. "Bunch of Flowers," Eisenberg 1940***
Manufacturer unknown for Eisenberg Jewelry, Inc.
   Gold-plated metal brooch with green enamel,
ruby red crystals, amethysts and rhinestones,
shaped like a bunch of flowers. 12x6.5cm.
   Marked Eisenberg Original.
   A more refined, sterling version of this item
was made in 1944 (E11.)

E11. "Bunch of Flowers," Eisenberg 1944****
Manufacturer Fallon & Kappel for Eisenberg
Jewelry, Inc.
Designer Ruth Kamke.
Not patented.
   Sterling brooch with amethyst crystals and
rhinestones, in the shape of a bunch of flow-
ers. 11.5x6cm.
Marked Eisenberg Original Sterling.

E12. "Bow," Eisenberg 1944***
   Manufacturer Fallon & Kappel for Eisenberg
   Jewelry, Inc.
   Designer Ruth Kamke.
   Not patented.

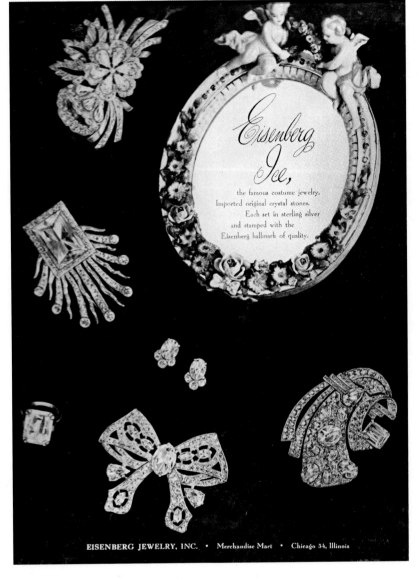

Vogue, September 15, 1944.

   Sterling brooch of a bowknot, with white and fumé crystals. 6.5x5.2cm.
   Marked Eisenberg Original Sterling.
   A picture of this brooch, together with other brooches, appeared in a *Vogue* advertisement on 15th September 1944. The advertisement stated that the items were made of sterling and marked with Eisenberg's quality mark. The trademark was Eisenberg Ice. The bowknot was a recurring motif in Eisenberg's as in precious and non-precious jewelry.

E13. "Spider," Eisenberg 1944***
   Manufacturer Fallon & Kappel for Eisenberg Jewelry, Inc.
   Designer Ruth Kamke.
   Not patented.
   Victorian style sterling pin clip with large hexagonal white crystal in the center, resembling a stylized spider. 7.3x5.2cm.
   Marked Eisenberg Original Sterling "2".
   The pin clip was fitted with a safety clasp which had a double hook cast onto the structure, into which the pin points could be inserted. This was a typical Eisenberg mechanism which was not a feature of the older items.

E14. "Decoration," Eisenberg
1946***
Manufacturer Fallon & Kappel
for Eisenberg Jewelry, Inc.
Designer Ruth Kamke.
Not patented.

Vogue, March 1946.

Sterling brooch resembling a decoration with a movable drop-shaped
pendant, with two large white crystals
and rhinestones. 8x4cm.
Marked Eisenberg Sterling.
This set of a brooch and earrings–
also with movable drop-shaped pendants– appeared in a *Vogue* advertisement in March 1946 and in *Harper's
Bazaar*, April 1946. The advertisement
specified that the set was made of sterling with hand-set imported stones.

E15. "Mayan Mask," Eisenberg 1940*****
Manufacturer unknown for Eisenberg Jewelry, Inc.
Gold-plated metal pin clip, red and green crystals, of a Mayan mask. 9.5x8cm.
Marked Eisenberg Original "N".

E16. "Sinbad," Eisenberg 1940*****
Manufacturer unknown for Eisenberg Jewelry, Inc.
Gold-plated metal pin clip, light blue and black enamel, various colored drop-shaped dangling crystals, turquoises and rhinestones, of a turbaned male head. 7.5x4.6cm.
Marked Eisenberg Original.
There are no documented references for the name "Sinbad."

E17. "Torso," Eisenberg 1940*****
Manufacturer unknown for Eisenberg Jewelry, Inc.
Rhodium-plated metal clip, with white crystal at the top and pink at the base, red cabochons, in the shape of a torso. 5.5x6cm.
Marked Eisenberg Original.

E18. "Egyptian," Eisenberg
1940*****
Manufacturer Unknown for Eisenberg Jewelry, Inc.
  Gold-plated pin clip with round emerald green crystals. The pin depicts an Egyptian holding a cornucopia with a large branch in bloom. 10x4.5cm.
  Marked Eisenberg Original.
  The trademark is stamped on a plaque cast on the base metal and the Eisenberg letters resemble the printing of the trademark on fabric.

E19. "Winged Creature," Eisenberg 1944*****
Manufacturer Fallon & Kappel for Eisenberg Jewelry, Inc.
Designer Ruth Kamke.
Not patented.
  Gold-plated sterling brooch with red and green enamel, oval green stone, portraying a winged figurine similar to the stone figures on the facades of late Romanesque or Gothic churches. 5x3cm.
  Marked Eisenberg Original Sterling.

E20. "Puss-in-Boots," Eisenberg 1940*****
Manufacturer unknown for Eisenberg Jewelry, Inc.
  Gold-plated metal pin clip, black enamel, red stones and turquoises, depicting a cat with boots, sword and hat. 8x7cm.
  Marked Eisenberg Original.
  This subject was probably inspired by Charles Perrault's fable "Puss-in-Boots".

E21. "Cleaning Woman," Eisenberg 1944*****
Manufacturer Fallon & Kappel for Eisenberg Jewelry, Inc.
Designer Ruth Kamke.
Not Patented.
   Gold-plated sterling pin clip, red enamel and rhinestones, portraying a cleaning woman with a bucket and a brush. 7.5x4cm.
   Marked Eisenberg Original Sterling.

E22. "Ballerina," Eisenberg 1944*****
Manufacturer Fallon & Kappel for Eisenberg
Jewelry, Inc.
Designer Ruth Kamke.
Not patented.
   Gold-plated sterling brooch with red stones and rhinestones, of a ballet dancer. 8x5cm.
   Marked Eisenberg Sterling "37".

E23. "Dancer," Eisenberg 1944****
Manufacturer Fallon & Kappel for Eisenberg Jewelry, Inc.
  Designer Ruth Kamke.
  Not Patented.
   Gold-plated sterling brooch, green and black enamel, green and white crystals, rhinestones, of a ballerina dancing with a ribbon in her hands. 9x5cm.
   Marked Eisenberg.

E24. "Dolphin," Eisenberg
1942****
Manufacturer Fallon & Kappel for
Eisenberg Jewelry, Inc.
Designer Florence Nathan.
Not patented.

Vogue, February 1, 1942.

Gold-plated metal pin clip, light blue crystals, red enamel and rhinestones, of a dolphin. 7.5x5.5cm.
Marked Eisenberg Original.
The same design appeared on a compact in an advertisement in *Vogue*, 1st February 1942, along with other pieces designed and patented by Florence Nathan.

E25. "Fish," Eisenberg 1944****
Manufacturer Fallon & Kappel for
Eisenberg Jewelry, Inc.
Designer Ruth Kamke.
Not Patented.
Gold-plated sterling
brooch, small white pearls
and rhinestones, in the
shape of a fish. 5.5x6cm.
Marked Eisenberg
Original Sterling.

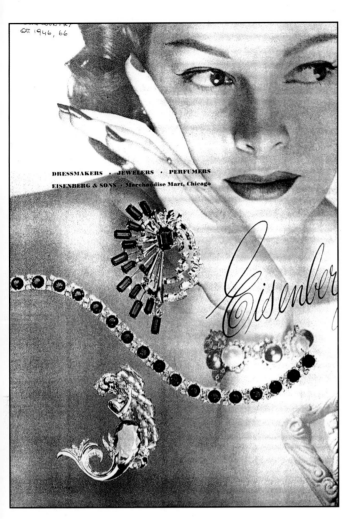

Town & Country, October 1946: "Mermaid" by Eisenberg.
Town & Country, November 1944: "Naiad Clip" by Verdura.

Gold-plated sterling brooch of a siren. Her body is made of a large topaz crystal and amber colored glass beads. Her hair and tail are ornamented with rhinestones. 8x7cm.
Marked Eisenberg Sterling.
There are other versions of this brooch with crystals and beads in different colors.
A picture of this brooch appeared in a Vogue advertisement on 1st October 1946, and in Town & Country, October 1946.
This item is a precise reproduction of a fine piece of jewelry by the Duke of Verdura; the "Naiad Clip," which was made of gold with an opal, pearls and diamonds, and appeared in an advertisement by Verdura Inc. published in Town & Country, November 1944. The price of this piece of jewelry was $2,500.

E26. "Mermaid," Eisenberg 1946*****
Manufacturer Fallon & Kappel for
Eisenberg Jewelry, Inc.
Designer Ruth Kamke.
Not patented.

E27. "Doe," Eisenberg 1944****
Manufacturer Fallon & Kappel for Eisenberg Jewelry, Inc.
Designer Ruth Kamke.
Not patented.

Leaping into Christmas spheres are Eisenberg's doe and reindeer of pageant-colored stones. At Carson Pirie Scott, Chicago; J. P. Allen, Atlanta; and Kerr's, Oklahoma City

Town & Country, December 1944: "Doe" and "Reindeer" (E28.) by Eisenberg.

Gold-plated sterling brooch, with red and black enamel and rhinestones. The brooch is of a doe wearing a beret. 7.5x5cm.
Marked Eisenberg Sterling.
A picture of this item appeared on p. 56 of *Town & Country,* December 1944, among the "Good Buys for Christmas" and was on sale at Carson Pirie Scott in Chicago, J. P. Allen in Atlanta and Kerr's in Oklahoma City.

E28. "Reindeer," Eisenberg 1944****
Manufacturer Fallon & Kappel for Eisenberg Jewelry, Inc.
Designer Ruth Kamke.
Not patented.
Gold-plated sterling brooch with red stones and rhinestones, of a reindeer. 6.5x5.7cm.
Marked Sterling "S".
A picture of this item appeared on p. 56 of *Town & Country,* December 1944, among the "Good Buys for Christmas" and was on sale at Carson Pirie Scott in Chicago, J. P. Allen in Atlanta and Kerr's in Oklahoma City.

E29. "Fighting Cock," Eisenberg 1945****
Manufacturer Fallon & Kappel for Eisenberg
Jewelry, Inc.
Designer Ruth Kamke.
Not patented.

Town & Country, March 1943: Fighting Cocks by Cartier.

Gold-plated sterling brooch with enamel, blue crystal and rhinestones, of a fighting cock. 3x6cm.
Marked Eisenberg Original Sterling.
A matching brooch of a second fighting cock facing the former one also exists.
This subject was inspired by the design of a piece of fine jewelry by Cartier ("Town & Country, March 1943) and also inspired Staret (Simons, *Costume Jewelry,* II ed., p. 135) and Coro.

E30. "Galloping Horse," Eisenberg 1940*****
Manufacturer unknown for Eisenberg Jewelry, Inc.
Gold-plated metal brooch of a galloping horse with red
enamel hooves, black enamel mane, eye and nostrils and
rhinestones with a star-like setting. 6x7.3cm.
Marked Eisenberg Original.
Eisenberg made at least another brooch of
a horse (Schiffer, *Fun Jewelry*, p. 83)
and another one of a horse's head
(Simons, *Costume Jewelry*, II ed.,
p. 94).

E31. "Flower Cascade," Eisenberg 1944****
Manufacturer Fallon & Kappel for Eisenberg Jewelry,
Inc.
Designer Ruth Kamke.
Not patented.
Gold-plated sterling pin clip with pink crystals and
rhinestones, of a flower cascade. 7.5x6cm.
Marked Eisenberg Original Sterling "N".

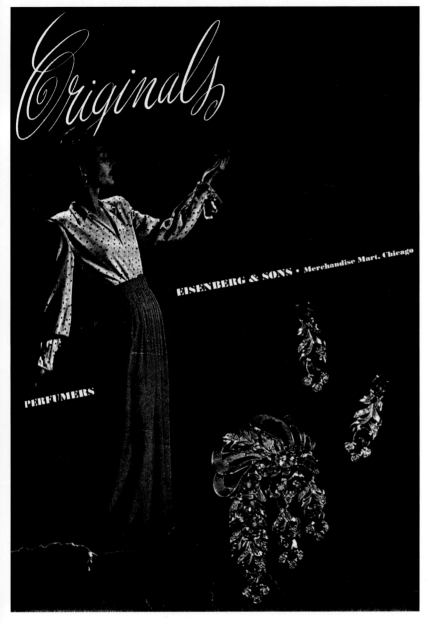

Vogue, May 1, 1946.

Set made up of gold-plated sterling brooch and bracelet. The brooch features movable pendants and measures 9.1x6cm. The bracelet is made up of hinged links, each measuring 1x3cm.

The brooch is marked Eisenberg Sterling E "4". The "E," in capital block letter appears on three links of the pendants. The bracelet is marked "E" in ornate capital italics, Sterling "U".

The simultaneous use of different marks is rather unusual, particularly in the case of the trademark "E," stamped both in block letters and in italics.

The last movable link of the brooch can be used as a bracelet link and as an earring pendant. Both the brooch and the earrings appeared in an advertisement in *Vogue,* 1ˢᵗ May 1946, and in *Town & Country,* May 1946.

E32. "Drop Set," Eisenberg 1946****
Manufacturer Fallon & Kappel for Eisenberg Jewelry, Inc.
Designer Ruth Kamke.
Not patented.

E33. *"Pitcher,"* Eisenberg
1944****
Manufacturer Fallon & Kap-
pel for Eisenberg Jewelry, Inc.
Designer Ruth Kamke.
Not Patented.

No woman ever has too much inci-
dental jewelry, which she is practically compelled to wear to distin-
guish her black dress from the
black dresses of a million other
females. As a Christmas gift, this
reduces the risk to nil. Eisenberg
designed these two clips, in gold-
finished sterling. The pitcher does
new things with bright stones and
black enamel. The spidery flower
is set with imported stones in amethyst and deep rose colors. Pitcher
about $25.50, flower around $33.50.
At Carson Pirie Scott, Chicago, Ill.

LAPEL WHIMSIES

Town & Country December 1944: "Pitcher" and "Poinsettia" (E34.) by
Eisenberg.

  Gold-plated sterling pin clip, blue enamel and rhinestones, in the
shape of a pitcher. 5x4cm.
  Marked Eisenberg Original Sterling.
  This item was featured in *Harper's Bazaar,* February 1945, (on sale
at Franklin Simon, New York, for $30) and also in *Town & Country,*
December 1944, (on sale at Carson Pirie Scott, Chicago, for $25.50
plus tax.)

E34. *"Poinsettia,"* Eisenberg 1944****
Manufacturer Fallon & Kappel for Eisenberg Jewelry,
Inc.
Designer Ruth Kamke.
Not Patented.
  Gold-plated sterling brooch, turquoise and red
cabochons, of a poinsettia. 9x7.5cm.
  Marked Eisenberg Original sterling.
  The brooch, together with the "Pitcher" (E33.),
appeared in Town & Country, December 1944,
and was on sale at Carson Pirie Scott, Chicago,
for $ 30.50 plus tax.

E35. "Star," Eisenberg 1947***
Manufacturer Fallon & Kappel for Eisenberg Jewelry, Inc.
Designer Ruth Kamke.
Not patented.
Star-shaped sterling pin clip and earrings with pale blue crystals and rhinestones. 7.5x7.5cm. Screwback earrings 2cm.
Marked Eisenberg Sterling.
The mark is on the pin clip together with the letter "N" and on both earrings together with the figure "2": both identify the stone setter. The pin clip has a double-hook safety clasp. The dating is based on the metal used, i.e. sterling silver, which means that the items date no later than 1948. At the same time the sterling used is very light and is of a lighter color than the sterling used in 1946. Another useful element for the dating of these items is the manufacturing technique used: the items are cast, but not very accurately finished. In appearance these items are still compact and "heavy," however the metal used was lighter both for economic reasons and to adapt to the fashionable lighter fabrics in use at the time.

E36. "Watch," Eisenberg 1949***
Manufacturer Fallon & Kappel for Eisenberg Jewelry, Inc.
Designer Ruth Kamke.
Not patented.
Gold-plated metal brooch, shaped like a pocket watch with mobile hands and the hours marked by white round, triangular and drop-shaped crystals. 6.8x5.3cm.
Marked "E" in ornate italics capitals.

ELZAC

In the years during the Second World War, California, which had a long tradition of producing novelties locally but was almost exclusively known in the rest of the US for jewelry made for cinema and also, from 1937, for the retail jewelry by Joseff of Hollywood, specialized in making costume jewelry with alternative materials that substituted metals subject to rationing at that time because of war needs. Ceramic, wood, plastic, horn, bone, cork, sponge, and fabric were used in the production of non-precious jewelry and experienced a real boom.

Some small Californian laboratories became particularly famous, e.g., Nancy Lee, Jane Whitmore, Francis Campbell, and Alice Johnson, as part of California Accessories, also, Yvonne of Hollywood, Margot Studio, Olga of Hollywood, and Jean Le Seyeux. This last designer who worked for the cinema, started his own retail business which went by the name of Jean Le Seyeux, and then joined the Leonard Hover Company, 1436 Beachwood Drive, Hollywood. Other manufacturers were Arnold Co., Frick Industries, Ernie Frank Co., which Marta Newman designed for, Frank Roger, which Anita Wallace designed for, Hedi Shop, Bauware, W. A. Curie, Continental Art Studios, Costume Accessories, Oliver Mfg. Co., Plastic Hollywood Arts, Salz Mfg. Co.

The items that these companies produced often appeared in *WWD* along with some advertisements (*WWD*, 3rd May 1940, 3rd December 1942, 19th March 1943, 10th September 1943). In New York many of these items were presented at only one showroom at 303 Fifth Avenue, which belonged to Rose Klipper Kantrow who was also responsible for the California Accessories group.

The most important and renowned company was definitely Elzac Inc. Manufacturers of Los Angeles, 447-453 South Los Angeles Street, with a show-room in Los Angeles, 607 S. Hill Street, and one in New York, first at 366 then at 347 Fifth Avenue.

The company was founded in 1941 by Zachary "Zac" Zemby and Elliot Handler, and the name comes from shortened versions of the two partners' names: EL(liot) and ZAC(hary).

Zac Zemby was a Russian immigrant, who already made watch crystals and other items for the jewelry business. Zemby had

been impressed by a brooch designed by Handler, of a miniature woman's hand with long fingers, which held a small vial with a little water and a flower. This brooch could be pinned to a lapel.

The piece had been such a success that Zemby found out who the designer was and immediately suggested that they set up a company manufacturing costume jewelry and novelties.

Elliot Handler was born in Denver, Colorado, where he grew up and attended school, and where he met the same aged Ruth Mosko (1916-2002), whom he married in 1937. Elliot went to art school, while Ruth worked as a secretary at Paramount Pictures. Elliot soon showed himself to be a talented designer, who was fascinated with the idea of creating new designs from new materials. One of his assignments in his industrial design class was to design items us-

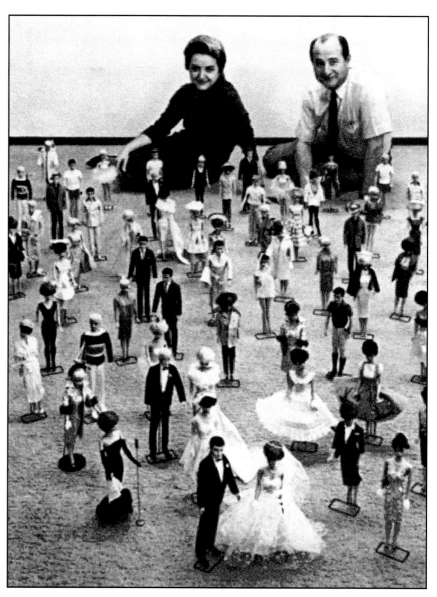

Ruth and Elliot Handler.

ing a recently patented (1937) acrylic plastic, called Lucite or Plexiglas. Eliot used his empty apartment which needed furnishing as inspiration, and he came up with a series of items, all in Lucite, which included coffee tables, lamps, and various accessories such as hand mirrors, trays, bowls, candelabras and cigarettes boxes. While keeping her job at Paramount, Ruth publicized and sold the items designed by her husband. However, money was tight at the time and for this reason they happily accepted Zemby's proposal.

Elzac specialized in making ceramic, wooden, and Lucite jewelry, with so much success that the company announced a 50% enlargement of factory space after only the first year in production and soon grew to employ over 300 workers and made gross profits of about two million dollars a year. Until he left the company in 1945, Zemby was president and sales manager, whilst Elliot Handler was the head designer and Harold "Matt" Matson, Handler's best friend, was production manager.

In 1943, due to increasing capital needs, Zemby brought three new investors into the company: H. Weiss, Z. Taube and A. Oben.

The most famous trademark was "Black Magic" in production from 1943, which focused on items where black prevailed. From 1942-1943 Black Magic included a most beautiful series of brooches of masks, faces, figures, animals and musical instruments. Most of them came from patented designs made by Elliot Handler. What set these brooches apart was the use of such materials as cloth, wood, fur, feathers, raffia, enamel and Lucite, which were added to the base design of the items. The faces look completely different depending on the color, make-up or headdress obtained with different materials. The line presented in the summer of 1943 contained over three hundred original creations and the average cost of the items ranged from $1 to $2.50 and cost a maximum of $8 for the most elaborate brooches. The line also included necklaces, bracelets and earrings in the same materials. Among the most curious items is the "Pooch," a joyful little dog with a curled Lucite tail, "Missouri Mule," a ceramic mule with long ears and a tail of Lucite, and a squirrel with a fur or curled Lucite tail.

The items were made and painted individually by hand and color was applied using a firing procedure. All the items had metal pin backs first welded in Lucite and then applied to the ceramic, which prevented them from coming loose or pulling off. The ceramic and the Lucite used were produced directly by Elzac and typical color combinations were brown ceramic with clear Lucite, and light green with pink, and yellow with blue.

These and other subjects with endless combinations and variations continued to be produced along with more traditional items made of Lucite and sterling in the subsequent years. In its most prominent period, Elzac, in addition to Los Angeles and New York, also had showrooms or sales offices in Chicago, Detroit, Atlanta, and Toronto and Vancouver in Canada.

The company frequently advertised in WWD and in the major magazines which published designs. This advertising is invaluable material in allowing for dating items, especially non-patented items.

The arrival of three new partners did not, however, bring luck to the company because they soon began arguing amongst themselves and with Zemby, Handler, and Matson. The main point of contrast being the fact that they did not want to introduce new products and lines, but, in contrast with their partners, simply wanted to exploit the existing stocks. In the end, Handler was not even allowed to design new products. These issues led to a split and, in 1945, first Handler and Matson, and then Zemby quit the company. Zemby set up his own company, Zemby & Co., and produced silver compacts, silver and 14K gold charms and Lucite and silver costume jewelry (WWD, 17th August 1945).

In the same year, Elliot and Ruth Handler together with Matt Matson, founded Mattel, once again using shortened versions of their names to name the company: MATT EL(liot). From then on the Handlers' story is the same as that of Mattel, the largest toy industry in the world.

The trend boom for Californian ceramic brooches stopped at the end of the War and already seemed in decline in 1945.

The last well-known collection made by Elzac, which then became Elzac California Jewelry & Gift Ware, was "Tiempo de Fiesta," a traditional line of necklaces, bracelets, earrings and brooches in geometrical designs made of gold-plated or rhodium-plated sterling, which was advertised in *WWD*, 2nd August 1946, also in *Vogue, Charm, Harper's Bazaar,* and *Glamour.*

There is no further information about Elzac from the beginning of 1947 and the company probably ceased before the end of the 1940s. Even production of the ceramic goods almost completely stopped although some ceramic items did appear in some lines produced shortly after 1946 by Californian manufacturers but just as a curiosity.

WWD, August 2, 1946: "Tiempo de Fiesta," Jewelry by Elzac.

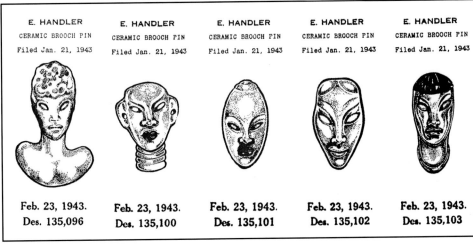

E. HANDLER	E. HANDLER	E. HANDLER	E. HANDLER	E. HANDLER
CERAMIC BROOCH PIN	CERAMIC BROOCH PIN	CERAMIC BROOCH PIN	CERAMIC BROOCH PIN	CERAMIC BROOCH PIN
Filed Jan. 21, 1943	Filed Jan. 21, 1943	Filed Jan. 21, 1943	Filed Jan. 21, 1943	Filed Jan. 21, 1943
Feb. 23, 1943. Des. 135,096	Feb. 23, 1943. Des. 135,100	Feb. 23, 1943. Des. 135,101	Feb. 23, 1943. Des. 135,102	Feb. 23, 1943. Des. 135,103

Hand painted ceramic brooch, light brown, red, green and black enamel, depicting a woman's face with an elaborate headdress made from leather, wood and plastic. 10x5.5cm.
Unmarked.
Also in the case of the numerous women's faces the basic design underwent many variations in make-up and hairstyles. This would explain the modern name "victims of fashion" which they are sometimes called, though no documented reference to this exists.

EL1. "South American Belle," Elzac 1943*****
Manufacturer Elzac, Inc., Los Angeles.
Designer Elliot Handler.
Patent n° 135,100 Elliot Handler, Los Angeles, February 23rd 1943, filed January 21st 1943.

EL2. "Black Face," Elzac 1943*****
Manufacturer Elzac Inc., Los Angeles.
Designer Elliot Handler.
Patent n° 135,102 Elliot Handler, Los Angeles, February 23rd 1943, filed January 21st 1943.
   Hand painted ceramic brooch, black, red, green and yellow enamel, depicting the face of a black woman with large hoop earrings, wearing a fabric turban decorated with a plate of fruit. 9x7.2cm.
   Unmarked.

EL3. "Ubangi," Elzac 1943*****
Manufacturer Elzac, Inc., Los Angeles.
Designer Elliot Handler.
Patent n° 135,100 Elliot Handler, Los Ange-
les, February 23rd 1943, filed January 21st 1943.
    Hand painted ceramic brooch, brown, red,
and black enamel, depicting an Ubangi woman
with elaborate headwear made of wood, raffia,
leather, coloured beads, mother of pearl and
sequins. 9.5x5cm.
    Unmarked.

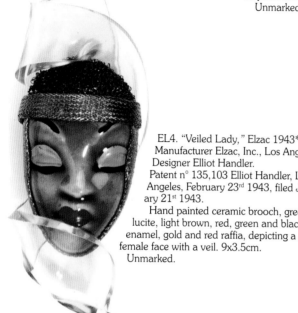

EL4. "Veiled Lady," Elzac 1943*****
Manufacturer Elzac, Inc., Los Angeles.
Designer Elliot Handler.
Patent n° 135,103 Elliot Handler, Los
Angeles, February 23rd 1943, filed January 21st 1943.
    Hand painted ceramic brooch, green
lucite, light brown, red, green and black
enamel, gold and red raffia, depicting a
female face with a veil. 9x3.5cm.
    Unmarked.

    Hand painted ceramic brooch, pink,
blue, and black enamel, wool and cloth,
depicting the head of a young girl with long
pig-tails wearing a beret and pom-pom.
9x4.5cm.
    Unmarked.
    The item was reproduced under the
name "Daisy" in an advertisement in
WWD, March 7th 1945.

EL5. "Daisy," Elzac
1943*****
Manufacturer Elzac, Inc.,
Los Angeles.
Designer Elliot Handler.
Patent n° 136,221
Elliot Handler, Los
Angeles, August 24th
1943, filed July 29th
1943.

EL6. "Smart Lady," Elzac 1943*****
Manufacturer Elzac, Inc., Los Angeles.
Designer Elliot Handler.
Patent n° 135,101 Elliot Handler, Los Angeles,
February 23rd 1943, filed January 21st 1943.
    Hand painted ceramic brooch, brown
lucite, white, red, black, blue and pink enamel,
depicting a female head with an elegant hat and
pom-pom made of wood and plastic, chinstrap of
silver raffia. 9x4.5cm.
    Unmarked.

New "Nonsense" in Plastic
Lapel Ornaments for Gifts

"Angel Face"
has flower petals
of colored Lucite
with the little
yellow-haired face
done in ceramics.

    The comic pup
is all-plastic —
—clear, with col-
ored "features."
The floppy ears
are movable.
From Elzac, Inc.

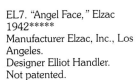

WWD, October 9 1942: "Angel Face" by Elzac.

    Hand painted ceramic brooch, green lucite, light
brown and yellow enamel, depicting a head inside a
corolla. 8x8cm.
    Unmarked.
    The design was featured with the name "Angel Face"
in *WWD,* October 9th 1942.

EL7. "Angel Face," Elzac
1942*****
Manufacturer Elzac, Inc., Los
Angeles.
Designer Elliot Handler.
Not patented.

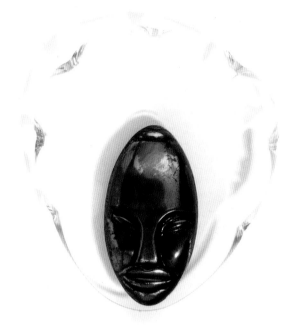

EL8. "Bonnet Head," Elzac 1943****
Manufacturer Elzac, Inc., Los Angeles.
Designer Elliot Handler.
Patent n° 135,101 Elliot Handler, Los Angeles, February 23rd
1943, filed January 21st 1943.

WWD, January 12, 1945: "Bonnet Head" and other pins
by Elzac.

Copper and lucite brooch depicting a mask.
7.5x6.5cm.
Unmarked.
The item was featured with the name "Bonnet Head"
in an advertisement in WWD, January 12th 1945.

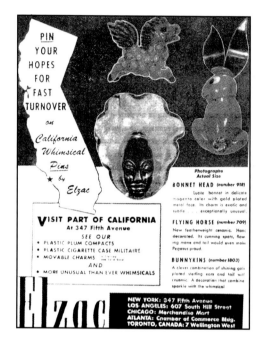

EL9. "Eliza,"
Elzac 1943*****
Manufacturer
Elzac, Inc., Los
Angeles.
Designer Elliot Han-
dler.
Patent n° 135,103 El-
liot Handler, Los Angeles,
February 23rd 1943, filed
January 21st 1943.
Hand painted ceramic brooch,
lucite, cloth, brown, blue, red and
black enamel, depicting a female
head with a large hat. 9x8cm.
Unmarked.
The item was featured with the
name "Eliza" in the Sears catalogue
Fall 1944, and was on sale for 85c.

EL10 "Face," Elzac 1943****
 Manufacturer Elzac, Inc., Los Angeles.
 Designer Elliot Handler.
  Patent n° 135,102 Elliot Handler, Los Angeles,
February 23rd 1943, filed January 21st 1943.
    Hand painted ceramic brooch, yellow lucite,
pink, red, lilac and black enamel, depicting a
woman's face with Lucite hair. 8.5x6cm.
    Unmarked.

EL11. "Asian Goddess," Elzac
1943*****
Manufacturer Elzac Inc., Los
Angeles.
Designer Elliot Handler.
Patent n° 135,103 Elliot
Handler, Los Angeles, February 23rd 1943, filed January
21st 1943.
   Hand painted ceramic
brooch, green lucite, red,
black and pink enamel, depicting an Asian female head
with veil. 8.5x5cm.
   Unmarked.

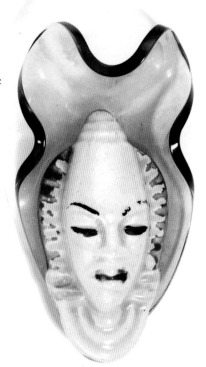

EL12 "Bolivian Woman," Elzac
1943*****
Manufacturer Elzac Inc., Los Angeles.
Designer Elliot Handler.
Patent n° 135,100 Elliot Handler,
Los Angeles, February 23rd 1943,
filed January 21st 1943.
    Hand painted ceramic brooch, green
chamois leather with a brown strip, cork,
wood, red and black enamel, depicting
the head of a Bolivian woman wearing
a traditional hat. 12x5cm.
    Unmarked.

EL13. "Inca Face," Elzac 1943****
Manufacturer Elzac, Inc., Los Angeles.
Designer Elliot Handler.
Patent n° 135,100 Elliot Handler, Los
Angeles, February 23rd 1943, filed
January 21st 1943.
    Hand painted ceramic brooch,
yellow lucite, wood and cloth, de-
picting an Inca head. 9x5cm.
Unmarked.

EL14. "Blue Lady," Elzac 1943*****
Manufacturer Elzac, Inc., Los Angeles.
Designer Elliot Handler.
Patent n° 135,103 Elliot Handler, Los Angeles,
February 23rd 1943, filed January 21st 1943.
Hand painted ceramic brooch, lucite,
blue enamel, copper color raffia, depict-
ing a female face with feathered hat.
10.5x6.5cm.
Unmarked.

EL15. "Indian Twins," Elzac
1943*****
Manufacturer Elzac, Inc., Los
Angeles.
Designer Elliot Handler.
Not patented.

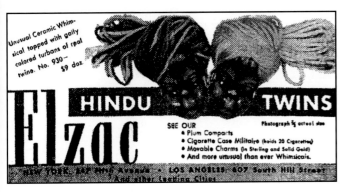

WWD, March 2, 1945: "Hindu Twins" by Elzac.

Hand painted ceramic brooch, wool and cloth
brown, red, white and green enamel, depicting an
Indian couple. 4x6cm.
Unmarked.
The same faces but with turbans and different
make-up were featured in an advertisement in
WWD of March 2nd 1945 as "Hindu Twins".

EL16. "Sheik," Elzac 1943*****
Manufacturer Elzac, Inc., Los Angeles.
Designer Elliot Handler.
Patent n° 135,096 Elliot Handler, Los Angeles,
February 23rd 1943, filed January 21st 1943.
   Hand painted ceramic brooch, multicolour
cloth with mother of pearl insertions, red and
black enamel, depicting a bearded man's head
with a turban. 7.5x3.5cm.
   Umarked.
   The pin was featured with the name "Sheik,"
in the Sears catalogue in fall 1944 and was on
sale for 85c.

EL17. "Hobby," Elzac 1942****
Manufacturer Elzac, Inc., Los Angeles.
Designer Elliot Handler.
Not patented.
   Hand painted ceramic brooch, yellow lucite, brown,
red and green enamel, depicting a horse with ears
made of brown cloth. 8x5.5cm.
   Unmarked.
   The item was featured with the name "Hobby" in the
Sears catalogue Fall 1944, and was on sale for 85c.

EL18. "Horse Head," Elzac 1942****
Manufacturer Elzac, Inc., Los Angeles.
Designer Elliot Handler.
Not patented.
   Hand painted ceramic brooch, pink lucite, blue,
red, yellow and black enamel, depicting a horse's
head. 6x7cm.
   Unmarked.

EL19. "Carousel Horse," Elzac 1943*****
Manufacturer Elzac, Inc., Los Angeles.
Designer Elliot Handler.
Patent n° 135,595 Elliot Handler, Los Angeles, April
27th 1943, filed March 29th 1943.

Hand painted ceramic brooch, pink lucite, white,
bordeaux and red enamel, gold colored leather,
feathers and sequins, depicting a merry-go-round
horse. 11x7cm.
     Unmarked.
     The basic designs were produced by Elzac in
numerous variations with additions of different ornamental elements and using various materials.
     The original design was featured in the Sears
catalogue, Fall 1944, under the name "Pegasus" for
sale at 85c.

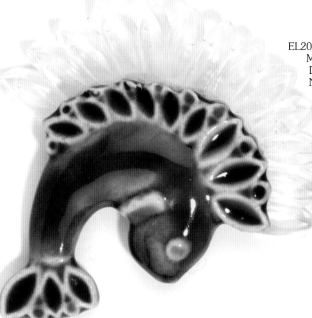

EL20. "Blue Dolphin," Elzac 1942*****
Manufacturer Elzac, Inc., Los Angeles.
Designer Elliot Handler.
Not patented.
     Hand painted ceramic brooch,
lucite, blue and brown enamel, depict-
ing a dolphin. 10x10cm.
     Unmarked.

ELZAC

EL21. "Shy Squirrel," Elzac 1943*****
Manufacturer Elzac, Inc., Los Angeles.
Designer Elliot Handler.
Patent n° 135,519 Elliot Handler, Los Angeles,
April 20th 1943, filed March 29th 1943.

Hand painted ceramic brooch, yellow lucite, blue, yellow, red and black
enamel, depicting a squirrel wearing
a leather beret with a cloth pom-pom.
7.5x3.5cm.
   Unmarked.

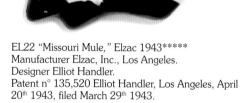

Hand painted ceramic brooch, lucite,
yellow, black and red enamel, depicting a
mule. 8x6.8cm.
   Unmarked.
   The item was featured with the name "Missouri Mule" in an advertisement in WWD,
October 2nd 1942.

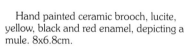

EL22 "Missouri Mule," Elzac 1943*****
Manufacturer Elzac, Inc., Los Angeles.
Designer Elliot Handler.
Patent n° 135,520 Elliot Handler, Los Angeles, April
20th 1943, filed March 29th 1943.

EL23. "Twin Horses," Elzac 1943****
Manufacturer Elzac, Inc., Los Angeles.
Designer Elliot Handler.
Not patented.
   Hand painted ceramic brooch, grey, yellow, sky-blue
and black enamel, depicting two galloping horses.
7x8.5cm.
   Unmarked.

EVANS CASE CO.

U1. "Portrait of a Woman,"
Unsigned 1942****
Manufacturer Evans Case Co.

WWD, June 26, 1942: Evans Case Co. Jewelry.

Sterling brooch, gold-plated in two different tones with blue cut-stones, of the face of a woman. 9x3.3cm. Marked Sterling.

The brooch, along with matching earrings, featured in *WWD*, 26th June 1942, which reported that "A small collection of exotically styled sterling Silver jewelry, chiefly big pins and matching earrings, is being introduced by Evans Case Co.". Jewelry production was an exception for Evans Case Co., which was specialized, as its name suggests, in compacts, cigarette holders etc. Very little information is available about the company, which started up in 1920 as the D. Evans Case Co. and then, at a later date, became a division of Hilsinger Corp., Plainville, Ms. The company was last cited in 1965.

LEO GLASS

Leo Glass & Co., Inc., was established by Leo Glass in September 1928 (*WWD*, 13th September 1928). Leo Glass had been working for several years in the field of costume jewelry before creating his own firm: he had spent ten years with Lisner as a sales rep in the Midwest. The company headquarters and showroom were first situated in 298, and then, from 1938, in 377 Fifth Avenue. Subsequently the firm moved to 31 West 47th Street (1947), and finally to 37 East 18th Street. The company went bankrupt in 1957 and its assets were auctioned off on 27th August 1957.

Initially the company was also an importer. Its first spring 1929 collections were called "Season's Sensation" and "Hawaiian Lei Motif Jewelry."

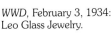

WWD, February 3, 1934: Leo Glass Jewelry.

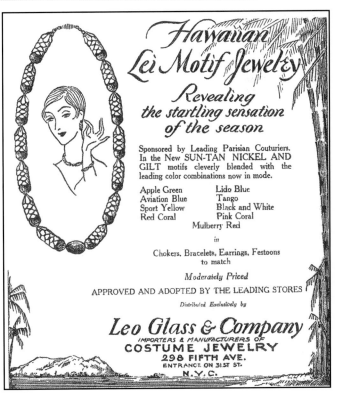

WWD, February 28, 1929: Leo Glass first collection.

In December 1930 *WWD* presented a three-strand necklace of white crystals separated by small imitation onyx grains and silver-plated metal in "Italian Renaissance" style. According to *WWD* of 29th December 1933, the company produced extraordinary fashion lines that could be purchased in every state and in all the best shops, including Bonwit Teller, Bergdorf Goodman, and Saks. Some collections of this period were documented in the papers and magazines of the time: for example the collection called "Felix the Cat," inspired by the cartoon of the same name, in the spring of 1932 (*WWD*, 11th February) and a collection inspired by the navy in the spring of 1934 (*WWD*, 15th June) including, among various items, a harpoon-shaped blue catalin brooch and a silver-plated chain bracelet with charms in the shape of small prystal fish-tanks with back-engraved fish. In 1938 *Vogue*, 15th February, presented the "Flashes of Wit" collection which consisted of brooches with large multicolored stones shaped like flowers, butterflies, spiders and birds, and in 1940 *Harper's Bazaar*, November issue, presented a series of gold-plated metal and glass bead necklaces on sale at Saks.

From the start, the company used all the usual materials for its jewelry production: metal, sterling, plastics, including Lucite, wood, and ceramic. During the war there was, for obvious reasons, a prevalence of non-rationed materials. An example of the production of this period is the "Starfish" set, composed of a brooch and earrings made of ceramic and pink plastic with white and pink stones, advertised in *Vogue*, 15th July 1943.

The Leo Glass company initially only advertised in *Women's Wear Daily*, but later also in *Vogue* and other national circulation magazines. Already in 1938, *Vogue* was presenting its jewelry in fashion reportages and in folders advertising the hottest items.

Until 1941 production was aimed at the most affluent clientele, however, with the fall 1941 collection, Leo Glass, according to *WWD* 27th June 1941, "enters the field of low-priced jewelry." In 1942, for one year, Leo Glass interrupted production, only to resume operations at the beginning of 1943 (*WWD*, 12th February 1943).

During the second half of the 1940s the level of product inventiveness and quality declined and the firm occupied a medium-low market position, with banal rhinestone jewelry, like those of its 1947 collection (*Vogue*, 15th March) or the rather insignificant Victorian style jewelry of the fall 1948 collection (*Vogue*, 15th October)

Designers for the company were Leo Glass, Anne Glass, and Beatrice Glass who only patented a series of designs with flowery subjects in 1948. In 1941, David Mir, who also worked for Trifari, designed jewelry inspired by the sea abyss for Leo Glass. The jewelry is mainly marked *Leo Glass* which is inscribed in italics in a polygonal plate and the trademark reproduced Leo Glass's signature

exactly how it appeared in the only patent registered in his name. The trademarks "Leo Glass Original" and "Courtly Jewels," the latter registered in 1948, were only used for advertising purposes.

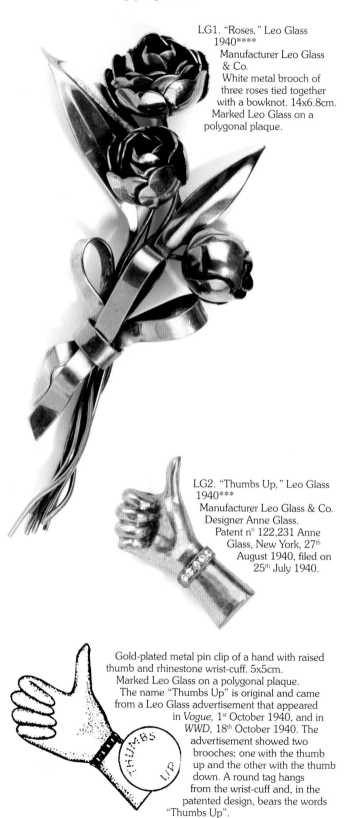

LG1. "Roses," Leo Glass 1940****
  Manufacturer Leo Glass & Co.
  White metal brooch of three roses tied together with a bowknot. 14x6.8cm. Marked Leo Glass on a polygonal plaque.

LG2. "Thumbs Up," Leo Glass 1940***
  Manufacturer Leo Glass & Co.
  Designer Anne Glass.
  Patent n° 122,231 Anne Glass, New York, 27th August 1940, filed on 25th July 1940.

Gold-plated metal pin clip of a hand with raised thumb and rhinestone wrist-cuff. 5x5cm.
Marked Leo Glass on a polygonal plaque.
The name "Thumbs Up" is original and came from a Leo Glass advertisement that appeared in *Vogue*, 1st October 1940, and in *WWD*, 18th October 1940. The advertisement showed two brooches; one with the thumb up and the other with the thumb down. A round tag hangs from the wrist-cuff and, in the patented design, bears the words "Thumbs Up".

LG3. "Fireworks," Leo Glass
1938****
Manufacturer Leo Glass & Co.
Red gold-plated metal
brooch of a bunch of flowers tied with a bowknot.
The flowers are made of
pear-shaped pearls and
oval faceted pink, blue,
azure and green stones.
13x6cm.
Marked Leo Glass on
a polygonal plaque. '
On 15th March
1938 Vogue pub-
lished the picture of
a Chanel brooch
called "Fireworks"
imported by Berg-
dorf Goodman.
This brooch might
possibly have served as
inspiration, since it is actually very similar to the one
designed by Leo Glass.

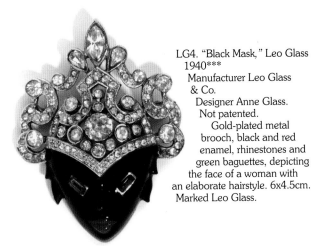

LG4. "Black Mask," Leo Glass
1940***
Manufacturer Leo Glass
& Co.
Designer Anne Glass.
Not patented.
Gold-plated metal
brooch, black and red
enamel, rhinestones and
green baguettes, depicting
the face of a woman with
an elaborate hairstyle. 6x4.5cm.
Marked Leo Glass.

MIRIAM HASKELL

Miriam Haskell was born in Cannelton, Indiana, on 1st July 1899, into a well-to-do family of Russian-German descent. She spent her childhood and youth in New Albany. Her father Simon ran a small firm and later helped his daughter start up her business in New York. Haskell regularly attended school until graduation and was enrolled at the University of Chicago for two years. In 1924, after moving to New York, encouraged by the success of her artifacts among her friends and high society acquaintances, she began to design and manufacture costume jewelry in a small workshop. In 1926 she opened a shop called "Le Bijoux de l'Heure" on the premises of the McAlpin Hotel, 103 16th Street. The shop did remarkably well and, possibly in 1929, Ms. Haskell moved to 411 Fifth Avenue, as advertised in WWD of 21st April 1929. At the time Mrs. Haskell also imported jewelry from France, as confirmed by an article in WWD, 8th August 1929, presenting some of her imported pieces.

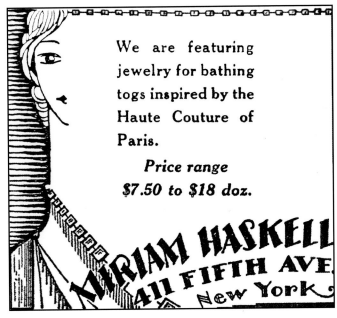

We are featuring
jewelry for bathing
togs inspired by the
Haute Couture of
Paris.

Price range
$7.50 to $18 doz.

WWD, June 6, 1929: advertisement by Miriam Haskell.

In the same year she opened a boutique on the premises of the Hotel Roney of Miami, Florida and, in 1932 (*WWD*, 25th November 1932), a new sales outlet opened in 7W 57th Street, New York. After a little while (1933) the firm moved again to 392 Fifth Avenue, first occupying only a single floor and then taking up a second and a third floor of the building.

Production was carried out by an average of eighteen specialized workers who assembled items completely by hand. It is not clear whether Frank Hess, Mrs. Haskell's right hand man and designer of practically all the jewelry, had already started cooperating with her from the beginning, in 1924, or in 1926, or in 1929-30. When Mrs. Haskell first "discovered" him, Hess was working as a window dresser at Macy's. His collaboration with Haskell Jewels continued after 1950, when Miriam Haskell had stopped running her company.

In 1950, following what was described as a severe nervous breakdown, Miriam Haskell withdrew from business and transferred the company – Haskell Jewelry Ltd. – to her brother Joseph, who ran the firm, together with Hess, until 1956, when he sold the company to Morris Kinzler who, in 1984, sold it to Sanford Moss, general manager of the company from 1956 and vice-president from 1983. The last ownership transfer is dated 1989, when the firm was purchased by Frank Fialkoff, president of Victoria International Inc., a manufacturer of costume jewelry of Warwick, Rhode Island.

The firm is still in business today at its New York headquarters with an annexed plant and employs about sixty-five people. Frank Hess was succeeded as company designer by Robert E. Clark (1960 – 1967), Peter Raines (1968 – 1970) and Larry Vrba (1970 – 1978). Haskell's head designer has been Camille Petronzio from 1980.

According to company sources reported in several books, Ms. Haskell continued to supervise production, even after she retired and until her brother's death in 1977. However, this is not the case, and, in reality, it was Hess alone who kept the "Haskell Style" alive and unchanged. Mrs. Haskell was thought of as a perfectionist who not only supervised each phase of jewelry production, from design to marketing, but also regularly visited the company suppliers in the USA and abroad. Miriam Haskell died on 4th July 1981 aged eighty-two and was buried in Louisville, Kentucky.

Much is known of Mrs. Haskell's life, and the many more or less scabrous details and anecdotes of her life could fill a book. However, this of course, would be of little interest to serious collectors, whose only interest lies in the attribution and dating of marked and unmarked items. In Haskell's case, there are no definitive documents to go by. The only existing documentation consists of original designs, provided they are dated, as well as publications and advertisements in the press. With these premises any "attributions," based principally on the

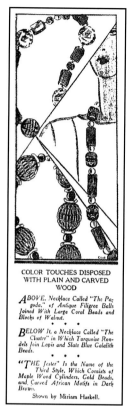

COLOR TOUCHES DISPOSED
WITH PLAIN AND CARVED
WOOD

*A*BOVE. Necklace Called "The Pagoda," of Antique Filigree Balls Joined With Large Coral Beads and Blocks of Walnut.

*B*ELOW It, a Necklace Called "The Cluster" in Which Turquoise Rondels Join Lapis and Slate Blue Calalith Beads.

"*T*HE Jester" Is the Name of the Third Style, Which Consists of Maple Wood Cylinders, Gold Beads, and Carved African Motifs in Dark Brown.

Shown by Miriam Haskell.

WWD, March 3, 1929:
Miriam Haskell Jewelry.

"unique" characteristics of items, are of a rather dubious nature, since they rely on subjective evaluations. The reproductions in books of "attributed" items, cannot be entirely relied on and one can only hypothesize about attribution and dating, but hypotheses should not justify high prices.

The facts on which any assessment should be based, are:

• No design by M. Haskell (if any), Hess, or any other in-house or free-lance designers has ever been patented. This means that there is no certain documentation on which to rely.

• The original designs supplied by the company appear, as far as can be inferred from their reproductions in books, to be undated.

• The company only started advertising nationally (*Vogue, Harper's Bazaar, Town & Country*) at the end of 1945.

• The first advertisement in *Women's Wear Daily* appeared in 1929. From this date onwards, the paper kept presenting – albeit at irregular intervals – Haskell's production, together with relatively few advertisements. This information gives an idea of Haskell's production between 1929 and 1942 and again from 1945 onwards.

Trademarks, as has previously been stressed, cannot be relied upon for the dating of jewelry. In Haskell's case, no trademark was registered until 1988, when the best-known one was registered with the name in block letters inscribed in an oval plate. As far as production was concerned, there is general agreement, in the books, that from the beginning of the firm's business, throughout 1938, jewelry was unmarked. According to Simons Miller (*Costume Jewelry*, II ed.) Haskell jewelry was sold in "lovely boxes with the name written in black art deco characters. Silver labels with the logo printed in black were also used." Baker in *Fifty Years of Collectible Fashion Jewelry*, p. 14-15 maintains that the trademark inside the oval plate first appeared at the end of the 1930s (possibly 1938), however hers is the only claim of this kind, since, according to most experts (for example Farneti Cera in *I Gioielli della Fantasia* and in *I Gioielli di Miriam Haskell*, Becker in *Fabulous Fakes*, Gordon in *Twentieth Century Costume Jewelry*), this trademark was first used at the end of the 1940s (possibly 1948), and definitely after the war. Consequently it

WWD, June 13, 1929: "The New Cork Jewelry" by Miriam Haskell.

WWD, November 7, 1929: "New Sunday Night Jewelry," by Miriam Haskell.

WWD, March 13, 1930: Miriam Haskell Jewelry.

can be said that Haskell's jewels were unmarked until at least 1946 or even 1950. The only exception might be represented by the "horseshoe" trademark, which was apparently used in 1944 (or 1945) for a collection manufactured exclusively for a Chicago (according to some a New England) boutique. A small bird appears on some jewelry, dangling from necklace clasps which is believed to symbolize the dove of peace, and was apparently used during the war. Yet, it was also found on necklaces with the oval trademark and even on more recent necklaces. The oval plate was also used as a sort of label, i.e. not imprinted on the jewels, but attached to them. Confusion reigns, and what data is available does little to clarify matters.

As to the unmarked pieces, a comparison between the images of those reproduced to date, and those directly examined, with those reproduced in *Women's Wear Daily* from 1929 to 1950 and with the advertisements published on national magazines from 1945 to 1950, leads to the conclusion that there is a remarkable similarity, if not complete identicalness in just two cases. In the first case the piece of jewelry is a brooch, whose picture appeared in *Bijoux* (Farneti Cera, p. 146): it is an unmarked brooch dating from the 1940s,

which is very similar to one published, together with other pieces of the same set, in *WWD*, 21st May 1937. However, the design presented in *WWD*, though very similar, exhibits some significant differences from the photographed item of jewelry. In this case two hypotheses can be formulated:

Either it is the same item of jewelry and is actually by Miriam Haskell, but underwent several rather important changes during production, or it is a contemporary imitation, which was a rather frequent occurrence, made easier by the fact that Haskell did not protect its designs in any way.

The same considerations can be applied to another brooch reproduced in *I Gioielli della Fantasia*, p. 175, n. 70: which showed a carved wooden turtle placed on a "nest" made of natural seashells. A similar design with even more differences than the previous one, was presented in *WWD*, 3rd and 7th July 1942 as part of a summer collection called "Walk a little faster" whose seashells were said to come from Cuba.

These examples demonstrates the need for caution when making attributions based on documentation, in Haskell's case.

WWD, May 1, 1930: Galalith Jewelry by Miriam Haskell.

SMALL AND LARGE GALALITH BEAD EFFECTS

The necklace above consists of crystal lalique beads interspersed with small jade colored beads.

The other necklace is of pear-shaped pink coral galalith beads offset by small ones in black and crystal.

Models from Miriam Haskell.

However, it has been maintained that identification is possible due to the "unmistakable" nature of the materials used and the manufacturing style. That is the jewelry – particularly the necklaces – are made of very peculiar materials. Glass beads of every shape, size and color, imported from Austria, France, Czechoslovakia, and Italy, used in the most disparate chromatic combinations, alone, or with other materials. Wood, seashells, mother-of-pearl, plastic (Bakelite, Lucite, etc.), fabric and metal are also variously combined. Another distinctive feature of Haskell's products, probably the best known, was the use of pearls, particularly of very tiny pearls (2 mm diameter), applied to the jewelry in very thick layers and, the use of baroque pearls especially after the war. Many of these materials were in use from the very start until the most recent production. The same applies to such "alternative" materials as wood, plastic, or seashells, which remained in use beyond the war period.

The items were often assembled to a metal base cast in such a way as to resemble a typical "open work" or filigree effect and gold plated with a special galvanic process that gave it an opaque finish called "antique Russian gold." The molding and gold-plating were mainly carried out in Providence plants, and were personally inspected by Haskell.

It is true that these characteristics can be found both in marked and unmarked Haskell jewelry, however these are the very features that are most likely to be copied, as was openly done by such major firms as Coro, De Mario, Eugene, and Robert-Fashioncraft, which stamped the items with their own trademarks. Therefore, it is highly probable that anonymous, perfect copies displaying excellent quality exist.

Crystal Grist Beads, and Multi-Strand Versions in Bright Colored Beads

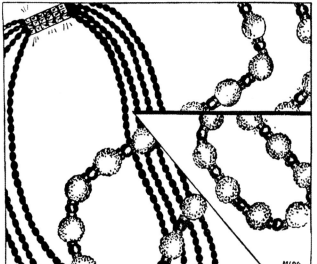

The necklace illustrated at left is a four-strand sports type of small lozenge-shaped beads in coral color, with a fastening of baguettes.

The other style is fashioned of "crystal grist" balls interrupted by small beads of turquoise color.
Models from Miriam Haskell.

WWD, December 11, 1930: Models from Miriam Haskell.

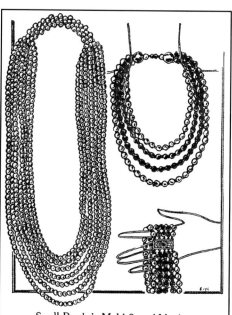

WWD, May 21, 1931: Models from Miriam Haskell.

Small Beads in Multi-Strand Versions

The necklace illustrated at left consists of seven strands of small glass beads in black, red, yellow or white, the new detail being the narrow woven section at back, which is slenderizing.

Next is a four-strand choker in various colors, the matching bracelet shown below.
Models from Miriam Haskell.

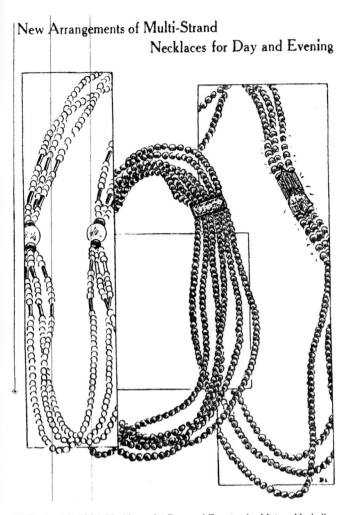

New Arrangements of Multi-Strand
Necklaces for Day and Evening

WWD, April 2, 1931: Necklaces for Day and Evening by Miriam Haskell.

Apart from some small corrections and a little additional information, little can be added to what was written about Miriam Haskell in 1997 in *American Costume Jewelry*. This is the case, in spite of further, in-depth research, because of the difficulties in dating and attributing this company's jewelry.

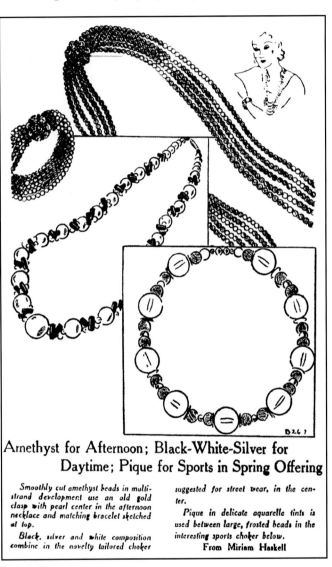

Amethyst for Afternoon; Black-White-Silver for
Daytime; Pique for Sports in Spring Offering

Smoothly cut amethyst beads in multi-strand development use an old gold clasp with pearl center in the afternoon necklace and matching bracelet sketched at top.

Black, silver and white composition combine in the novelty tailored choker

suggested for street wear, in the center.

Pique in delicate aquarelle tints is used between large, frosted beads in the interesting sports choker below.

From Miriam Haskell

WWD, February 2, 1932: Jewelry by Miriam Haskell.

The complexity of the situation impacts also on the dating of the items, usually encompassing a whole decade – the 1930s, 1940s, 1950s – which, in a production period spanning less than thirty years (those in which Haskell was directly present, 1924-1950), practically means no dating at all, since, for a collector, it obviously makes a difference if a piece in the style of the "1940s" is made at the beginning or at the end of the decade. This is even more the case for pieces dating from the 1950s, since Mrs. Haskell left the company in 1950.

In conclusion, Haskell's production, which mostly consisted of necklaces, but also included the usual costume jewelry arsenal of bracelets, brooches, earrings, rings and combs, is rather abundant on the market and, though much of the jewelry is really beautiful, in the end a sense of repetitiveness and also of "pretentiousness," rather than elegance prevails. In choosing an item of Haskell jewelry, a collector should not be guided by the mere beauty of the item, but also by those elements that have been objectively illustrated here, to ascertain whether it belonged to the period in which production was directly supervised by Mrs. Haskell, without forgetting that, certainty is improbable as far as the unmarked pieces are concerned.

Two monographs have been written about Haskell's jewelry: *I gioielli di Miriam Haskell* by Deanna Farneti Cera (1997) and *Miriam Haskell Jewelry* by Gordon & Pamfiloff (2004). Both were based on the analysis of available material and on interviews with family members and collaborators. Hundreds of marked and unmarked pieces were described, together with an analysis of materials, components, styles and mechanisms. However, much uncertainty remains concerning the pieces belonging to the period under review in this book (1935-1950); a period which coincides with the time when Miriam Haskell was head of the company.

Hand-Made Jewelry That Is Different

ENSEMBLES in crystal—designed to brighten up the first fall Black—is being featured in the handmade line of Miriam Haskell. There is at great deal of detail on delicate pins, earrings, necklaces and bracelets.

Featured is the leaf pin with or without the large pear-shaped crystal drop. Earrings are outstanding: Some extra large drops outstanding for their fine craftsmanship, and others moderate-sized with crystal detail. Coil bracelets with elaborate ornaments are lovely complements to the pins and earrings as it a novel double-clip necklace. This consists of a few strands of beads with a clip at each end, which can be tied and worn in many ways. It adapts itself to any type of neckline.

Chrysoprase and coral are two colors combined for another striking ensemble. Pins, earrings, bracelets and necklaces are available—all noteworthy for their delicacy and intricate work.

This firm also has a large selection of ornamented combs, with intricate lacework, elaborate floral patterns and wing motifs.

WWD, August 4, 1944: Hand-Made Jewelry by Miriam Haskell.

It is an almost certainty that jewelry was never marked at least before 1948, or, most probably, until 1950. Even the "horseshoe mark," contrary to what has been a widespread belief up to now and to what was claimed in the previous paragraph, was never used before these dates, whereas it did appear on items manufactured in the 1960s. Other features, such as the ornaments of closures and clasps, like the doves which were believed to be symbols of peace and consequently dated from the war period, were used as decorations of more recent products and are therefore unhelpful in allowing for the correct dating of Haskell jewelry. For these reasons the jewelry is dated by five and ten year periods. The only exceptions are represented by some more recent items, whose designers – Frank Hess's successors – are known. However, even in these cases, it is still impossible to give a precise dating for the items. The few patent numbers that have been found, refer to the mechanisms used and are therefore of no use, either for dating purposes or the attribution of unmarked pieces, since the same patented mechanisms were also used by other manufacturers. The advertisements in period papers and magazines allow for a precise identification of only a few pieces, some of which were unmarked and therefore date from the 1924-1950 period, while for the most part the items are recent. Moreover, the watercolors attributed to Larry Austin are of little use, since they are not dated and illustrate jewelry items that only vaguely resemble the items that were actually manufactured.

In conclusion, the only items that are definitely Haskell's are the marked pieces, but they all belong to a later period than the one being reviewed in this book. Nevertheless a section has been dedicated to Miriam Haskell, because she was an important figure in the field of costume jewelry and her creations are still sought after collector's items today. The items have been re-dated and others have been added. Two of the jewelry items added to the list are unmarked, and therefore can only be tentatively attributed: they probably belong to the 1950-1960 decade, when Frank Hess, the real inventor of the Haskell style, was still with the company.

Vogue, November 15, 1946: "Portrait Jewels" by Miriam Haskell.

The "Parure," MH10, offers an excellent example of the difficulties in dating and attributing jewelry items to various designers. In *American Costume Jewelry* the set had been dated from 1946, the year when it was thought that the introduction of jewelry marking took place. In the same year, the first advertising campaign at national level began. The comparison with the items presented in advertisements of that period and the patent of the earring clip, issued in 1946, was also crucial in dating the set, although utility patents were known to be used for their whole duration (17 years) and sometimes beyond expiry. Now it seems that this patent, for a combination of clip and screw, began to be used only in 1960. This decision was taken by Sanford Moss, as he himself admitted, following many customer complaints about the uncomfortable nature of the so-called French clips. Thus, the set should be dated after 1960 and, based on a comparison with other pieces, it should be dated from Robert Clark's time (1960-1967). However, Larry Vrba, who the author of this book met in New York during the Triple Piers 2002, claims to be the inventor of the design, and maintains that the design dates from 1970-1978. It has been repeatedly stated that evidence supplied by prominent figures in the world of costume jewelry, is not always reliable. However, in this case, there is no reason to doubt Vrba's word, which means that there is a thirty year difference between the first and the last dating of the set. Confusion is generated by the fact that the company, especially when it started being administered according to managerial criteria, always asked its designers to express their own inventiveness in the traditional vein of Haskell's style.

MH2. "Black Necklace," Miriam Haskell 1950-55****
Manufacturer Miriam Haskell Jewels Ltd.
Designer Frank Hess.
   Gold-plated metal filigree necklace with jet black glass beads, semicircular pendant with twelve leaves with black glass seed bead pavé and central flower with central glass bead and rhinestone rose montée. The hidden clasp is made of metal filigree leaves with rhinestone rose montée. The four glass bead strands are separated by gold-plated metal flowers with glass bead and rhinestone pavé. Length: 29cm; pendant: 7x4.5cm.
   Marked Miriam Haskell in an oval plaque engraved in the metal of the clasp.

MH1. "Pink Necklace," Miriam Haskell 1950-55****
   Manufacturer Miriam Haskell Jewels Ltd.
   Designer Frank Hess.
      Necklace with pendant, with five fine gold-plated metal threads and a strand of pink glass beads alternated with rhinestone washers. The pendant is made of two clusters of pink glass beads with two metal flowers and central rhinestone, projecting from an elaborate rhinestone-studded motif. Pendant length: 8.5cm.
      Marked Miriam Haskell on an applied oval plaque.
      This is a typical example of the amount of manual work that went into Haskell's jewelry, which was completely manufactured by hand, from the stringing of the stones to the assembly of the metal components.

MH3. "Rose Necklace," Miriam Haskell 1940-1945****
Manufacturer Miriam Haskell Jewels Ltd.
Designer Frank Hess.
   Glass bead necklace with engraved glass pendant shaped like a rose with two overlapping gold-plated metal leaves. Cylindrical screw clasp. Length: 25cm, pendant: 5x4cm.
   Unmarked.

MH4. "Dove Necklace," Miriam Haskell 1950-55****
Manufacturer Miriam Haskell Jewels Ltd.
Designer Frank Hess.
   Choker with gold-plated metal filigree pendant with large orange glass paste oval stones. The clasp is surmounted by a small metal dove. Pendant: 5x6cm.
   Marked Miriam Haskell on an applied oval plaque.

MIRIAM HASKELL

MH5. "Pendant Necklace," Miriam Haskell 1950-55****
Manufacturer Miriam Haskell Jewels Ltd.
 Designer Frank Hess.
    Gold-plated metal filigree necklace, with pink glass beads,
 semilunar pink glass, pendant in the shape of a flower with
 pink and clear glass seed beads and charm made of five
 gold-plated metal chains with five pink glass beads at the
 end. Gold-plated metal hidden closure shaped like a flower
 with pink glass seed beads. Length: 35cm; pendant with
 charm: 11x4.5cm.
    Marked Miriam Haskell in an oval plaque engraved in
 the metal of the clasp and in an oval plaque applied to the
 pendant.

MH6. "Citrine Earrings," Miriam Haskell 1950-55***.
Manufacturer Miriam Haskell Jewels Ltd.
Designer Frank Hess.
    Gold-plated filigree clip earrings, with glass beads, citrine
 stones and a topaz. 2.5x3.5cm.
    Marked Miriam Haskell in an applied horse-shoe plaque.

MH7. "Sunburst," Miriam Haskell 1949***
Manufacturer Miriam Haskell Jewels Ltd.
Designer Frank Hess.
    Gold-plated filigree brooch with marquise- and rose-cut crys-
 tals and rhinestones, depicting a bursting sun. Diameter: 6.2cm.
    Marked Miriam Haskell in an applied horse-shoe plaque.
    This is probably Haskell's version of the "Sunburst" motif that
 was popular in the fine jewel version designed by the Duke of Verdura, which was interpreted many times by different costume jewelry
 manufacturers. The mark, inscribed in a horseshoe plaque, apparently dating from 1945, was applied to a line of products sold exclusively
 to a Chicago or New England store (according to more recent research,
 this mark dates from after 1949-50).

MH8. "Green Parure," Miriam Haskell
1950-1955*****
Manufacturer Miriam Haskell Jewels Ltd.
Designer Frank Hess.
   Set composed of an asymmetric
choker, a bracelet and clip earrings
with green glass beads (of differing
sizes in the choker), green stones
and rose montée with rhinestones
and baguettes on the hidden
clasps and on the star-shaped
earrings. Choker: 19cm (closed);
bracelet (closed): 5cm; earrings:
2.5x2.5cm.
   Marked Miriam Haskell in an
oval stamped on choker and
bracelet and on the button at
the base of the earring clip.

MH9. "Sautoir," Miriam Haskell 1946-1949****
Manufacturer Miriam Haskell Jewels Ltd.
Designer Frank Hess.
  Four strand pearl necklace with two pendants with
pearl pavé and six pearl strands. The lock is made of
gold-plated filigree with pearls, seed pearls and rhinestones. When open, one of the two necklace extremities
can be inserted. Length: 34cm.
  Unmarked

MH10. "Parure," Miriam Haskell 1970-78*****
Manufacturer Miriam Haskell Jewels Ltd.
Designer Larry Vrba.

Set composed of necklace, brooch and earrings made of polished white metal and rhinestones: the necklace is made of square filigree links with a central motif consisting of three rhomboid plaques shaped like fleur-de-lis at the base and central rhinestone-studded umbo. Each plaque measures 5.5x5.5cm.

Round brooch with central umbo and margins with rhinestone-studded chains. Diameter: 5cm.

Clip and screwback dangle earrings, with rhinestone-studded rhomboid plaque, 5cm.

Marked Miriam Haskell on an applied oval plaque. All items are marked, and the earrings also bear the patent number of the mechanism, Pat. n. 2,400,513. The patent was assigned to Marcus Jellinek, Larchmont, NY., on 21st May 1946 and filed on 4th October 1944. However, according to Sanford Moss, it was only used by the company from 1960.

HESS-APPEL

In 1940 Lester L. Hess was working for Nat Levy – Urie Mandel, Corp., for which he designed and patented two pins portraying band leaders (NLUM1.). Soon after the company folded, in July 1942, Hess and Jack H. Appel established Hess-Appel with company headquarters at 309 Fifth Avenue, New York. Hess-Appel was already in business in June 1943, when Hess took a leave of absence due to receiving a government appointed position as production officer at Fort Monmouth, NJ, although this did not prevent him from continuing to design for the company (WWD, 4th June 1943). At this time, the firm already owned the trademark Jollé, although it was not yet impressed on the jewelry. On 30th July 1943 WWD presented with much fanfare the "Russian Dancers" (HA2.) which was also shown in a picture together with a brooch of a peacock.

Hess-Appel's best production features sterling and, frequently, enamel jewelry and dates from the first years of the company (1943-1946). The Jolle trademark (which was without the accent, unlike the version of the word used in advertisements) began to be regularly stamped on Hess-Appel items from 1944.

The company Jelly Bellies, like those manufactured for the spring 1945 collection (WWD, 16th March 1945), which included a "Heart Bird," an apple, a fish and a winged insect, were stamped with the Jolle trademark.

Another designer who worked for the company, in addition to Lester L. Hess, was George E. Fearn (HA1.), a freelancer who also collaborated with Kaufman & Ruderman (Karu).

WWD, July 30, 1943: "Russian Dancers" and peacock by Hess-Appel.

Twin lapel ornaments, dancing Russian figurines, masculine and feminine, are luxuriously detailed with colored enamel and rhinestones, in sterling silver, gold-plated.

The graceful peacock with high coiling tail feathers also uses rhinestones, with rich, dark blue tones on the breast. These are high quality pieces from the new line of Hess-Appel.

HA1. "Card Dancers," Hess-Appel 1947****
Manufacturer Hess-Appel, Inc., New York.
Designer George E. Fearn.
Patents n° 146,467, (man), 146,468 (woman), George E. Fearn, New York, 18th March 1947, filed 28th May 1946, assignor to Hess-Appel, New York, a firm composed by Lester L. Hess and Jack H. Appel.

Pair of gold-plated sterling brooches, with red and black enamel, pearls and rhinestones, depicting two dancers wearing costumes with the four playing card symbols: hearts, diamonds, spades and aces. The man is holding a stick with a heart at the top. Man: 6.5x5.3cm; woman: 6x4.5cm.
Marked Jolle Sterling (both).
George E. Fearn was a freelance designer who also worked for Kaufman & Ruderman (Karu).

Gold-plated sterling brooches, red, pink, yellow and blue enamel, rhinestones, of a couple of Russian dancers. Lady: 4.8x2.9cm, Man: 4.9x3.7cm. Marked Sterling Pat'D 110202 (both).
This does not refer to the patent number but to the provisional number assigned to the application.
The "Russian Dancers" featured in an advertisement in *WWD,* 30th July, 1943.

HA2. "Russian Dancers," Hess-Appel 1943****
Manufacturer Hess-Appel, Inc., New York.
Designer Lester L. Hess.
Pat. Lady 136,741 Lester L. Hess, New York, 30th November 1943, filed on 13th May 1943, Man 138,056 Lester L. Hess, New York, 6th June 1944, filed 13th May 1943.

HOBÉ

The history of the Hobé family, who were possibly of Hungarian or German descent, began in Paris, France, where, around the year 1848, the goldsmith master Jacques Hobé was working.

Vogue, March 1, 1948: "Jewelry of Legendary Splendor" by Hobé.

According to information supplied by the company itself, there was a trademark featuring the name Hobé inscribed in a lily which was already in use before 1868, although it is not known whether it was stamped on the jewelry or not. After 1868 the company used a different trademark which featured the name of the company inscribed in a five point crown. From 1883 to 1902 a newly designed trademark was used: it featured the company name surmounted by two crossed swords. From 1903 to 1917, the trademark in use was the company name inscribed in an oval. Unfortunately there is no trace of production with this trademark, which probably consisted of precious jewels manufactured in France and Germany. For this reason, any information relating to Hobé trademarks should be dealt with cautiously.

Around 1889 one of Jacques's children, who was also called Jacques, came up with the idea of using the new techniques arising from the industrial production of jewelry which were being tested in the States, particularly in Providence, to manufacture precious jewelry at lower prices, thus making them accessible to a larger public.

US immigration Office documents provide more precise information about Jacques II and his son, William W. According to these documents, the latter was in the United States four times, twice in 1910 (18th March and 23rd October), once in 1922 (4th August) and once in 1923 (16th October).

The 1910 documents report that William was a German citizen, born in 1881 in Berlin, where his father Jacques, a "merchant" by profession, lived, and that he was a non-immigrant alien, with a house in New York. Interestingly, in these documents William was once registered as being "single," on 23ʳᵈ October 1910, and once as being "married," on 18ᵗʰ March of the same year. 1910 was probably the year in which he married Silvia. On 10ᵗʰ January 1922, by decision of the District Court of New York, William became an American citizen, living in New York, at 700 Broadway Embassy Hoke. In 1923 he was still living in New York, at 219 W. 37ᵗʰ St.

Before setting up his own company, William worked in a firm owned by Jacques Fath, Philippe Mangone, and Pierre Hobé (his uncle) which manufactured embroidered dresses and theatre costumes. It was while working as a salesman for this company, that, around the mid-1920s, William met the famous impresario Florence Ziegfeld, who, in addition to ordering costumes, ordered jewelry to go with them. This meeting marked the beginning of William's fortune, and, in 1927, he opened a workshop for the production of costume jewelry (and accessories, including buttons. William patented the design of a button on 26ᵗʰ July 1927 n. 73,130, based on an application dated 16ᵗʰ March 1925). The company was called Hobé Cie Limited and had offices in New York, 10 E. 49ᵗʰ St. The company still exists today and, until some time ago, was run by members of the same family. The plant, which is still situated at Mount Vernon (N.Y.), presently employs about eighty workers and the company has showrooms in New York, Los Angeles, and Dallas.

Nothing is known about Hobé production between 1927 and 1938. On 22ⁿᵈ February 1938, William Hobé patented his first three designs; two brooches, one shaped like a shield, the other round, and a bracelet with large squares combining Egyptian inspired motifs and filigree.

The *Jewelers Circular Keystone* of March 1938 featured an advertisement for Hobé offering jewelry of his own design. His jewelry was made of sterling silver and semi-precious stones and was entirely hand-made by a group of artists and master artisans. Its prices ranged from $1 to $10 a piece – and it was characterized by the use of precious metals, 14K gold and silver, and semi-precious stones, jewelry made entirely by hand, sometimes with the assistance of Hobé himself, and antique jewelry inspiration. These remained constant features of Hobé's production throughout the period being considered and also account for the very high sales prices of the items, the differences between the artifacts and the patented designs and their present rarity. William Hobé was an antique jewelry collector and a scholar who lectured on Medieval Art at the Sorbonne, in Paris.

On 15ᵗʰ October 1939 *Vogue* featured an extraordinary bib necklace with matching brooch, earrings and bracelet with "wet moss" colored stones set in gold-plated silver.

Vogue, October 15, 1939: Hobé sterling jewelry.

From then on and up to 1ˢᵗ February 1949, William Hobé patented for the two traditional seasons of spring-summer and fall-winter, 108 designs including the three mentioned above. The designs mainly featured brooches with vegetation motifs, particularly bunches of leaves and flowers, shuttle brooches, bows, baskets, hearts. The designs included only a few figurative subjects, such as a "Tibetan" chessman (1944), a theme that was developed in unpatented designs (H12. and H14.), a bracelet with a clasp in the shape of a hand and a heart-shaped pendant, a brooch of three doves in flight, and again a bracelet with two charms in the shape of a coach and a star.

Hobé's jewelry was mostly made of silver, and many items were gold-plated (20% 14K gold), a typical feature of Hobé's creations which makes his products refined and precious. This particular gold finish was achieved by means of a proprietary electrolytic process called "Formula 70." The items that were gold-plated in this way, usually bore the words "1/20 14K on sterling" inscribed in a rectangular or square plate, together with the usual Hobé trademark. At the beginning and at the end of the period being reviewed in this book, Hobé also made some metal items. The most valuable Hobé jewelry featured a combination of metal or sterling with stones of various sizes, cuts, and colors.

From May 1948 to 7ᵗʰ September 1948, the company patented a series of beautiful designs by Sylvia Hobé, William's wife, who had become a partner in the company in 1943 together with their sons Donald and Robert. The patented designs include an extraordinary series of oriental figures called "Ming," with faces and bodies made of sealing wax red plastic in imitation of a Chinese wood called "bandora." Sylvia also designed "chessman," albeit a smaller version than William's. Other subjects were cameos and of vaguely Victorian figurines. Many pieces, in particular the oriental figurines, were still made of silver with the usual 1/20 14K golden finish. Another designer, Lou Vici, is known to have collaborated with Hobé from the 1930s to the 1970s, but there are no documents of his work.

The trademark stamped on jewelry of the period being reviewed here, is just Hobé, sometimes inscribed in rectangular plates or in plates shaped like obtuse or acute triangles which were applied or stamped. Sometimes the name Hobé was accompanied by the words Sterling, Design. Pat., 1/20 14K.

Several sources reproduce a diagram, possibly coming from the firm itself, reporting all its trademarks with the relevant periods of use. Unfortunately this diagram is not reliable, as shown both by the trademarks of the patented items, and by the blatant errors it contains, such as the dating from 1918-1932 of the trademark Hobé Design. Pat. inscribed in an obtuse triangle. This date precedes any patent by Hobé and even the production of costume jewelry by the firm (which began in 1927).

H1. "Shield Clip," Hobé 1939*****
Manufacturer Hobé Cie, Ltd.
Designer William W. Hobé.
Not patented.
Antique gold-plated metal filigree clip with gold-plated metal flowers, central blue lucite cabochon, surrounded by three transparent lucite cabochons, variously cut, blue, red and white stones, in Empress Eugenie style. 6.5x5cm.
Marked Hobé on an applied rectangular plaque.

H2. "Heart," Hobé 1946****
Manufacturer Hobé Cie, Ltd.
Designer William W. Hobé.
Patent n° 145,214 William W. Hobé, New York, 16th July 1946, filed on 27th August 1945.

Gold-plated metal heart-shaped brooch, surmounted by a plume with a large heart shaped aquamarine at the center, surrounded by variously cut white and azure stones of different sizes. 7x4.7cm.
Marked Hobé on an applied rectangular plaque.
The brooch is part of a set including earrings and a ring.

H3. "Square Brooch," Hobè 1945****
Manufacturer Hobé Cie, Ltd.
Designer William W. Hobè.
Patent n° 141,303 William W. Hobè, New York, 22nd
May 1945, filed on 8th March 1945.

Sterling brooch with gold-plating 1/20th
14K gold, with amethyst color crystal in
the centre. 5.5x6.5cm.
Marked Hobé 1/20th 14K ON STER-
LING DESIGN PAT'D.

H4. "Square Pin & Earrings," Hobé 1939*****
Manufacturer Hobé Cie, Ltd.
Designer William W. Hobé.
Not patented.
   Set of antique gold-plated metal brooch and earrings. The set is made of filigree
with a minute patterns of leaves and flowers and a large rectangular amethyst at
the center, surrounded by citrine stones and amethysts. Brooch 4.8x5.4cm; screw-
back earrings 2.4cm.
   Marked Hobé on an applied rectangular plaque. The earrings are unmarked.

H5. "Pendant Brooch," Hobé 1945****
Manufacturer Hobé Cie, Ltd.
 Designer William Hobé.
  Not patented.
   Sterling brooch with gold plating
1/20th 14K, pink and amethyst stones.
10x4.7cm.
   Marked Hobé 1/20th 14K ON STER-
LING DESIGN T'D.

H6. "Brooch and Earrings," Hobé
1946****
Manufacturer Hobé Cie, Ltd.
Designer William W. Hobé.
Patent n° 143,486 William W. Hobé,
New York, 8th January 1946, filed on
22nd August 1945.

Gold-plated metal brooch and earrings, blue crystals and
rhinestones. Brooch 6x7.5cm, earrings 3x2.8cm.
Brooch marked Hobé, earrings unmarked.

H7. "Arrow with Hearts," Hobé
1945***
Manufacturer Hobé Cie, Ltd.
Designer William W. Hobé.
Patent n° 141,344 William W.
Hobé, New York, 22nd May 1945,
filed on 8th March 1945.

White and gold-plated sterling brooch, with 1/20th 14K gilding, depicting two hearts pierced by an arrow. The hearts are ornamented with
gold foil leaves and flowers and feature a central heart-shaped green
stone. The hearts are welded to the arrow. 10x3cm.
    The brooch is unmarked possibly due to the loss of the usual
triangular plate applied to Hobé items in this period. In this
particular case the mark must have been Hobé Sterling 1/20th
14K. However, the correct attribution of this item is made possible because of the manufacturing and gilding techniques used and
comparisons with items created at the same time and with the patent.

H8. "Sapphire Set," Hobé 1945*****
  Manufacturer Hobé Cie, Ltd.
  Designer William W. Hobé.
  Not patented.
    Set composed of white and gold
  plated sterling necklace and two
  bracelets, with 1/20 14K gilding. The
  items feature sapphire blue square and
  rectangular stones.
    The necklace has a large hinged link
  chain and a large round pendant entirely
  ornamented with an intricate pattern of
  roses and leafs. A sapphire is set at the center.
Length 49cm, pendant diameter 5.5 cm.
    Bracelet made up of five oval links joined
  by a small sterling ring, ornamented with
  gold-plated leaves and square sapphires. The
  bracelet has a hook clasp. Length 19cm, width
  2.5cm.
    Bracelet made up of seven square links joined
  together, with leaves and flowers and a rectangular
  sapphire at the center. Length 19cm, width 2.5cm.
    Marked Hobé STERLING 1/20 14K in an engraved
  triangle. The same mark appears on all the items.
    The items can be precisely dated to the spring of 1945
  since they compare with designs that were patented in
  that period.

H9. "Navette," Hobé 1942***
Manufacturer Hobé Cie, Ltd.
Designer William W. Hobé.
Not patented.
     Shuttle shaped sterling brooch with engraved leaves and relief flowers. 6.8x3.5cm
     Marked Hobé STERLING on an engraved triangular plaque.

H10. "Bunch of Flowers," Hobé
     1942***
     Manufacturer Hobé Cie, Ltd.
     Designer William W. Hobé.
     Patent n° 132,323 William Hobé,
     New York, May 5th 1942, filed
     March 31st 1942. See also n°
     132,324, same date.

     Sterling brooch of
a bunch of flowers and
leaves tied with a bowknot.
8.5x4.4cm.
     Marked Hobé STERLING on an
applied rectangular plaque.
     This brooch is a synthesis of two
patented design, as is often the
case with Hobé's floral items of this
period.

H11. *"Bracelet,"* Hobé 1941****
Manufacturer Hobé Cie, Ltd.
Designer William W. Hobé.
Patent n° 126,785 William W. Hobé, New York, 22nd April 1941, filed on 19th March 1941.

Sterling bracelet with chain links and leaf and flower decorations. High 4cm.
Marked Hobé STERLING DESIGN PAT'D.

Sterling brooch with 1/20 14K gilding, ivory and green stones, depicting an oriental figurine described as a Tibetan by the company in an advertisement of the time. The figurine is an ivory statuette stapled onto the brooch base, wearing a large crown of golden leaves and placed on a pedestal made of golden leaves and green stones. 9x5.5cm.

Marked Hobé STERLING 1/20 14 on a pentagonal plaque.

In September 1944 Hobé patented the only design of a series of chessmen, whose total number is unknown. The patented chess piece, possibly a bishop, was given design patent n° 138,939 on 26th September 1944, in response to the application filed on 8th August 1944. Another chess piece appeared in an advertisement published by the company with the following description: "Jeweled Tibetan Chessman. Ancient Tibetan figure carved from antique ivory" (Simons, *Costume Jewelry*, II ed., p. 127, with erroneous dating from the 1920s). The advertisement referred to the showroom in Los Angeles, 311 North Beverly Drive, where the item was on sale at the relatively high price of $55, although such a price tag was justified due to the use of semi-precious materials as ivory. The brooch here reproduced could possibly represent the king, on account of its clothes and the use of a crown and scepter. Other pieces are of a pawn, a smaller sitting figure, the queen, the knight and the tower.

It has been suggested that these items were heavily influenced by, if not imitations of, Japanese "netsuke," which were wooden or ivory plaques with refined, sometimes figurative engravings. These were attached to the strings used to hang pouches and other objects from the obi, the sash worn on the kimono which originally had no pockets. Hobé was a scholar of ancient jewelry of various provenance and therefore this source of inspiration is a distinct possibility and cannot be discounted, although no documented evidence exists to support such a thesis.

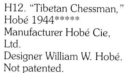

H12. "Tibetan Chessman," Hobé 1944*****
Manufacturer Hobé Cie, Ltd.
Designer William W. Hobé.
Not patented.

H13. "Red Bandora," Hobé 1948****
Manufacturer Hobé Cie, Ltd.
Designer Sylvia Hobé.
Not patented.

White and gold plated sterling brooch of an oriental face, made of sealing wax red plastic, with an elaborate headdress made of leaves and pink and citrine stones. The brooch is made of three parts applied to a sterling template. 8x5cm.

Marked Hobé 1/20th 14K ON STERLING DESIGN PAT'D on an applied square plaque.

This item, albeit not patented in this form, was certainly based on design n° 149,495 of 4th May 1948 by Sylvia Hobé, to which it is identical, except for the addition of a square piece in the end part.

H14. "Tibetan Chessman," Hobé 1944*****
Manufacturer Hobé Cie, Ltd.
Designer William W. Hobé.
Not patented.
Sterling brooch with gold plating 1/20 14K gold, ivory and green stones, in the shape of an oriental figure defined by the company in an advertisement of the time as being a "Tibetan" figure. 8.5x5cm.
Marked Hobé STERLING 1/20 14K.

H15. "White Bandora," Hobé
1948****
   Manufacturer Hobé Cie, Ltd.
   Designer Sylvia Hobé.
   Patent n° 149,753 Sylvia Hobé,
   New York, May 25th 1948,
   filed March 4th 1947.

H16. "Red Bandora," Hobé
1948****
   Manufacturer Hobé Cie, Ltd.
   Designer Sylvia Hobé.
   Patent n° 149,493 Sylvia
   Hobé, New York, May 4th
   1948, filed February 28th
   1947.

   Sterling brooch with gold plating
1/20th 14K gold and white plastic,
depicting a farmer. 6.8x4cm.
   Marked Hobé 1/20th 14K STER-
LING DESIGN PAT'D.
   From May 1948 to September
1948 Sylvia Hobé patented a series of
designs of oriental figures with white or
sealing wax-colored faces and bodies, which were made of plastic
that looked like "Bandora" a Chinese wood. This series has been
called "Ming" although the name "Bandora" was used by the
company itself to indicate these items within a group of items being auctioned at Christies.

   Sterling brooch with gold
plating 1/20th 14K gold and
wax-colored plastic, depicting
an oriental figure sitting under
some trees. 5x5.5cm.
   Marked Hobé 1/20th 14K
ON STERLING DESIGN
PAT'D.

IMPERIAL PEARL CO., INC.
See also Mrl1 (Marleen).

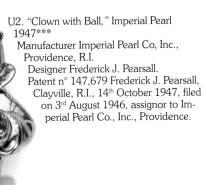

U2. "Clown with Ball," Imperial Pearl
1947***
   Manufacturer Imperial Pearl Co, Inc.,
   Providence, R.I.
   Designer Frederick J. Pearsall.
   Patent n° 147,679 Frederick J. Pearsall,
   Clayville, R.I., 14th October 1947, filed
   on 3rd August 1946, assignor to Im-
   perial Pearl Co., Inc., Providence.

   Gold-plated metal brooch with pink, blue
and clear rhinestones, depicting a running
clown clutching a large ball which is a faux
pearl. 6.9x4.1cm.
   Unmarked.

Mrs1. "Owl," Marslieu 1947***
Manufacturer Imperial Pearl Co., Inc.
Designer Frederick J. Pearsall.
Pat. n° 146,775 Frederick J. Pearsall,
Clayville, R.I., 13th May, 1947, filed
on 27th May 1946, assignor to Imperial Pearl Co., Inc., Providence.

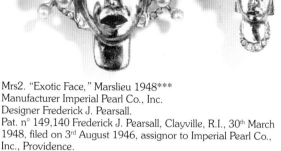

Gold-plated
sterling brooch,
glass and
rhinestones, in
the shape of an owl.
5.2x4cm.
Marked Marslieu
Sterling Pat.Pend.

Mrs2. "Exotic Face," Marslieu 1948***
Manufacturer Imperial Pearl Co., Inc.
Designer Frederick J. Pearsall.
Pat. n° 149,140 Frederick J. Pearsall, Clayville, R.I., 30th March
1948, filed on 3rd August 1946, assignor to Imperial Pearl Co.,
Inc., Providence.

Gold-plated sterling brooch and earrings,
white pearls and rhinestones, depicting an
exotic face with an elaborate hairstyle. Brooch
5x4.3cm, earrings 2.8x2cm.
Marked Marslieu Sterling Pat. Pend. (both).
The earrings are identical to the patent, while
the head is a different version.

JOSEFF

Eugene Joseff was born in Chicago on 25th September 1905 into a family of Austrian origin. He did not follow a regular course of studies, but went from one school to another, showing a certain skill for mechanics and design. He was hired as an apprentice at a foundry and later became a camshaft draughtsman in the car industry. According to Joseff, both working experiences were very useful for his future career as a jewelry manufacturer and, later on, as a manufacturer of components for the aeronautic and electronic industries. However, his first real job was in advertising, in Chicago.

The Great Depression of 1929 and ensuing unemployment, prompted Joseff to move to California in 1930, to Hollywood, Los Angeles. The state of California had not been affected by the Great Depression and there Joseff continued to work in advertising, every now and then trying his hand at costume jewelry making, although with scarce success. Among the new friends he made in those years, one would prove to be very important for his future: Walter Plunkett (1902-1982), one of the most successful cinema costume designers, who, in 1939, designed the costumes for *Gone with the Wind*. Plunkett, on hearing Joseff's criticism of the jewelry worn by Constance Bennet in *The Affairs of Cel-*

lini, 1934, as being in complete contrast to the costumes worn by the actress, invited him to make costume jewelry more in keeping with the costumes. Thus, Joseff's wonderful career actually began in 1935 in a small, highly specialized workshop, in 1609 Cahuenga Boulevard, Hollywood, called The Sunset Jewelry Shop, and later Sunset Jewelry Co. From the start Joseff chose not to sell the jewelry he made for the movies, but to lease it, so that it could be used again for other movies. In 1937 Joseff was already known nationwide. The New York-based *Women's Wear Daily* (29th October 1937) dedicated an article to him, in which it briefly outlined his story, and mentioned the most successful movies in which his jewelry had appeared. In the article, special mention was made of an extraordinary necklace worn by Greta Garbo in *Camille* 1936, the boxes and Tibetan rosary beads of *Lost Horizon,* 1937, the tiara worn by Madeleine Carrol in *The Prisoner of Zenda,* 1937, the cross with square crystals worn by Loretta Young in *Wife, Doctor and Nurse,* 1937, and the chain with faux precious stones, the crown, and crucifix worn by Katharine Hepburn in *Mary of Scotland,* 1936. The article stated that Joseff was the author of some designs, but he mainly worked on the ideas of the movies' art directors, such as, among others, Plunkett of MGM and Royer of Twentieth Century Fox. The article ended by stating that Joseff had a project to make costume jewelry for retail sale, based on some of the designs made for the cinema and also on some of his own original designs.

In effect, retail sale production began in the spring of 1938. One of the first successful costume jewelry items made for retail was the "Head Hunter" (J1.), which was made of black tenite with golden rings in the nose and ears and chains dangling from the rings. An English silver necklace featured a pendant in the shape of a small Buddha. A heavy silver chain with charms of a gladiator's medal, a lily flower, and a Buddha was said to have been worn as a bracelet by Heather Thatcher in *Fools for Scandal,* 1938. The turtle was also made to be worn as a single brooch (J2.). Among the reproduction of items originally made for the movies, was a cross made for Loretta Young in *Wife, Doctor and Nurse,* which was made of Sheffield plate with large ruby-colored stones.

Other items made for successful movies were the ornate head-dress worn by Virginia Bruce in *The Great Ziegfeld,* 1936, and Madeleine Carrol's tiara, necklace and bracelet worn in *The Lloyds of London,* 1936. This information comes from another article published in *Women's Wear Daily* on 15th April 1938, which stated that "Joseff plans to reproduce some extraordinary costume jewelry items made for movies and to sell them to wholesalers for distribution to a limited number of outlets throughout the country. Each item will bear the trademark 'Joseff-Hollywood'. To cope with the increasing volume of production, there are plans for the construction of a new building at the back of the existing one and for the purchase of new equipment." From this quote from the article, it might be reasonable to presume that the Joseff-Hollywood trademark would only be stamped on reproductions of the items made for the cinema, but in practice, the trademark was stamped on all Joseff costume jewelry made in this period.

The outlets chosen by Joseff were mainly the great department store chains, particularly Bullock's, which organized the launch of Joseff's jewelry in style, with daily displays and color advertisements. In addition to Bullock's, other Joseff distributors were Altman, Buffum, Julius Garfinkel, Pogues, Neiman-Marcus, Wanamaker's, and Marshall Field's.

On 7th October 1938 *Women's Wear Daily* mentioned a few items for retail sale copied from movie originals, such as the "Empress Eugenie" jewelry designed by Royer and manufactured by Joseff for Loretta Young, who played Napoleon III's wife in the film *Suez* (1938) and the jewelry made for Barbara Stanwyck in *The Mad Miss Manton* (1938). One item in particular became very popular: It was a heart-shaped ring, like the one made for Norma Shirer in *Marie Antoinette,* (1938), inscribed with the words "Everything leads me to thee."

WWD, March 24, 1939: Anita Louise in the photograph, Twentieth Century Fox featured player, wears jewelry designed for her by Royer and made by Joseff of Sunset Jewelry, Co., Hollywood. The pieces sketched are also in leather designed by Valle and distributed by California Accessories, Inc., Los Angeles.

The costume jewelry items that Joseff made for the company's first presentation in New York at the McAlpin Hotel were quite formal. They included: a long lariat necklace with metal chains, epaulets which could be pinned to the shoulders or to the front of dresses or be worn like brooches, and plastic flowers. The latter were probably reproductions of a Hawaiian flower called "lei no ka oe." They were made of tenite in various colors (red, black, white, green, and grey) with gold-plated central pistils, and probably date from 1939 (J3.). All these items were marked with the words Joseff or Joseff-Hollywood written in block letters.

The Joseff trademark written in italics first appeared in 1938 and was soon used in advertisements and, later on, was stamped on jewelry. Unlike the Joseff-Hollywood trademark, which was never registered, the Joseff trademark was registered on 29th August 1947.

In 1941 Joseff opened a store at 3324 Wilshire Boulevard, Hollywood, which sold precious platinum and diamond jewelry and costume jewelry, while production was moved to a new larger plant in Burbank, California, which is still operative today. Possibly at the same time as the move, the company changed its name from Sunset Jewelry Co. to Joseff Hollywood Inc.

In 1942 the Joseff plant, like other costume jewelry companies, was almost totally converted to war production, in particular the production of airplane components. *WWD* of 6th October 1944, informed its readers that, after over two years dedicated exclusively to the production of precision components for the government, Joseff intended to go back to designing jewelry. Joseff himself stated that jewelry production would begin only when the necessary materials were available, but that he was going to start designing his first post-war collection straightaway.

At the end of the war, Joseff continued its airplane component production, progressively replacing its war-time military customers with civil aviation customers. Nowadays, this production, together with aerospace and electronic industry supplies, makes up almost the whole company business.

Glitter for the stars

American Magazine, September 1948:Eugene Joseff and Linda Darnell.

On 18th September 1948, at forty-three years of age, Joseff died in an airplane crash a few minutes after taking off from Los Angeles airport in his personal plane with destination Prescott, Arizona, where he had opened a store in 1946 and where he had recently purchased a ranch. After the death of its founder, leadership of the company was taken up by his widow, Joan Castle Joseff. The company is still in business today and it deals almost exclusively in the production of components for the civil aeronautic and space industry, as well as the electronic industry.

Until his death, the only designer of Joseff retail sale items was Joseff himself. No other designer names are known, but it is likely that the jewelry made after Joseff's death was inspired by items designed by cinema costume designers.

The company jewelry trademarks are: "Joseff" or "Joseff Hollywood" written in block letters from 1938 to 1941. It is unknown however, when the trademark "*Joseff*" written in italics and reproducing the designer's own signature started being stamped on Joseff items or on a plate which was usually round. This trademark had been in use for advertising purposes and had even been reproduced on package paper from 1938, but it was only registered in 1947. Two hypotheses can be made about this:

1) The old trademark was abandoned at the beginning of 1942, when production was moved to Burbank, the company name was changed to Joseff Hollywood, Inc., and production was converted to war supplies. In 1945, when the company resumed its costume jewelry production, the new trademark which was already well known due to advertisements, came into use.

2) The second, less plausible hypothesis, suggests that the new trademark began to be used at the same time as its registration in 1947.

This would make a correct dating of pieces with the Joseff trademark in italics a difficult task, particularly because they also include newly produced items, or rather, reproductions of older items. For this reason each Joseff item should be individually assessed and dated.

Production for the cinema continued until the end of the 1960s with a continued policy of leasing the items. Among the most successful items which were copied for retails sale, are Grace Kelly's earrings in *High Society*, (1956), and the jewelry worn by Elizabeth Taylor in *Cleopatra* (1963). In these cases, as in the past, the designs were made by movie costume designers, while the company staff was responsible for transforming them into industrial designs.

Generally Joseff's costume jewelry, which was very showy and large, was made of metal, typically with a matt yellow gold plating or burnished silver finish. Compared to other costume jewelry makers, Joseff made rather little use of rhinestones, privileging instead medium-large faceted stones or cabochons, reproducing topazes, amethysts, turquoises, rubies, emeralds and sapphires. Sterling and other materials like ceramic were also little used. The items were manufactured by casting or molding.

J1. "Headhunter," Joseff 1938*****
Manufacturer Sunset Jewelry Co., Hollywood.
 Designer Eugene Joseff.
    Black tenite brooch of a head, similar to a headhunter's trophy, with large golden nose ring and long loop earrings with gold plated metal fringes. 12x5cm.
    Marked Joseff in block letters.
    The brooch belonged to the first collection made by Joseff for retail sale, which was made up of original designs and items made for the cinema. Among these was a charm necklace made of heavy silver-plated metal with several charms, worn as a bracelet by Heather Tatcher in the film Fools for Scandal (1938) and the cross designed for Loretta Young in Wife, Doctor and Nurse (1937). The "Headhunter," the original name of one of the most successful items (*WWD*, 15th April 1938) was exclusively designed for J. W. Robinson Co., Los Angeles store, and was on sale for $6.95. The model was made both in black and white tenite. Tenite is a thermoplastic material available in all colors, which had been patented in 1934 by Eastman Tennessee Co., a subsidiary of Eastman Kodak Company, Kingsport, Tennessee.
    It is an interesting point that Joseff had just one design patented - a ring – and all his other designs were unpatented. Another point of interest is the fact that he made use both of casting and molding techniques, especially for his later items. Only the molded items are specified on the cards since all the non-specified items are cast items.

J2. "Turtle," Joseff 1938***
Manufacturer Sunset Jewelry Co., Hollywood.
Designer Eugene Joseff.
Molded gold-plated metal brooch of a turtle. 5x3.8cm.
Marked Joseff-Hollywood.
    The turtle was made to be worn as a charm on a necklace which also had the following charms: a medal with the image of a gladiator, a lily and a Buddha. The necklace could also be worn as a bracelet as Heather Tatcher did in the film Fools for Scandal (1938).

J3. "Lei no ka oe," Joseff 1939****
  Manufacturer Sunset Jewelry Co., Hollywood.
   Designer Eugene Joseff.
     White tenite brooch of a Hawaiian lei no ka oe flower, with tenite petals and burnished gold-plated metal pistils in relief. Diameter: 7.5cm.
     Marked Joseff-Hollywood.
     This item was described in *Women's Wear Daily*, 7th July 1939, as being part of the fall collection presented at the McAlpin Hotel of New York. The model was made in several color variants. The petals used were also used as pendants in bracelets and necklaces.

J4. "Choker," Joseff 1939*****
Manufacturer Sunset Jewelry Co., Hollywood.
Designer Eugene Joseff.
   Heavy burnished white-metal choker with double braided chain with engraved links.
Length: 42cm, width: 2.5cm.
   Marked Joseff-Hollywood.
   A gold-plated metal version of the same model was also made. It had been designed for the personal wardrobe of actress Kay Francis and was also worn by the actress Mary Astor in the movie Woman against Woman, a provisional title taken from the Joseff archives, the final version of which is unknown. A picture of this item was published in Glamour, May 1939. The choker was on sale at J. L. Hudson, a Detroit store.

Glamour, May 1939. Joself

J5. "Fish," Joseff 1938****
Manufacturer Sunset Jewelry Co.,
Hollywood.
Designer Eugene Joseff.
Gold-plated metal brooch in the shape of a fish. 3.5x3.8cm.
Marked Joseff Hollywood.

J6. "Owls," Joseff 1938**** Manufacturer Sunset Jewelry Co., Hollywood. Designer Eugene Joseff.

Pair of gold-plated metal brooches, of two owl heads, one larger one smaller. 3x3.7cm, 2x2.5cm. Marked Joseff Hollywood.

J7. "Belle Watling Bell Earrings," Joseff 1942**** Manufacturer Joseff of Hollywood, Inc., Burbank. Designer Walter Plunkett.

Gold-plated metal earrings in the shape of bells with mobile dong. 3x2cm. Marked Joseff.

These earrings were worn by Belle Watling in the film "Gone With The Wind" in the scene where Rhett Butler bids her farewell. The original design was probably made by Walter Plunkett, costume designer of the film. Joseff later manufactured these earrings for retail trade.

Jewelers' Circular Keystone, May 1939

The necklace and armband set was designed for the actress Joy Hodges who wore them in the film "They Asked For It." Vera West, of Universal Studio, designed a powder blue knit ensemble.

J8. "Amethyst Pin," Joseff 1947-50**** Manufacturer Joseff of Hollywood, Inc., Burbank Designer Eugene Joseff.

Burnished and engraved gold-plated metal brooch with large faceted, rectangular, amethyst crystals. The brooch is of a twig with leaves and flowers. 12x7cm. Marked Joseff in italics on a round plaque.

As the brooch size and its mark suggest, it was probably made after a 1940 model.

J9. "Oak Necklace," Joseff 1939***** Manufacturer Sunset Jewelry Co., Hollywood. Designer Eugene Joseff. Gold-plated metal necklace with oak-leaf motif chain and pendant in the shape of oak leaves and acorns. The pendant made to be worn also as a brooch. 7x6.5cm. Marked Joseff Hollywood.

J10. "Elephant Head," Joseff 1947-50****
Manufacturer Joseff of Hollywood, Inc., Burbank.
Designer Eugene Joseff.
     Burnished gold-plated metal brooch, with
pearls and variously colored rhinestones,
depicting an elephant's head.
5x4cm.
     Marked Joseff in italics
engraved on metal.
     This item belonged to
a set including a neck-
lace with pendants
and earrings.

J11. "Camel," Joseff 1947-50****
Manufacturer Joseff of Hollywood, Inc., Burbank.
Designer Eugene Joseff.
     Burnished gold-plated fretwork metal brooch, with cabo-
chons and variously colored rhinestones, depicting a saddled
camel. 7.7x6.2cm.
     Marked Joseff in italics on a round plaque.

J12. "Renaissance Choker," Joseff 1950****
Manufacturer Joseff of Hollywood, Inc., Burbank.
     Burnished gold-plated metal choker with tubular chain and large pen-
dant held in place by a baroque style barrette. The medallion features
an outer frame made of small spheres joined to the central rosette by
four rectangular azure stones. The rosette features a relief subject of
cherubs with flower garlands on a lace-like engraved background.
The relief was designed to resemble the style of Luca della Rob-
bia. Medallion diameter: 11cm.
     Marked Joseff in italics on a round plaque.
     This item could well verify Joan Castle's statement concern-
ing the assembly of existing components for Joseff items. The
same tubular chain had indeed appeared in *WWD*, 19th July
1940, and again in 1941 around Lucille Ball's neck in an
advertisement for the movie Look Who's Laughing. It is an
open choker that ends with two spheres that have hanging
fringes. The choker has an identical bracelet. The chain appears again with the same ends as those of the "Renaissance
Choker" in two bracelets worn by Marlene Dietrich in the film
Kismet (1944).
     WWD, 25th August 1950, featured the "Renaissance" collec-
tion, which included the choker, with the following words: "The
Italian Renaissance period reflected in baroque motifs, cherubs,
serpents and filigree designs, is the big story at Joseff-Hollywood.
Featuring antique gold and silver finish metals, the costume pieces
included in the group are sometimes accented with small pearls, gold
beads and polished Czechoslovakian crystals. Clip on belt ornaments and
oversize, lightweight pins are especially new, although the drop earrings,
bracelets and pendant-type necklaces on heavy chains are all interesting."

In 1944 two new jewelry lines were introduced: "Toddle-Tot," a line of children's jewelry, made of 14 and 10 carat gold and silver, and "Walburt" (*WWD*, 9th June 1944), named after Walter's two sons, Walter, Jr., and Burton. The person responsible for the line, whose slogan was "Style interpreted in Jewels," was Maybelle Manning, while Ira Barzilay, who had acquired much experience working independently in the field of costume jewelry, was in charge of sales. "Walburt" had a showroom at 48 W48th Street, where Lampl had its headquarters. The line was discontinued in 1946.

On 6th August 1945 Walter Lampl died of a heart attack at 50. The company however remained in business under the leadership of Walter's wife Sylvia and son Walter, Jr., until its closure in 1959.

Jewelry was designed by company staff, including Nat Block and June Redding, but all designs had to be examined and approved by Walter Lampl, who was also the holder of all patents.

The trademarks used were WALTER LAMPL or LAMPL or, occasionally, WL, in block letters; by Lampl, in italics and, more frequently, WL inscribed in a shield. Some items are not marked but can be recognized by the fact that they are identical to patented designs.

WL2. "Chinese Maid," Walter Lampl 1940****
Manufacturer Walter Lampl, New York.
   Not patented.
   Gold-plated metal pin clip, green, pink, red and black enamel, small stones in various colors, rhinestones, of a Chinese maid with a traditional dress and fan. 7.5x3.5cm.
   Unmarked.
   This design is not patented but is certainly a variant of Des. No. 120,462, 7th May 1940 by Walter Lampl (WL1.).

WL1. "Chinese Couple," Lampl 1940****
Manufacturer Walter Lampl, Inc.
Designer Walter Lampl.
Patent n° 120,446 (man), n° 120,462 (woman), Walter Lampl, New York, 7th May 1940, filed on 30th March 1940.

WL3. "Watch Pin," Lampl 1941***
Manufacturer Walter Lampl, Inc.
Not patented.
   Gold-plated relief metal brooch, of a convex fretwork box with fringes. The box is open and inside it is a watch marked Imperial. 3.4x6.4cm.
   Marked Walter Lampl.
   Lampl's brooches with hidden watch are mentioned in *WWD*, 3rd October 1941, together with the picture of a palm-shaped brooch with watch.

   Pair of gold-plated metal pin clips with pink, green, black and yellow enamel and rhinestones, depicting a Chinese man and woman. The man is holding a flower with a red stone in the middle, a possible gift for the woman. Man: 5x2.9cm; woman: 5.1x1.5cm.
   Marked Patent Pend. (both).

LISNER - SCHIAPARELLI
See also Jelly Bellies in Volume 2.

WWD, January 1, 1930: V-shaped Necklaces by Lisner.

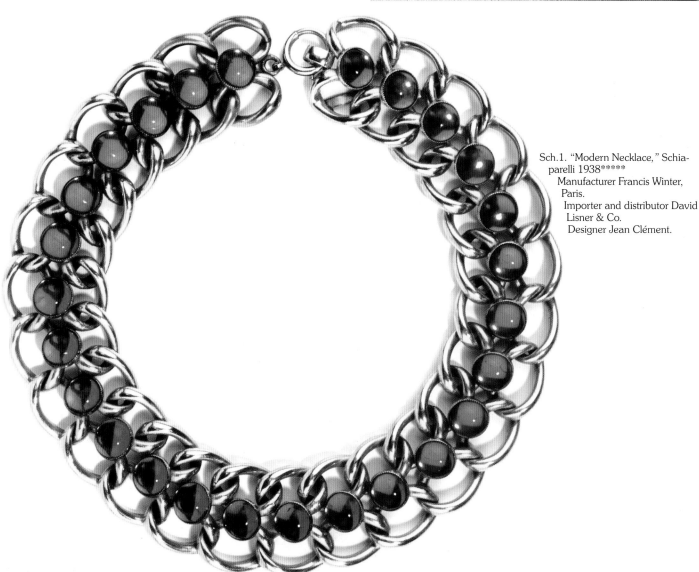

Sch.1. "Modern Necklace," Schia-parelli 1938*****
   Manufacturer Francis Winter, Paris.
   Importer and distributor David Lisner & Co.
   Designer Jean Clément.

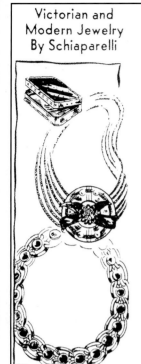

Victorian and Modern Jewelry By Schiaparelli

Examples of period and modern costume jewelry from a collection designed by Schiaparelli and now being distributed here under the couturiere's label. Victorian pieces in black enamel and gold are strongly represented in the collection. Two examples are the saccharine box sketched here — which might be used for aspirin or vitamin capsules — and the choker necklace in flexible gilt chain with jeweled cluster at the throat. Below, a modern necklace in gold links set with cabochon stones.

Also in this collection and not illustrated here, are pieces of Louis XIV inspiration — pendant necklaces, chatelaines, bracelets in leaf designs — "East Indian" jewelry in massive, stone-set pieces, and a variety of other modern pieces in metal and stone.
From D. Lisner & Co., authorized agent.
Distributed through D. Lisner & Co.

WWD, August 19, 1938: Schiaparelli jewelry imported and distributed through D. Lisner & Co.

Gold-plated metal knitting design necklace with sapphire-blue cabochons. Cm 3.3h stitch.
Marked Schiaparelli.
Although designed and produced in France for Schiaparelli, this necklace can rightfully be described as being American costume jewelry because it was imported and distributed by David Lisner & Co., Schiaparelli's authorized agent in the United States. The necklace was featured in *WWD* 19th August 1938 with this information.
David Lisner & Co. was one of the most important producers of costume jewelry at the time. The company, (which was based in New York, 303 Fifth Avenue) was founded in 1904 by Sidney Lisner and Saul Ganz.

NAT LEVY-URIE MANDLE CORPORATION – URIE F. MANDLE

WWD, January 13, 1956: Urie F. Mandle.

In 1937 Urie F. Mandle, who was born in 1876 and had worked for Coro (1901-1926) and Lisner (1926-1937), joined Nat Levy & Co, a company established in 1931 by Nat Levy, before Wertheimer, Levy & Co. From then on, the company name was Nat Levy-Urie Mandle Corporation, with offices in New York, first at 302 and later at 411 Fifth Avenue.

In 1938 the company obtained an exclusive license for the production of charms of the famous Tony Sarg puppets (Anthony Frederick Sarg 1881-1942), which proved to be a commercial success. In 1940 Lester L. Hess worked for the company as a designer. Between the end of 1942 and the beginning of 1943, together with Jack H. Appel, he founded the firm Hess & Appel. In 1940 Hess designed and patented for Nat Levy-Urie Mandel two pins representing a "Band Leader" (NLUM1.).

In July 1942 the company went into liquidation due to a lack of raw materials caused by wartime rationing, as stated by the partners in an open letter published in *WWD*, 17th July 1942.

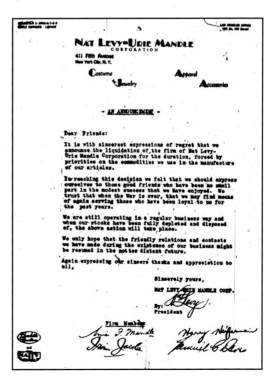

WWD, July 17, 1942: letter announcing the liquidation of Nat Levy-Urie Mandle Co.

WWD, February 18, 1938: Tony Sarg Marionette Charms by Nat Levy-Urie Mandle Co.

In effect the two former partners went on working, though separately: Nat Levy with Nat Levy & Co. advertised in *WWD*, 21st May 1943, presenting, among others, a brooch patented in his own name (Des. 135,782 of 8th June 1943. See also Des. 135,780 – 781 – 783). His company ceased operations probably towards the end of the 1940s.

Urie Mandle, after a short period in which he shared an office with the staff of Heller-Deltah, 411 Fifth Avenue (*WWD* 12th December 1942), founded the firm Urie F. Mandle Co., opening a showroom at 411 Fifth Avenue. This company distributed under the trademark "Uro Creations" costume jewelry manufactured and supplied by several firms.

WWD, January 1, 1947: Uro creations by Urie F. Mandle Co.

These included S. J. Bush, Inc., New York, an importer of Sterling Mexican Jewelry; Mandel Bead & Import Co., New York, a manufacturer of the "Karen Lyne Creations" jewelry, as well as other unknown manufacturers of costume jewelry from California and Florida. The company also distributed products of firms from other sectors, including Kroywen Pottery Inc., New York, a manufacturer of artistic ceramics. Later advertisements published in *WWD* indicated the names of the other represented firms, including, among costume jewelry manufacturers: Leonard Hover Co. of Los Angeles Ca., with creations by Jean Le Seyeux; Ernie Frank of Los Angeles with "Macaroni Jewelry," and Burger Specialty Co., of Miami, Florida.

WWD, February 4, 1944: advertisement showing the firms represented by Urie F. Mandle Co.

Among the companies represented by or manufacturing for Urie F. Mandle was Goldseal Manufacturing Jewelers, a manufacturer who owned the Murray Slater (UM2., UM3., UM4., UM5.) patents. The Murray Slater – Urie F. Mandle connection was based on the fact that Slater's "Dagger" (UM2.) was manufactured for Urie F. Mandle Co., as indicated in an advertisement published in *WWD*, 1st March 1946.

Urie Mandle continued to work independently until 1955 when, after his company went into liquidation, at almost seventy years of age, he was hired as sales manager by Paulette Jewelry.

On 21st September 1976 Urie F. Mandel died at ninety years of age. At the time he was a retired salesman for R. Mandle Inc., 389 Fifth Avenue, New York. This company which was established by his son in 1957, was joined immediately by his father on the strength of his seventy-five year career in the field of costume jewelry. He left, besides his son Robert, his wife Dora and a daughter of the same name.

NLUM1. "Band Leaders," Nat Levy-Urie Mandle 1940****
Manufacturer Nat Levy-Urie Mandle Corporation, New York.
Designer Lester Hess.
Patents n° 119,857 (man), 119,858 (woman), Lester Hess, New York, 9th April 1940, filed 15th February 1940, assignor to Nat Levy-Urie Mandle Corporation, New York.

Pair of gold-plated metal pin clips with pink, blue, white and red enamel and rhinestones, of two "Band Leaders"; a man and a woman. 6x3.5cm. Marked Patent. Pend.

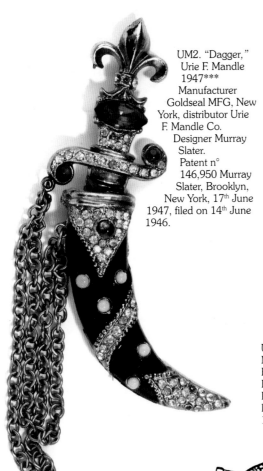

UM2. *"Dagger,"* Urie F. Mandle 1947*** Manufacturer Goldseal MFG, New York, distributor Urie F. Mandle Co. Designer Murray Slater. Patent n° 146,950 Murray Slater, Brooklyn, New York, 17th June 1947, filed on 14th June 1946.

Double gold-plated metal and enamel brooch shaped like a dagger and sheath, joined by a chatelaine. The brooch could be worn both with the dagger in the sheath or separate from it. The hilt of the dagger is ornamented with a lily, a sapphire blue marquise cut stone, rhinestones and two small cabochons. The sheath is black enameled with turquoises and rhinestone arabesques. 11x3.5cm.

Unmarked .

A metal and a sterling version of this item were made, and for this latter version, the item bore the mark Sterling.

The "Dagger" design with Urie F. Mandle's name, featured in *WWD*, 1st March 1946.

UM3. *"Dragon Head,"* Urie Mandle 1948**** Manufacturer Goldseal MFG, New York, distributor Urie F. Mandle Co. Designer Murray Slater. Patent n° 149,095 Murray Slater, Brooklyn, New York, 23rd March 1948, filed on 18th October 1946.

Relief sterling pin clip with red and white enamel, red and green stones, a triangular amethyst violet stone and rhinestones, depicting a dragon's head. 6.2x2cm.

Marked Sterling Pat. Pend.

As usual, this item was assigned the date of the patent, however this was a time in which long periods, even more than a year, elapsed from the filing of a patent application and its granting and the Pat. Pend. mark indicates that it had definitely been manufactured after 1946.

UM4. *"Cards King and Queen,"* Urie F. Mandle 1946**** Manufacturer Goldseal MFG, New York, distributor Urie F. Mandle Co. Designer Murray Slater. Patents "King" n° 145,462, "Queen" n° 145,463 Murray Slater, Brooklyn, New York, 20th August 1946, filed on 11th January 1946.

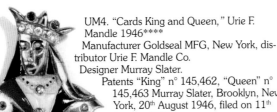

Pair of pink gold-plated sterling brooches with enamel in various colors, of a king and a queen. "King": 5x3.8cm; "Queen": 4.5x3.5cm.

Marked Sterling Pat. Pend.

The patented series included a crown with the symbols of playing cards - hearts, spades, diamonds, aces and the "Jack" and a bracelet with thin lozenge shaped links with the playing card symbols, all made in 1946. There was also an unpatented "Joker".

The brooches, joined to the playing card symbols by a chatelaine, were presented by Goldseal, a manufacturer for the wholesale market and patent holder, in the *Jewelers' Circular Keystone*, March 1946.

UM5. "Columbine & Harlequin," Urie F. Mandle 1947****
Manufacturer Goldseal MFG, New York, distributor Urie F. Mandle Co.
Designer Murray Slater.
Patents "Columbine" n° 146,751, "Harlequin" n° 146,752 Murray Slater,
Brooklyn, New York, 6ᵗʰ May 1947, filed on 14ᵗʰ June 1946.

Pair of gold-plated sterling brooches of a Columbine listening to Harlequin singing and playing the mandola. Their faces and the box of the
mandola are made of white and pale green moonstones, respectively. Columbine is wearing a dress with a rhinestone pavé bodice, pink rhinestone
collar and long black enamel gloves. Harlequin is wearing his trademark
costume with multicolored lozenges, a cocked hat with two red rhinestones,
a green rhinestone collar and clear rhinestone sleeve puffs. Columbine:
6.8x3cm; Harlequin: 6.5x5.3cm.
Columbine is marked Sterling Pat. Pend. Harlequin is marked Sterling.
At the back, the brooches feature a small ring that allows for them to
be joined together or to other musical symbols such as a treble clef by a
chatelaine. At the beginning of 1947 Urie F. Mandle publicized a line called
"Moonglo," as the largest moonstone collection of the season. Harlequin
and Columbine might possibly belong to this series.

MARLEEN

Mrl1. "Pirate Head," Marleen 1945***
Manufacturer Marleen Costume Jewelry Com-
pany, Providence, Rhode Island.
Designer Frederick J. Pearsall.
Patent n° 144,579 Frederick J. Pearsall,
Clayville, Rhode Island, 30ᵗʰ April 1946, filed
on 21ˢᵗ August 1945, assignor to Marleen
Costume Jewelry Company.

Gold-plated sterling brooch and earrings, of a pirate head. Brooch 4.8x4.5cm. Screwback ear-
rings 2cm.
The brooch is marked Marleen Sterling Pat. Pend. D. 121564 on an applied square plaque.
The earrings are marked Sterling.
Rather unusually, the patent application registration number was impressed on the item.
Therefore this item can be dated from 1945. This was a period in which many months,
sometimes more than a year, elapsed between the filing of a patent application and its granting.
The set is part of a series with pirate subjects, for which Pearsall submitted a patent application on behalf of Marleen in August 1945. Other subjects in the series are: a pirate ship, a
pirate hat and sword, the figure of a pirate with a wooden leg and sword, a gun. The "Pirate
Head" featured, together with the wooden-legged pirate, in WWD, 30ᵗʰ August 1946, in an
advertisement for Fineman & Co., Jolly Jewels of Baltimore. In the advertisement the two pirates
are described as "Swashbucklers".
Pearsall was a freelance designer who also patented other designs, which shared the trademark
feature of having small and large pearls. He did this for the Imperial Pearl Company, Inc., of Providence, R.I., which used the trademark Marslieu that was also stamped on their jewelry (Mrs1. & 2.).

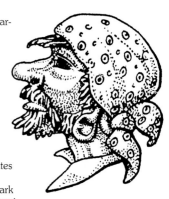

MAZER

The Mazer parents and their seven children, moved from Russia to the States some time between 1917 and 1923. The names of four of the seven brothers are known: Joseph, Louis, Abe, Harry.

Mazer's first business – apparently set up by Joseph and Louis – was the manufacturing of shoe buckles, which continued production until at least 1929 (*WWD*, 25th April 1929). The production of costume jewelry started in 1927, apparently after advice from Marcel Boucher, who, at the time, was working for Cartier New York, and from Orenstein, an importer of jewels, who was a supplier of Mazer's.

There is no evidence to sustain the theory (Farneti Cera, *I gioielli della fantasia*, p. 217) that the Mazers started their business in 1917 in Philadelphia, as Franco-American Bead and Novelty Company, manufacturing shoe buckles for Wise Shoes, before moving to New York in 1926. In reality, as stated by Joseph Mazer to *WWD*, 23rd May 1941, the business started in 1923.

Certain data concerning Mazer includes the registration of the Mazer Brothers trademark in New York on 25th June 1929 and of the names of two lines "Sea Foam" ad "Sea Maze," which were registered on 26th June 1929. Around the same time (in August 1929) the first advertisement for the company appeared in *Women's Wear Daily*. In this advertisement the firm is called Mazer Bros. and is described as a manufacturer and importer of costume jewelry, with offices at 6 West 32nd Street, NY. The firm advertised its marcasite and rhinestone baguette jewelry items, some of which were reproduced in *WWD* of 15th August.

In 1930 (*WWD*, 24th July and 31st August) the company used the trademark Mazer Brothers written in full for its advertisements; the address was the same, but the company no longer described itself as being an importer and manufacturer of costume jewelry, but only as a manufacturer of *"Fine Sterling Jewelry."* Afterwards both trademarks – Mazer Bros. (the more used) and Mazer Brothers – were alternately used in advertisements. The collections of this period were clearly inspired by European models.

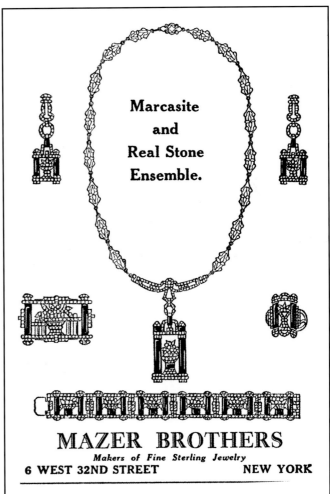

Marcasite
and
Real Stone
Ensemble.

MAZER BROTHERS
Makers of Fine Sterling Jewelry
6 WEST 32ND STREET   NEW YORK

"WWD" July 24, 1930: Jewelry by Mazer Brothers.

Probably sometime in 1930, Marcel Boucher, having left Cartier, began to collaborate with Mazer, and continued working with them until March 1937, when Boucher established his own firm. As regards the patents confirming the collaboration between Boucher and Mazer, reference is made to these in the section dedicated to Boucher.

The company was headed by Louis Mazer with the collaboration of his brothers Joseph, Abe, and Harry and, from the very start, there was a definite focus on the production of high-quality "real look" jewelry,

Numerous New Creations in Marcasite Rings with real stones. Necklets and Bracelets to match.

Mazer Brothers
6 WEST 32nd STREET, N.Y.C.

WWD, September 26, 1929: Marcasite Rings by Mazer Brothers.

with rare excursions into the field of figurative subjects, which were few and did not appear before 1939.

Mazer patented only a few designs, almost all of which were designed by Louis Mazer, except for a few items by Boucher and Joseph Wuyts (M2. and M4.), who also worked for Trifari.

Louis Mazer first patented a design of "an article of jewelry" (pat. n. 1,981,521 of 20th November 1934), and then (pat. n. 2,153,022 of 4th April 1939 filed on 28th August 1937) a mechanism to "combine" two clips into a single brooch, which, together with similar mechanisms patented for the company by Boucher, was Mazer's answer to Coro's Duette and Trifari's Clip Mates. Then, on 31st May and 21st June 1938, Louis Mazer patented a series of floral designs for four brooches and a bracelet, respectively. Two designs date from 25th April 1939, one of them being of a funny frog. Afterwards, Louis Mazer only patented five designs, two on 10th December 1940, two on 8th April, and one on 30th December 1941. The designs are of wonderful brooches shaped like masks (M1., M6., and M7.). No other design was patented between 1941 and 1949. Between 1949 and 1951 four designs of earrings and a necklace were patented for Mazer Bros. by André Fleuridas (not Fleurides, as it is sometimes written) from Westport, Connecticut, formerly with Van Cleef & Arpels, who was company head designer at the time. In 1950 Fleuridas also designed an unpatented set of a necklace, a bracelet, and earrings, called "Trianon" which Joan Crawford wore in the film *The Damned Don't Cry* of the same year.

Joseph Mazer also patented a machine to expand rings (ring expander, pat. n. 1,830,235 of 3rd November 1931, filed on 13th June 1929).

From 1929 onwards, Mazer's jewelry was advertised once in a while in *Women's Wear Daily*, whereas the first advertisements in *Harper's Bazaar* and *Vogue* appeared in 1946 and 1947, respectively. In 1941 the company moved to 20 West 33rd Street, New York. According to Joseph Mazer, who at the time was vice president of the company, the new, larger headquarters which accommodated the plant, offices, and five showrooms, were an innovative example of production organization expanding horizontally on the same floor. The plant, employing about 100 workers, was equipped with a modern dust trapping system, while the electroplating machinery was steam driven.

At the end of 1948 Louis and Joseph Mazer separated. Louis with his son Nat continued the Mazer Bros. business, as a joint stock company (Mazer Bros. Inc.) and it remained in business until its closure in the first half of the 1950s.

Joseph and his son Lincoln, born in 1924, in partnership with Paul A. Green, who had worked for 16 years at De Rosa's, began manufacturing costume jewelry under the name of Joseph J. Mazer & Co., Inc., New York 29 West 36th Street. In reality, a firm with the name of Joseph J. Mazer had already been registered on 28th September 1932. This would demonstrate that, on that date at least, Joseph had his own business in the field of precious stones and that, after separating from his brother, continued to operate with the same company name as a joint stock company, this time in the costume jewelry sector. The showroom opened in January 1949 and the first collection was the fall of 1949 collection. The first items by Joseph J. Mazer & Co. publicized in *Women's Wear Daily*, was a set of pineapple-shaped brooch and earrings with a dome shaped ring. Joseph J. Mazer, better known as Jomaz, like the trademark stamped on the items, remained in business until 1980, when it was mentioned for the last time in the *"Jewelers Board of Trade Directory."* Jomaz" production belongs for the most part to a period not considered in this review.

The trademarks stamped on the Mazer Bros items were: MAZER, in block letters, from the start of the company until the first half of 1948, when the two brothers went their separate ways; MAZER BROS., also in block letters, from the second half of 1948 until the company ceased to exist.

The trademark *Mazer* in italics surmounted by a lily flower was used as a trademark only in advertising at least from 1946 and was apparently registered in 1949.

Mazer's collections, often named with elaborate names, were mainly copies of precious jewels. The materials used were the usual ones: gold or rhodium plated metal before and after the war, sterling silver during the war and, until 1946, imported stones, often by Swarovski, and enamel. The quality of the items was always high, both in terms of materials and manufacture. There were very few figurative subjects, but they were always very beautiful (in addition to the above mentioned masks, see also M2., M3., M4., M5., and M12.). However, the constant imitation of precious jewels, especially in the second half of 1940s, created a feeling of repetitiveness, especially when, towards the end of the period herein reviewed, creative spirit and imagination began to dwindle.

M1. "Blackamoor," Mazer 1941*****
Manufacturer Mazer Brothers, New York.
Designer Louis Mazer.
Patent n° 130,951 Louis Mazer, New
York, 30th December 1941, filed on
29th October 1941.

Rhodium plated metal
pin clip, red, brown,
green and black
enamel, red and blue
stones, rhinestones,
of a blackamoor
head with a turban.
4x4cm.
Marked "12".

Gold-plated metal
pin clip with green, black
and red enamel and
rhinestones, of a seated
Maharajah with a bag
in his hands. 5x2cm.
Marked Pat. Pend.

M2. "Maharajah," Mazer 1939*****
Manufacturer Mazer Brothers, New York.
Designer Joseph Wuyts.
Patent n° 114,801 Joseph Wuyts, New York, 16th
May 1939, filed on 28th March 1939, assignor to
Mazer Brothers, New York, a copartnership.

M3. "Cambodian Dancers," Mazer 1941****
Manufacturer Mazer Brothers, New York.
Designer Louis Mazer (?)
Not patented.
Pair of gold-plated metal brooches with
green baguettes and rhinestones, depicting
two Cambodian dancers. Woman dancer:
6.4x4.2cm; male dancer: 5.2x2cm.
Marked Mazer.

M4. "Whispering of Good and Evil," Mazer 1941*****
Manufacturer Mazer Brothers, New York.
Designer Joseph Wuyts.
Patent angel n° 124,521, devil n° 124,522 Joseph Wuyts,
New York, 7th January 1941, filed on 16th October 1940,
assignor to Mazer Brothers, New York, a copartnership.

Gold-plated metal pin clips with rhinestones, of an angel
and a devil, whispering good and evil. Devil 2.7x7cm, angel
2.7x6.8cm.
Marked devil Mazer "13," angel Mazer.
The patents refers to the earrings which were
published in *Town & Country*, December 1940,
in an advertisement by Bergdorf Goodman,
as "Whispering of Good and Evil," on sale
at $10.

M5. "Black Woman," Mazer 1940*****
Manufacturer Mazer Brothers, New York.
Rhodium plated metal pin clip, black, red, yellow and ochre enamel, carved rose-cut blue and pink stones, rhinestones, depicting a black woman carrying two trays of flowers. 8.5x5.5cm.
Marked Mazer "R".

M6. "Venetian Mask," Mazer 1940*****
Manufacturer Mazer Brothers, New York.
Designer Louis Mazer.
Patent n° 123,911 Louis Mazer, New York, 10th December 1940, filed on 27th September 1940.

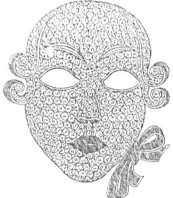

Rhodium plated metal pin clip with rhinestone pavé, red and black enamel, depicting a Venetian mask with a bowknot at the side of the neck. 6.5x4.8cm.
Marked Mazer.

M7. "Oriental Mask," Mazer 1940*****
Manufacturer Mazer Brothers, New York.
Designer Louis Mazer.
Patent n° 123,910 Louis Mazer, New York, 10th December 1940, filed 27th September 1940.

Rhodium plated metal pin clip with rhinestone pavé, red, green and blue stones, black and red enamel, depicting an oriental (Balinese) mask. 6x5cm.
Marked Mazer "13".

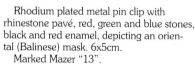

M9. "Fan," Mazer 1944***
Manufacturer Mazer Brothers, New York.
Gold and rhodium plated sterling brooch with fake turquoise cabochons, red stones and rhinestones shaped like a fan. 5.5x5cm.
Marked Mazer Sterling.

M10. "Butterfly," Mazer 1944***
Manufacturer Mazer Brothers, New York.
Gold-plated sterling brooch of a butterfly with citrine stone at the center of the body, marquise cut topazes and rhinestones on the wings. 5.3x5.8cm.
Marked Mazer Sterling.

M8. "Tribal Mask," Mazer 1941****
Manufacturer Mazer Brothers, New York.
Designer Louis Mazer (?)
Not patented.
Gold-plated metal pin clip, with red, green and blue navettes and oval stones and rhinestones, depicting an African tribal mask. 6.5x4.8cm.
Marked Mazer.

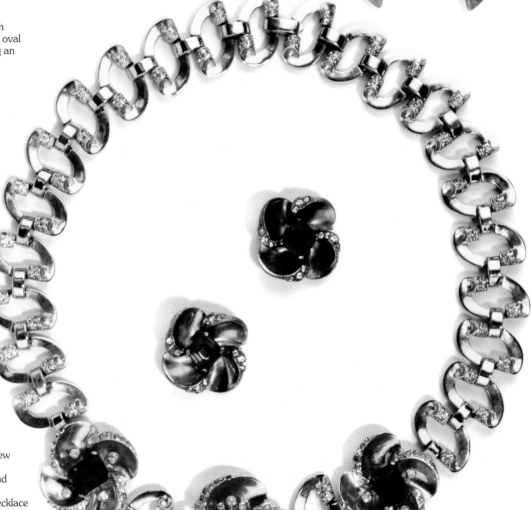

M11. "Rose Set," Mazer 1940****
Manufacturer Mazer Brothers, New York.
Gold-plated metal necklace and earrings, square red crystals and rhinestones with a rose motif. Necklace 3.5x11.5cm (central motif). Earrings 2x2cm.
Necklace marked Mazer, earrings unmarked.
A very similar set called "Solitaire" was reproduced in *WWD*, 25th October 1940.

M12. "Humming-bird," Mazer 1941****
Manufacturer Mazer Brothers, New York.
    Rhodium plated metal brooch with enamel, large amethyst stones and rhinestones, depicting a hummingbird in flight. 8x8cm.
    Marked Mazer "12".
    The spring 1941 collection (*WWD*, 3rd January 1941) included flowers, animals and birds, and its trademark was the use of enamel and the presence of a large central stone.

M14. "Flower Spray,"
Mazer 1941****
Manufacturer Mazer Brothers, New York.

WWD, August 29 1941: "Flower Spray" by Mazer.

    Rhodium plated metal brooch, sky blue and blue stones, rhinestones, in the shape of a flower spray. Matching earrings. Brooch 10.5x5.5cm, earrings 2.5x2.5cm.
    Brooch marked Mazer, earrings unmarked.
    The design of the brooch was reproduced in *WWD*, 29th August 1941.

M13. "Duck and Ducklings," Mazer 1941***
Manufacturer Mazer Brothers, New York.
    Rhodium plated metal brooch, yellow enamel, pink crystals, blue baguettes and rhinestones, depicting a duck with its ducklings. 3x5.5cm.
    Marked Mazer.

M15. "Crown Jewels," Mazer 1949****
Manufacturer Mazer Bros., Inc., New York.
    Pair of gold-plated brooches with amethyst cabochons, small red, green and blue stones, topazes and rhinestones. The brooches represent the British royal crown. "King" 6.2x5.4cm. "Queen" 4x4.3cm.
    Gold and rhodium plated brooch with green, red and blue stones, amethyst-like lucite cabochons, pearls and rhinestones, depicting the British royal globe topped by a cross. The sphere surface features an engraved motif of leaves and flowers. 8x5cm.
    Marked Mazer Bros.
    Amethysts on crowns symbolize the color of penitence, which, together with the red of martyrdom, is the color of the fabrics with which the crown is lined. The color of the lining is chosen by the new monarch.

MOSELL

Mo1. "Ram," Mosell 1941****
Manufacturer Mosell Costume Jewelry, Inc.
Designer Frederick Mosell.
Patent n° 127,708 Frederick Mosell, New York, 10th June 1941, filed on 21st January 1941.

Gold-plated metal brooch and faux turquoise stones, of a ram. 8x6.5cm.
Marked Mosell.
Only one other design, in addition to the Maltese dogs (Mo3.) and this ram, was patented by Frederick Mosell, immediately after founding the company, on 10th December 1940 (filed on 22nd October 1940), with n° 123,912. This design was one of the 'mirrors', which are among the most significant items of the 1941 spring collection.

Mo2. "A Night at the Opera," Mosell 1941*****
Manufacturer Mosell Costume Jewelry, Inc.
Designer Frederick Mosell.
Not patented.
Gold-plated relief metal brooch, with pink, black, green, white and red enamel, central clear faceted crystal and red and green rhinestones set in the metal. The brooch is of a theater stall with a man and a woman wearing, respectively, a tuxedo and an evening dress, watching a theater performance through binoculars. The man is holding an opera booklet in his left hand. 5.2x6.5cm.
Marked Mosell.

Mo3. 'Couple of Maltese Dogs', Mosell 1941****
Manufacturer Mosell Costume Jewelry, Inc.
Designer Frederick Mosell.
Pat. n° 126,403 Frederick Mosell, New York, 8th April 1941, filed on 21st January 1941.

Gold-plated metal pin clips with red enamel, of a couple of Maltese dogs. 5.8x3.4cm.
Marked US Patent Office D- 126403.
Mosell Costume Jewelry, Inc. was founded in the fall of 1940 in New York by Frederick Mosell. Its first collection for spring 1941 (which the Maltese dogs are a part of) was featured in *WWD* April 4th 1941. This first collection also included brooches in the shape of mirrors, hearts, birds, butterflies etc. Mosell was a small company with a medium to high quality range of products. Frederick Mosell was the company designer, as well as being the owner.

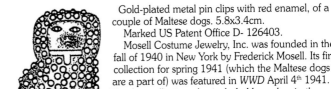

INDEX OF NAMES AND COMPANIES

Go-Gay Products Corp., ii-57 [ES1]
Goebel Porzellanfabrik GMBH KG Germany, ii-161 [U12]
Goddard, Paulette, ii-159 [U7]
Goldseal Mfg. New York, i-237 [UM4]
Goldstein, Louis, ii-163 [U16]
Gordon, Angie, i-200; ii-37
Gordon, Kathy, i-203
Granger, Stewart, ii-9 [U4]
Green, Paul A., i-156, i-240
Grosse, Heinrich, i-87

H
H.M. Schrager & Co. Inc. , ii-50ff
Handler, Elliot, i-184, i-187 [El1]
Handler Mosko, Ruth, i-184
Har – Hargo Creation, New York, i-10
Harrison, Sue, ii-51
Hartigan, John P. (Judge), i-76 [Ca2]
Hartnell, Norman, ii-59
Harry Brisbane Dick Fund, ii-213 [JB100]
Harves Jewelry, New York, ii-32 [R38]
Haskell, Miriam, i-199ff
Hattie Carnegie, i-74ff
Hawes, Elizabeth, i-76
Head, Edith, i-29
Hedi Shop, i-184
Heilbronner, Joseph, i-10
Heller-Deltah Co, Inc., ii-18
Henkel & Grosse, i-87
Hepburn, Katharine, i-36, i-222
Herbert, Sidney, ii-18
Hess – Appel, i-211ff
Hess, Frank, i-199, i-210
Hobé, i-212ff
Hodges, Joy, i-227 [J9]
Hollywood Jewelry Products Inc., i-7, i-25
Hoover, Herbert C., ii-247 [Psi30]
Hover, Leonard, i-184
Hugo, François, i-29
Hummel, Berta, ii-161 [U12]

I
Imperial Pearl Co. Inc. , i-221ff
Iribe, Paul, i-29

J
Jacques Kreisler Manufacturing Corporation, i-232ff
Jaffe, David, i-10
Jellineck, Marcus, i-210 [MH10]
Jelly Bellies, ii-172ff
Johnson, Alice, i-7, i-184
Joseff, i-222ff

K
Kamke, Ruth, i-4, i-22, i-163 – i-183
Kappel, August, i-165
Katz, Adolph, i-84 – i-91, i-155
Kaufman, Irving R. (Judge), i-12
Kaufman & Ruderman (Karu), i-211 [HA1]; ii-219 [JB120]
Kelly, Grace, i-224, i-231 [J17]

Kelly, Orry, i-25
Kimball, Abbot, ii-62
Kinnaird, Lady, ii-247 [Psi29]
Kinzler, Morris, i-200
Kipling, Rudyard, ii-35, ii-39 [RW8]
Klein, Sol, ii-45
Klipper Kantrow, Rose, i-184
Knudsen, William, ii-250 [PU38]
Korda, Alexander, ii-35 – ii-39, ii-51
Korda, Zoltan, ii-35, ii-37 [RW1], ii-39 [RW8]
Koslo Costume Jewelry Co.; i-71 [B81]
Kramer, Louis, i-10
Kraus, Abraham, i-85

L
La Fayette, Marquise de, i-6
La Tausca, ii-18
Lake, Veronica, ii-231, ii-245 [Psi25]
Lamarr, Hedy, i-231 [J17]; ii-37
Lampl, Walter, i-232ff
Lane, Kenneth J., i-10
Lancret, Nicolas, i-154 [C146]
Landaman, Irving, i-10
Lanvin, i-59
Lee, Nancy, i-184
Leigh, Vivian, i-36; ii-9 [U4]
Lelong, Lucien, i-8, i-29, i-30, i-87; ii-61
Leo Glass, i-197ff
Le Seyeux, Jean, i-184
Levey, Robert (Robert – Fashion Craft), i-10
Levitt, Edith, i-10
Levy, Harry, i-23
Levy, Nat, i-161, i-235ff
Lindbergh, Charles, i-86; ii-60
Lisner, David, ii-173
Lisner –Schiaparelli, i-234ff
Lisner, Sidney, i-234 [Sch1]; ii-173
Luster, E. J., i-65 [T5]
Lustig, Harry, ii-163 [U16]

M
MacArthur, Douglas, ii-36
MacNeil, Stanley, ii-160 [U9]
Maison Drecoll, ii-65 [T5]
Malard, Michel, ii-65 [T5]
Mandle, Robert, i-236
Mandle, Urie, i-235ff
Mangone, Philippe, i-213
Manning, Maybelle, i-233
Manzer, A., i-88
Marcel Boucher, i-40ff
Mark Louis C., ii-35-40
Markle, Willard, i-75, i-76
Margot Studio, i-184
Marleen, i-238ff
Marshal, O. Robert, ii-247 [Psi29]
Mason, Anita, i-6
Matta, Serge, ii-65 [T5]
Mattel, i-185
Mattson, Harold, i-185
Mature, Victor, ii-37
Maubussin, i-8; ii-40 [RW11]
Mayo, Virginia, i-230 [J15]
Mazer, i-239ff

McAdoo, Cynthia, i-89
McCardell, Claire, i-30, i-31
McCormick, Elsie, i-21, i-24, i-76 [Ca1], i-152 [C141], i-156; ii-136 [T182]
McDonald, Carol, i-92
McGowan, Beatrice, Grace, ii-48
McNellis, Maggie, i-89
Meadow, Noel, ii-18
Mellerio, i-119 [C54]
Milne, A. A., i-87
Mir, David, ii-61, ii-62
Miriam Haskell, i-199ff
Monet, i-14, i-16, i-27; ii-59
Moonan, Joanne, i-76
Moore, Melvin W., i-132, i-133 [C94]; ii-31 [R34], ii-166 [U25]
Morehouse, Eugene, i-132, i-133 [C94]; ii-31 [R34], ii-166 [U25]
Mori, Gioia, ii-41 [RW13]
Morris Mann & Reilly, Inc. Chicago, i-7
Mosell, i-245ff
Moss, Sanford, i-200

N
Napier Co. i-7, i-14, i-27
Nascia, Giuseppina, ii-58
Nat Levy – Urie Mandle Corporation – Urie Mandle, i-235ff
Natacha Brooks, i-72ff
Nathan, Florence, i-4, i-22, i-165, i-168 [E6], i-169 [E8, E9]
Nelson, Horatio, i-36
Nettie Rosenstein, ii-44ff
Newman, Marta, i-184
Norato, Grayce, ii-166 [U25]
Norma Jewelry Corp., i-5ff

O
Oben, A., i-185
Ogden, Jack, ii-213 [JB100]
Olga of Hollywood, i-184
Oliver Mfg. Co., i-184
Olivier, Laurence, i-36
Oppenheimer, Jerome, i-89
Ora, i-160 [DR8]
Orenstein, i-239
Oval Manufacturing Co. New York, ii-19, ii-24 [R16]

P
S. Packales & Co., ii-187 [JB35]
Palissy, Bernard (Ecole), i-40
Pamfiloff, Sheila, i-203
Panetta, i-165
Paris, Jean, ii-62
Pascal, Gabriel, ii-9 [U4]
Paschman, Morris, ii-164 [U20]
Patou, Jean, i-8, i-28, i-86, i-87
Patriotic Jewelry, ii-231
Paul, Michel, i-72, i-74
Pauzat, Charles, i-92, i-142 [C118]
Pearl, Joseph M., i-88
Pearl, Sidney, i-92
Pearsall Frederick J., i-221, i-238
Pennino, ii-5ff
Pepys, Samuel, i-95 [C2]
Perrault, Charles, i-174 [E20]
Petit, Marie, ii-166 [U26]
Petronzio, Camille, i-200

Philippe, Alfred, ii-58 – ii-156
Philippe, Jacques, ii-62
Phinney, Elisha A., i-9, i-103, i-104 [C19, C20, C21]
Piccard, Lucien, i-76
Pierangeli, Anna Maria, i-230 [J15]
Placco, Oscar, i-38 [BB1, BB2], i-92
Plastic Hollywood Arts, i-184
Plunkett, Walter, i-25, i-29, i-222, i-227 [J7]
Poiret, Paul, i-87
Poland, James, ii-243 [PGP19]
Polk, James Knox, ii-247 [Psi30]
Polignac, Comtesse de, ii-59
Porter, Cole, i-59
Powell, Michael, ii-37 [RW1]
Price, Francesca, ii-134 [T177, T178], ii-138 [T186]
Providence Jewelers Inc. , ii-9ff

R
Rains, Claude, ii-9 [U4]
Rainwater, Dorothy, ii-222 [JB126]
Ralph De Rosa, i-156ff
Ranieri of Monaco, i-231 [J17]
Rapphel Jewelers, i-148 [C129]
Rebajes, ii-10ff
Redding, June, i-233
Réja, ii-18ff
Regelmann, William, ii-160, ii-161 [U10, U11, U12]
Reines Peter, i-200
Reiter, Philip, i-60 [B49]
Rettenmeier, Frederik W., i-8, i-22
Rettenmeier, William, i-8, i-22
Revere, Paul, i-37 [AM1]
Ricarde of Hollywood, i-7, i-25
Ricciardi, Frank M., i-90
Rice & Hochster, ii-58
Rice-Weiner (Korda, McClelland Barclay) , ii-34ff
Richter's New York, ii-218 [JB117]
Rimsigeur, Charles, i-89
Rochas, Marcel, i-29
Rodriguez, José, ii-167-ii-168 [U29, U30, U31]
Rockwell, Norman, ii-233, ii-234
Roedelheimer, Edgar, i-35
Roosevelt, Franklin Delano, ii-247 [Psi30], ii-250 [PU38]
Roosevelt, Eleanor, ii-237 [PC2]
Rosenberger, George, i-89
Rosenblatt, Henry, i-85, i-89
Rosenblum, M., i-23
Rosenstein, Nettie, ii-44ff
Ross, Irwin, i-21, i-86, i-91, i-133 [C94], i-142 [C116]
Rouff, Maggy, ii-65 [T5]
Roxee Corp., i-71 [B81]
Royer, i-29, i-223
Ruben, John, i-154 [C146]
Rubin, Samuel, ii-51, II-52 [Si3]

S
Sabu, ii-36, ii-39 [RW8]
Salz Mfg. Co., i-184
Sandor, ii-47ff
Sarg, Anthony, i-235
Schiaparelli, Elsa, i-29, i-30, i-87,